THE MAVERICK MOUNTAINEER

The Remarkable Life of George Ingle Finch:
Climber, Scientist, Inventor

ROBERT WAINWRIGHT

ALLEN&UNWIN

First published in Great Britain in 2016 by Allen & Unwin

Originally published in Australia in 2015 by HarperCollins*Publishers* Australia Pty Limited

Allen & Unwin
c/o Atlantic Books
Ormond House
26–27 Boswell Street
London WC1N 3JZ
Phone: 020 7269 1610
Fax: 020 7430 0916
Email: UK@allenandunwin.com
Web: www.allenandunwin.co.uk

A CIP catalogue record for this book is available from the British Library.

Hardback ISBN 978 1 76011 192 2
Ebook ISBN 978 1 92526 843 0

Typeset by Kirby Jones in Adobe Caslon Pro
Printed in Great Britain by Bell and Bain Ltd, Glasgow

Cover images courtesy Mrs A. Scott Russell

10 9 8 7 6 5 4 3 2 1

To my wonderful sons,
Stevie and Seamus

contents

PART I

1.

TO SEE THE WORLD

George urged his pony up the steep slope. He could feel the animal's laboured breath beneath him, its flanks glistening with sweat as they pushed higher and higher, through the stands of crouching snow gums and silver-leafed candle barks that clung to the side of the long-extinct volcano.

The boy would remember the morning that would come to define his life as dewy. It was early October in 1901, one calendar month into spring, and the Australian bush around the inland New South Wales town of Orange – higher, wetter and cooler than the land to the west or the east – was still thawing from the winter, the mornings dark and frosty.

He had been up for hours, riding out from the family property to hunt for wallaby before the sun crested the surrounding ranges to melt the overnight frost and wash the countryside in pale gold. He might have woken his younger brother, Max, but had thought better of it, preferring to be alone in the waking bush with the utter sense of freedom that it brought.

Tall, lean and physically mature beyond his thirteen years, George had skirted the sleeping town and headed for Mount Canobolas, the highest inland point of the tablelands, a dozen or so miles to the south-west, where he was confident he would find the kangaroo-like marsupial feeding in mobs as the day warmed.

He and Max had hunted in the lower reaches of Canobolas many times before, but had never been interested in venturing up the towering rise, let alone pondering the origins of its name, a rather loose attempt at replicating the local Aboriginal word meaning a twin-headed beast.

They would come here to hunt, skinning and stretching the pelts of the animals they shot so they could be sold to dealers for four-pence each, and then using the money to buy fresh ammunition. But it wasn't the financial reward that drew George, who once sewed his mother a blanket from the six wallaby hides of a successful hunt. The money was simply a means to an end for a boy from a well-off family who relished the challenge and strategy of the hunt itself.

On this day George had found the wallabies easily enough – a mob of them at a waterhole in the virgin bush. He had waited, patient and content in the silence, for an opportunity, but when it came the flash of his gun barrel in the morning sun had stirred the animals and they'd scattered into the trees. Instead of following and perhaps scaring them further, George had decided to get to higher ground so he could spy where they had settled and try again.

There had never been a reason to climb even the lower reaches of Canobolas, and its freshness was intoxicating. The air was cooler up there as the mountain continued to shed the remains of its white winter coat. Small patches of snow still weighed down the boughs of some trees, ready to fall, melt and pool in the rock gullies where it would feed the flush of an Australian spring already evident in tiny flowers of kunzea, fringe myrtle and mirbelia that would soon explode into a blaze of white, yellow, red and violet.

It was mid morning when George reached a point high enough to be able to spot the wallabies again but he did not stop, instead choosing to keep going, the hunt all but forgotten as he sought the peak. One challenge had been replaced by another.

When it got too steep he searched for alternative routes where his pony, sturdy and sure-footed, could tread. At last he broke free of the dense foliage and reached a vast rocky outcrop that tapered into a stepped chimney to the summit, a series of upright rectangular blocks of stone that might have been placed there by a giant hand. His mount could go no further but, eager to continue, George dismounted and scrambled to the top in a few minutes, barely raising a sweat – then stood transfixed at the sight before him.

He hadn't stopped to consider what he might see from the summit or how his perspective of the world might change simply by viewing it from above. His eyes roamed across the scene in front of him, unable to pause even for a moment, such was the surreal nature of the view. Olive-green fingers of bushland reached out from Canobolas as if trying to claw back the plains of yellowed farmland that spread toward the Great Dividing Range, its rolling curves layered in hues of brown, blue and purple as they stretched to the horizon.

When he lowered his eyes and squinted into the still-rising sun, George could make out the glinting galvanised-iron rooftops and whitewashed walls of the houses of Orange, positioned in neat rows beside wide dirt roads crafted like ruled pencil lines, which led, ultimately, to the jewelled city of Sydney, 150 miles to the east. Years later he would recall the moment as clearly as if he was still standing there: 'The picture was beautiful; precise and accurate as the work of a draughtsman's pen, but fuller of meaning than any map. For the first time in my life the true significance of geography began to dawn upon me, and with the dawning was born a resolution that was to colour and widen my whole life.'

George remained atop Mount Canobolas for what seemed like hours, eventually tearing his eyes from the view and reluctantly climbing back down the stone steps to retrieve his pony. The boy would return home empty-handed several hours later but it mattered little, the spoils of a hunt replaced by a vision of his future: 'I had made up my mind to see the world; to see it from above, from the tops of mountains whence I could get that wide and comprehensive view which is denied to those who observe things from their own plane.'

George Finch, a boy who until then had only seen his world from the height of a saddle, wanted to be a mountaineer.

2.

A BOY FROM DOWN UNDER

Early in the summer of 1891, a few months after his son had turned three, Charles Edward Finch picked up the boy, dangled his legs over the side of a small wooden dinghy and plopped him into the calm, crystal waters of Sydney Harbour with the simple instruction, 'Swim, George, swim.'

The boy would do as he was told, fighting his way back to the surface and furiously dog-paddling to the gunwale, where he was plucked to safety by those same strong hands. George Finch would tell the story many times over the years, always fondly, dismissing any outrage among the listeners by arguing that his father had acted not out of cruelty but love, believing that in order to survive and thrive his son had to learn early to take care of himself.

The legacy of self-reliance that Charles Finch wanted to pass on to his children was not surprising given his heritage. His father, a redcoat soldier named Charles Wray Finch, the son of a far from prosperous clergyman, had arrived in Sydney aboard the convict ship *Hercules* in 1830 after a harrowing five months at sea. Once in New South Wales he was quickly promoted to the rank of captain, although he was not interested in a military career, and when the opportunity arose he resigned his commission to take up an appointment as a police magistrate. It was the beginning of a social and economic climb that would eventually make him one of the most prominent men of the colony, and his prospects were boosted by his marriage to Elizabeth Wilson, eldest daughter of the colony's powerful police magistrate, Henry Croasdaile Wilson.

The Finches soon quit Sydney and helped lead the push inland from the main colony, accepting Crown grants to develop the fertile agricultural and pasture land west of the Dividing Range. It was on a sheep station in the Wellington Valley that Finch called Nubrygyn Run (based on an Aboriginal phrase meaning the meeting of two creeks) that he not only made his fortune but, with Elizabeth, raised a family of nine children.

The station, running more than 12,000 sheep and 800 cattle, was a lush, blooming oasis in an otherwise harsh landscape, its homestead a sprawling stone building with seven bedrooms for family members and guests and large drawing and dining rooms for entertaining, leading onto a broad timber verandah with views across tended lawns to a creek that fed the paddocks. There were extensive vegetable gardens and an orchard with grapevines and over three hundred trees – peaches, cherries, apples, pears, plums, nectarines and apricots among them.

The gardener lived in a stone cottage, as did the station overseer, and there were separate quarters for household staff and the twenty-five farmhands, stockmen and shearers needed to run the operation. At the back of the house stood the stables and horse paddocks, to the side a massive brick woolshed with a 30-foot shearing floor and boasting the only hydraulic wool press in the district.

Charles Wray Finch would live at Nubrygyn for fifteen years before selling part of the property and securing a manager to run the large parcel of land that remained. He took his large family and fortune – 'estates of several thousand acres in extent in the county of Wellington and house, cottages and town allotments at Parramatta' –

and settled back in Sydney where he was welcomed into business and political circles, becoming a founding member of the Australian Club, joining the committee of the Royal Agricultural Society and being elected to the New South Wales Parliament. He was the parliamentary sergeant-at-arms, keeping order in the House, when he died suddenly in May 1873.

Charles Edward was his third child and second-oldest son, brought into the world in the main bedroom of Nubrygyn in 1843 and spending the first dozen years of his life on the station, until he was sent off to the King's School in Parramatta, making the journey on the back of a bullock wagon hauling wool bales to the city. Although he was ingrained with life on the land, the family's move to Sydney in 1855 shifted his expectations from the hardy life of a farmer to a privileged city existence and career. He graduated from high school with good grades, but surprisingly chose to bypass a university education in favour of a position with the New South Wales public service as a draughtsman. With diligence, and aided by the standing of his father, Charles worked his way through the ranks to become a district surveyor.

In 1885 Charles Finch would return to the Wellington Valley when he was appointed chairman of the Land Board at Orange, presiding over disputes concerning the Crown Lands Act, the guiding document in the division of New South Wales's vast tracts of arable land. In this role he would become more powerful than his father in many ways. He was a physically imposing man, tall and square-jawed, his neatly trimmed white beard contrasting with his dark, prominent eyebrows. His manner complemented his physical appearance: regarded as an uncompromising but fair man, he was a stickler for the rules and famous for once successfully defending a decision before the Privy Council in London, for which he earned the nickname 'King'.

Charles had never quite lost touch with his farming background. As the oldest surviving son (his elder brother had died in a farming accident), he inherited Nubrygyn when his father died and assumed the role of gentleman farmer, adhering to the strictures of Victorian morality and fashion, and donning formal dress for dinner, even in the heat of an Australian summer. He had married in 1870, aged twenty-seven and well set in his career, 21-year-old Alice Sydney Wood, the only daughter of a prominent family in a ceremony presided over by the Lord Bishop of Sydney. The marriage was widely reported in colony newspapers, as was Alice's sudden death just a year later, most probably in childbirth.

The loss of his young wife seemed to traumatise Charles because he remained widowed for the next sixteen years. He was finally married again in 1887, two years after moving back to Nubrygyn, this time to nineteen-year-old Laura Isobel Black, a woman twenty-five years his junior, who quickly bore him three children before he turned fifty.

George was the oldest, born on August 4, 1888, as Sydney celebrated the centenary of the First Fleet's arrival, while the rest of the populace, scattered across the vast southern land, grappled with the notion of a unified nation rather than a collection of independent states. By the time George Finch climbed Mount Canobolas on his pony thirteen years later, the Federation of Australia had been created, sparking the beginnings of a national identity that would be tested and refined by a world war that would soon devastate the fledgling nation with the loss of more than 60,000 lives.

* * *

Learning to swim was not the only lesson he received from his father, as George would recount in the last years of his life on a few pages of handwritten memories, the pencilled words fading on yellowed paper found lying at the bottom of a suitcase filled with his personal files. Titled 'The Boy from Down Under and his Adventures and Life', it is a statement not only of the significant early influences on what would be an extraordinary journey, but of his clear sense of identity as an Australian, even at the end of a life that took him to the other side of the world.

As much as Charles Finch expected his children to play responsible and productive roles in life, he also wanted them to leave their own mark, which might not necessarily align with his own, on the world. As George reminisced: 'Our father taught us from our earliest years to love the open spaces of the earth, encouraged us to seek adventure and provided the wherewithal for us to enjoy the quest and, above all, looked to us to fight our own battles and rely on our own resources.'

Some lessons were admonishments for stupidity – pointing an unloaded gun at a friend's head or attempting to lure out a deadly black snake sleeping beneath the floorboards of his bedroom with a bowl of milk. More profound were the encouragements to explore the natural environment, from the virgin land beyond the boundaries of their rural homestead to the waters of Sydney Harbour where George and Max and their sister, Dorothy, spent summer holidays in the bay below the house their grandfather had built at Greenwich Point, swimming behind shark-proof nets and sailing dinghies across the harbour to the chimney-topped city in the distance.

At its peak in the middle of the nineteenth century, Nubrygyn boasted a schoolroom, general store, blacksmith's shop and a hotel which the bushranger Ben Hall and his gang once held up, spending a night of merriment on stolen liquor in front of bemused residents. But by the early 1890s, when George was ready to start school, the village cemetery with its handful of gravestones was all that was left besides the still-grand homestead and its prosperous acreage.

The nearest large town was Orange, the birthplace of Banjo Paterson and named incongruously after the King of the Netherlands, formerly the Prince of Orange. George made the twenty-mile round trip each day on his pony to Wolaroi Grammar School, rewarding his steed with Tasmanian apples, but struggling himself to concentrate on the tedious formulated lessons. It was an eternal frustration for his parents who could sense a promising intellect behind the poor grades.

Things were different out of the classroom where George was a natural on a horse – 'dropped in a saddle at birth', as his father put it. He and Max were taught how to break and care for horses – they were to be curry-combed gently, brushed, fed and watered before the rider looked after himself, because 'a good horse is never to be treated as a machine but always as the rider's best friend'. They were expected to help muster cattle and sheep and ride the boundary fences to repair wires, strung low and tight to keep out the hordes of rabbits that ranged across south-east Australia threatening to destroy threadbare pastures.

George took his father at his word and explored the country every chance he got, often returning late at night and once riding as far as the Blue Mountains, falling asleep in the saddle on the return journey and relying on his horse to deliver him safely to the homestead as dawn broke the next morning.

He quickly became a crack shot with his .410 shotgun, practising on anything that was deemed a pest, from snakes to dingoes, and establishing a flourishing trade in pelts. The brothers even panned for gold in the streams around Mount Canobolas, once finding enough colour and small nuggets to buy new saddles and bridles.

George's love of adventure also extended to the water, not just the summer expeditions sailing dinghies back and forth across Sydney Harbour, but the romance of the open ocean. As an eleven-year-old he was riveted by newspaper accounts of a North Sea confrontation between the pride of the British navy, the battleship *Revenge*, and her Russian counterpart, the *Czar*. During an earlier summer he clambered aboard the famous wool clipper *Cutty Sark* as she lay at Circular Quay and, much to his mother's chagrin, asked for a job as a cabin boy. Despite her forbidding it, he sneaked aboard the next day and was given a trial, clambering easily into the rigging but upending a pot of tar – carried aloft by deckhands to coat the ropes and make them waterproof – which smashed onto the polished deck and ended his chance of a life on the high seas.

But Charles Finch's lessons and expectations went beyond mastering the outdoor skills of rural life, and he encouraged George to read the extensive range of books, mainly legal texts, he kept in his study, hoping it might pique a desire for what he called a 'serious future'. The boy read, or at least made an effort to plough through, a tome called *The Lives of the Chief Justices of England*, which extolled the virtues of a law-abiding society and the heroic lives of those who protected it, but it was the science books on his father's library shelves, collected during his days as a public servant, that caught George's attention.

George had continued to struggle at school to this point, the lessons in mathematics, French and Latin uninspiring to a youth who yearned to be outside on his horse, but he was suddenly captivated by the experiments created by his father during his days in the field as a surveyor: 'They awakened in me an abiding interest in science,' he later wrote.

In particular, he was engrossed by the art of navigation and the use of a sextant for surveying on both land and water. During holidays at Greenwich Point, he would wait expectantly for the sound of cannon fire across the waters of Sydney Harbour to signal that the Sydney Observatory had dropped its 1pm 'time ball', the only accurate measure of time in the colony and a navigation aid with which mariners could keep track of Greenwich Mean Time, regulated half a world away on a hilltop in south London. George was equally fascinated by his father's Atwood machine, a wooden pendulum designed in the eighteenth century to explain Newton's laws of motion and inverse square laws of attraction and repulsion. What should have been a complex subject for a boy who struggled at school had sparked his brain into action.

Although their age disparity was more akin to that between a grandfather and grandson, the bond between father and son was intensely close. George was imbued with resourcefulness and a desire for achievement, sensing that his character and interests were strongly congruent with his paternal line and, in particular, with his grandfather Charles Wray Finch whose questing journey halfway across the world was a source of wonderment and inspiration.

By contrast, George's relationship with his mother was, at best, distant. The story of his maternal family was murky and held little interest for him or relevance to his rough and tumble upbringing. He tended to disparage Laura Finch's fondness for the arts, making this clear in his late-life memoir that paid homage to his father's influence while scarcely mentioning his mother other than with a backhanded compliment about her singing: 'My mother was a good and attractive singer but rather over-fond of Mendelssohn's songs without words but at her very best with Schubert's songs.'

It would be a misplaced sense of identity, however. Although he clearly embodied his paternal grandfather's pragmatism and sense of adventure, George also had an ear for language, played the piano skilfully and later discovered a love of reading musical scores as others might read a book. There were physical similarities as well: he inherited Laura's searing pale-blue eyes and fine-boned features, not to mention her stubborn nature and razor-sharp tongue.

3.

A NEW HEMISPHERE

By her own account of their union, Laura Isobel Black was married off to Charles Edward Finch in 1887 to settle a financial debt owed by her bankrupt father. As outrageous as it sounded and without any evidence to suggest a financial link between the two men there was, nonetheless, a ring of truth to her claim.

The beginning of Philip Barton Black's story was a little like Charles Wray Finch's, although Black's journey to Australia was for different reasons and would have a very different outcome. He was the son of a successful Glaswegian cloth merchant, born in 1841 and the youngest of twelve children who, rather than find a place at the back of a queue of siblings, chose to accompany an uncle and emigrate to Australia. At first his enterprising nature seemed to pay off: he registered as an attorney and worked in Melbourne where he found himself a wife named Catherine Cox. Life seemed fabulous until he overreached.

In 1866 Black secured a Crown grant in Queensland on land opened up by the doomed explorer Ludwig Leichhardt, moving his new wife more than 1200 miles north to a property outside Rockhampton where their first child, Laura, would be born the following year. It seemed a strange shift, given that he had no experience on the land let alone the harsh environs of Australia's north, but most probably he had been enticed by the discovery of gold and later copper which drew men in their thousands, hoping to strike it rich.

The reality must have struck home quickly because within a year he had given up the idea of mining or running cattle and sheep, instead opening a legal office in the tiny town of Clermont that had flourished in support of the human stampede. But the gold seams rapidly ran dry and the town economy stagnated, the law business foundered and by 1869, just as Catherine delivered their second child, Philip Black was in serious financial difficulties. He closed the office and declared PB Black and Co insolvent, quitting the property and moving back to Victoria to be close to his wife's parents and beneath their financial umbrella.

But the change of scenery did nothing to stem the tide and the money problems grew, just as the family did. By 1877 there were five children (four sons came after Laura) and they moved again, this time to Orange where the New South Wales gold rush had begun and appeared to be more sustainable.

Black registered a new business entity, this time as a commission agent, a middleman specialising in rural property and commodities. Despite his struggles the family maintained a veneer of success, with Laura, then aged ten, taking singing and harp lessons as well as learning French and painting – the sort of skills expected of a young lady of means.

There are few records to shed a light on her father's business activities other than accounts of court appearances which show his efforts were of little avail. The gold rush had peaked and was now in decline and Philip Black slipped further into debt, his failure as an entrepreneur contrasting sharply with his success as a breeder of children. The combination proved disastrous and in 1881, just before the birth of their eighth child, the courts came to a conclusion about Philip Black and forced him to register debts of £1331 balanced against assets of just £125. He left town.

The family moved once more, this time to the inner-west Sydney suburb of Annandale, but it was a similar sad tale, Black ending up in a legal battle over the ownership of land in the centre of Melbourne – a battle he would ultimately lose. By the time he was finally declared bankrupt in 1892, Philip Barton Black was father to ten children – seven sons and three daughters.

Laura was fourteen when the family moved to Sydney from Orange. Bright and industrious and perhaps driven by the instability caused by her father's money troubles, she would opt for a career rather than a husband and entered teachers' college after finishing high school, graduating in 1886 and immediately finding work as a primary school teacher in Orange.

Dark-haired and exotic with alluring eyes and a sharp intellect, Laura Black would have been the centre of social attention in a town packed with mining men and farmhands. Charles Finch, by contrast, was older, authoritative and a man of some importance. Where and how they met has been lost in time but their courtship would be brief. For a young woman to marry a man only two years younger than her own father suggests that there were extraordinary circumstances at play, and lends weight to Laura's insistence that she was a sacrifice to her father's sorry financial history.

Whatever the reason for their marriage, it was clear that Charles Finch was besotted with his young wife, not just for her beauty but for her intelligence and presence. Apart from her love of the arts, Laura was a gregarious hostess even though the opportunities for entertaining in Orange were limited. Charles made every effort to turn his somewhat spartan homestead into a home befitting a woman who saw herself as a lady with a social position to uphold. The house at Greenwich Point offered some respite, but it, too, was relatively isolated, one of just a dozen or so houses in a bushland setting with grand verandahs and views across the water to the city, a lengthy boat ride away.

Laura relished her husband's insistence on formality in the household but without a sufficiently scintillating social and cultural sphere in which to shine, particularly as a mother of three young children, she became increasingly disenchanted until the night in September 1894 that she went to Sydney with friends to listen to a lecture by the controversial English theosophist Annie Besant.

Besant had been a prominent member of the National Secular Society in England and an outspoken women's rights activist before finding fame by championing the rights of the match girls of East London in their strike of 1888. Her popularity grew as she became a leading member of the Theosophical Society, its name taken from the Greek phrase meaning wisdom of the gods. The society preached universal unity and dedicated itself to 'the comparative study of religion, science and philosophy and the art of self-realisation'.

Besant's tour of Australia was a sell-out, her lecture in the then Sydney Opera House – a private theatre at the corner of King and York Streets – reduced to standing room. The small figure of Besant stood alone on the stage and lectured for ninety minutes on 'the dangers that threaten society', citing the unequal distribution of wealth as a particular evil and the need for a society without distinctions based on social status, sex or race. Mainstream religion was a destructive force, she argued, and should be discarded for the virtues of philosophy and science and the latent powers of man (or woman).

On the surface, at least, the message appeared to be at odds with the philosophy of Laura Finch and her desire for social recognition (she allegedly carried around a silver box once owned by Charles Wray Finch's father-in-law, Henry Croasdaile Wilson, containing a stale piece of Melba toast which she would present to hotel staff to indicate how she wanted her breakfast prepared). But the lecture that night clearly challenged her view of the world and she recognised in Besant a kindred soul disillusioned with the status quo. Certainly that was the story perpetuated in family circles: that she sat, mesmerised by Besant's charisma, and at the end of the lecture whispered the words, 'I agree with every word you said.'

Within a year Laura found a stage of her own in Sydney (belying her son's later dismissive judgment), appearing as a soprano soloist 'before a fashionable audience at the YMCA Hall', as reported by the *Sydney Morning Herald*:

> Mrs Charles Finch, a new amateur soprano with a fine
> platform presence, essayed the aria 'Vers nous Reviens
> Vainqueur' ('Aida') but was better suited by the valse air
> from 'Mireille'. In response to the applause which followed
> her interpretation of the Gounod melody, Mrs Finch added
> Meyer-Helmund's charming song 'Mother Darling'. A cordial
> feeling pervaded the concert room throughout the evening
> and the audience, which was a friendly one, included the
> Consul-General for France, M. Biard d'Aunet.

The two events would fuel a determination in Laura Finch to escape the isolation of Nubrygyn and she began studying the texts of Besant and her theosophist mentors. Frequent trips to stay with her parents or friends in Sydney once promised an exciting release from the boredom of the bush but, as the new century beckoned and Laura turned thirty, even the music halls and society events in the city seemed to be merely the fringe of possibilities.

Her husband was approaching his mid fifties, a kindly man but set in his ways and social sphere, making the difference in their ages and interests even more apparent. Charles Finch may have been content with his life but his wife wanted to explore the world outside. Europe beckoned and Charles knew he had no choice but to take her.

* * *

Charles Finch had other reasons for promising Laura that they would embark on a grand tour of Europe: while his wife's desire was to explore her potential, he wanted to discover his past. Unlike his father, who had become a soldier and travelled halfway around the world to escape his English legacy, Charles was fascinated by the family, history and determined to reclaim what he could of its status, even though the money, manor house and lands at Little Shelford near Cambridge that flowed from the highly successful ironmongering business of his forebears were now long gone. It fed his sense of place as a man of position and was also embraced eagerly by Laura, herself proud of her maternal link to an ancient titled Scottish family, the Maxwells of Bredieland, after whom her younger son had been named.

So, in August 1902, having secured generous leave from his position at the Land Board, Charles Finch bought tickets for his wife and three teenage children and headed for Europe aboard the steamship *Galician*. He imagined it would be a twelve-month trip, even describing himself as a 'tourist' on immigration documents. Instead, only two of the Antipodean branch of the Finches of Cambridge would ever return to Australia.

4.

WHYMPER'S PATH

The gendarmes, necks craned skywards, watched as the two figures inched their way past the famous parapet gargoyles toward the centre of the main face of the great Parisian cathedral of Notre-Dame. It was impossible to identify the climbers, silhouetted against the November moonlight, other than to note they were obviously fit and agile young men who were risking their lives and, more to the point, breaking the law.

Still, it was hard not to be impressed by the feat, the partners in crime climbing straight up the west wall like a pair of spiders, finding hand- and foot-holds in the ancient and pitted stonework. It made interesting an otherwise humdrum evening dealing with street drunks, bar fights and domestic disputes around the 4th arrondissement.

The officers were not the only spectators. A priest stood next to them, transfixed by the scene above. He might have been angry that a pair of fools was desecrating this grand monument to God; instead, he seemed amused by the events.

The two men were both near the top of the towers now, more than 200 feet above the cobbled forecourt. From their lofty position they had sublime views across the twinkling city but their attention was drawn to the knot of spectators gathering below, among them the dark blue cloaks of the police. One of them acknowledged the audience with a wave, prompting a sharp, demanding call: 'Descendez! Descendez!'

The taller of the two responded cheerfully: 'Oui, monsieur, nous serons dans un moment.'

Foreigners, probably Englishmen, although the accent was strange. Perhaps they should face charges, or at least a night in the cells to teach them a lesson. The priest seemed to read the change of mood and shook his head. He just wanted them down safely.

The officers weren't about to challenge a priest from the city's iconic cathedral. Instead, they watched in amazement as the climbers swiftly made their way back down the wall, hardly out of breath when they reached the pavement a few minutes later.

George and Max Finch grinned, aware of the risk they had taken but politely brushing aside the official admonishment, as they had a few weeks earlier when they'd scaled the 1500-foot chalk headland called Beachy Head, near Eastbourne on the south coast of England. On that occasion the law had been waiting at the top of the climb, at a notoriously dangerous spot known as the Devil's Chimney, bearing rope and rescue tackle and fearing the daredevils would tumble down the fragile cliff face to their deaths.

It seemed a strange disregard for the law by a young man so attuned to his father's wishes and principles, but it showed George Finch's true character: that he would challenge authority when he regarded it as overly bureaucratic, irrelevant or standing in the way of what he wanted to do.

There was a purpose behind the brothers' madness. George had recently discovered a book called *Scrambles Amongst the Alps* by the British mountaineer Edward Whymper, famous for being in the first party to climb the fearsome Matterhorn that rose like a stone arrowhead on the border between Italy and Switzerland. The book was regarded as one of the classics of mountaineering literature and George regarded Whymper as his hero, inspired by the Englishman's well-told stories and determined to emulate his feats, including Whymper's early jaunts climbing Beachy Head and Notre-Dame.

Although he hadn't been on the climb of Mount Canobolas that had inspired his brother, Max had willingly taken up the challenge and had proved a nimble and capable compatriot. It would be the beginning of a joyful sibling partnership as they turned from seaside cliffs and city buildings to the real challenge – the mountains of the Alps.

Their rebellious exploits had provided them with a welcome distraction from frustrations within the family. When they'd landed in England in the spring of 1902, the family had stayed near Cambridge, close to Charles's ancestral home but, despite an initial delight in her husband's pedigree – including immediately adopting the use of the name Ingle Finch, as borne by the English branch of the family – Laura was not interested in rural English life. She'd pressured Charles to move them to Paris where the theosophist movement was based, particularly as it had become clear that George, who for once sided with his mother, was finding it difficult to settle into the English public school system.

Charles had eventually relented and they'd moved into a grand apartment at 1 rue Michelet, in the heart of the university district, overlooking the spectacular Jardin du Luxembourg. It was the world of which Laura had dreamed while closeted by the stone walls, rough timber boards and dirt roads of Orange. Already a fluent French speaker, she was immediately at home, her entry to French society guided by influential theosophists including the scientist and Nobel Laureate Charles Richet. Within months she was hosting intimate soirées for the city's bohemian arts community, where her languid beauty and dreamy ways soon became famous.

While his much younger, beautiful wife slipped comfortably into the free-wheeling and decadent lifestyle of Paris, Charles Finch struggled. He was a socially rigid man who was used to being the centre of attention and in control of his environment. In Paris he was lost, nearing sixty and with little purpose other than as an uncomfortable and unwanted chaperon. It was clear that Laura would not easily be moved so, disillusioned, he decided to return to Australia alone.

It is doubtful that Charles sought to discuss the decision with his children or considered taking them home with him. It was clear they were content in their new environment, finally doing well at school, and the boys were excited by the prospect of exploring the mountains of Europe. George never commented about his father's departure, although the fraught relationship with his mother spoke volumes about the loss.

By April 1903 Charles was back at the New South Wales Land Board, but at the Goulburn office, where he would work for another decade. The newspaper reports of his retirement as a celebrated public servant in 1913 made no mention of a family and none attended the event. Charles Finch would live for another two decades, moving back into the Greenwich house that held only memories of happy summers with a family now settled on the other side of the world.

He would correspond with his children and send money to his estranged wife but he never returned to Europe and did not see Laura or his sons again. Only his daughter, Dorothy, would go back to Australia, in 1925. She would remain unmarried and live with her father for a time before moving to Inverell in northern New South Wales where she worked as a nurse.

Soon after her husband's departure from Paris, Laura took up openly with a French painter named Konstant and in 1904 gave birth to a son whom she named Antoine Konstant Finch. But who was the father? Certainly not Charles Finch who had left before Laura became pregnant, even though he was noted as Antoine's father on the birth certificate. The painter was a possibility, as was Professor Richet. For Charles Finch, Antoine's birth was the insulting coda to a trip that began as a unifying family adventure but ended up with its destruction.

George, then sixteen years old, was devastated and angered by the unravelling of the family and the departure of his father whom he loved. Even though he had no interest in pursuing connections with his father's English relatives and ingratiating himself with the British establishment, the young man did not understand or approve of his mother's lifestyle either and regarded her friends mostly as charlatans and theosophy as spiritualist mumbo-jumbo. It's unlikely he was impressed by Laura's writings, which included an article titled 'Should the Dead be Recalled?', published in the *Annals of Physical Science* newsletter, and another called 'The Tendencies of Metapsychism' in which Laura argued that religion had provided no definitive answers and that science in its various forms was too rigid: 'Who can say if some day prayer, ecstasy and especially intuition may not take the place of observation, experiment, logic and calculation? We dare affirm nothing, or rather we only affirm that this time has not yet come.'

George derided dialectic argument and philosophy, both pillars of theosophy, accusing Plato and Aristotle of spectacular drawings and lazy observations that relied on 'preconceived ideas of how things and men ought to behave', such as the ignorant belief that the heavier an object the faster it fell to earth. If only Aristotle had asked *how* rather than *why* an arrow flew:

By and large, all that mankind inherited from Aristotle's
barren inquisition into first causes was his voice of authority;

a voice that was to drown out the achievements of Archimedes and the now famous words of Horace ... and hold back the progress of man for more than two thousand years until Copernicus, Kepler, Galileo and Newton at last began to break down the wall of the Aristotelian authority. Man is ill-served by dialectics which is the art of proving anything. No wonder Dante consigned Socrates, Plato, Aristotle and others of that philosophical family to the first circle of Hell.

The relationship between mother and son would always be strained, at best, as shown by his terse description of her singing in his late-life reminiscences, and her disloyalty to his father must have been in the back of his mind when he faced a similar situation years later.

Yet as free-spirited as Laura Finch appeared to be, she could also be strict. When the children were young she would insist that they eat whatever food was put in front of them, no matter how long it took. If their morning porridge wasn't finished, the leftovers would be placed before them for lunch or as their evening meal until they were consumed. The nauseating memory of cold, lumpy porridge would stay with George, even in later life when he often regaled dinner guests with tales of hardship, including the story of the week that he and Max, then in their late teens, were left in Paris to fend for themselves while Laura went away with her friends.

The boys had very little money and ended up at a backstreet restaurant in a less-than-pleasant area of the city where prices were cheap and they could afford to share one of the meat dishes. The meal was surprisingly good so they returned the following night. The same dish, while still tasty, was not as good. Still, it was cheap and satisfying so they returned for a third night. This time, the meal was inedible. They stormed into the kitchen seeking answers and were confronted with the upper part of a human corpse with one arm hacked off. They both vomited before fleeing. As unlikely as it seems, his friends believed the tale to be at least close to the truth from a man not inclined to exaggeration.

Despite incidents like this, the move to Europe benefited George in a significant way. He had struggled in the Australian and English school systems but in Paris his mother found a tutor who was not only able to help him to eventually complete high school but to learn French well enough to qualify to study at the Faculté de Médecine. The transformation of George Ingle Finch (as his mother now insisted on referring to him) from struggling student to academic achiever had begun.

* * *

George was still following Whymper's path in January 1905 when he and Max took a train to the village of Weesen in north-east Switzerland. They were aiming to climb a nearby mountain known as the Speer, as their first tentative step into the Alps. At 'barely 6000 feet' it was a relatively modest challenge, but the brothers would soon learn one of the most important lessons in mountaineering – never be complacent.

After buying a map in the village they set off toward the mountain, a popular climb during the summer months when it was regarded as a realistic six-hour hike to reach the summit. But they had arrived in the dead of a European winter and, despite worsening weather and wearing little more than street clothes and shoes, they continued upwards through knee-deep snow. The wind rose after lunch but still they pressed on into the afternoon, even when it became clear that they could not reach the summit before nightfall, let alone return to the safety of the village.

It was 5pm, with darkness descending and their ignorance becoming life-threatening, when they stumbled across a disused wooden hut. The building was almost covered in a thick layer of snow, making it impossible to get through the door, so they forced their way inside through the chimney hole in the roof.

They would spend a sleepless night there, shivering inside the snowbound hut with no warmth and wet clothes and staring at the star-filled skies through holes in the roof. As soon as the sun appeared the next morning they staggered out, stiff and sore, yet not down the mountain, as one might have expected, but continuing upwards. They were determined to succeed, particularly as the weather had cleared and the sun was warm on their sodden backs. The reward was great, as George would later describe in loving detail:

> There, bathed in the warm sunshine, all the hardships were
> forgotten, and we gazed longingly over the ranges of the Tödi
> and the Glärnisch – real snow and ice mountains with great
> glaciers streaming down from their lofty crests. Thence the
> eye travelled away to the rich plains, the gleaming lakes and
> dark, forested hills of the lowlands, until details faded in the
> bluish mist of distance.

George was reliving the revelations of Mount Canobolas, only this time he was on the doorstep of his dream to climb the 'real' mountains of the Alps. Later that day, after they had descended safely and recovered from their chilling bivouac, the realisation set in that they had learned the first of many valuable lessons: 'This escapade taught us that mountaineering is a hungry game; that boots should be waterproof, and soles thick and studded with nails; that a thick warm coat can be an almost priceless possession.'

The lessons would come thick and fast over the next few years, as George and Max 'scrambled' among the lower slopes of the Alps, usually accompanied by experienced guides – a requirement demanded by their mother. Still, youthful enthusiasm led to a series of close calls from which George was learning the skills that would one day allow him to tackle peaks far higher than the 10,000-foot limit that Laura had also set for her sons.

Both were still studying under tutors so there was a certain freedom in their movements around Europe which fed their growing interest in climbing. Even during a sailing trip around Majorca in the summer of 1906, George and Max spent days scouring the rugged cliffs and mountains of the island while their yacht remained anchored in the bays below.

But their eyes were always on northern Europe where the real challenges lay, and they persuaded their mother to allow them to take a tutor to Switzerland where, between lessons, they climbed Mount Pilatus, a peak just shy of 7000 feet which overlooks the city of Lucerne.

As they climbed higher and higher, the brothers made mistakes that on occasion resulted in serious and even potentially fatal accidents – once almost plummeting to their deaths after slipping on wet limestone slabs, their fall halted by ropes – and yet their survival only added to their youthful disregard for mortality. It didn't mean that George ignored the lessons of his mistakes: when to climb with nailed boots and when to shed the footwear because 'stockinged feet' gave better purchase on the rocks. He grew to appreciate how to use his body, discovering that his legs were his most important asset, providing the muscle power to ascend, and that vice-like fingers to grab hand-holds were preferable to well-developed bicep muscles.

Half a century later, in a speech to the members of the Alpine Club in London, George Finch would reflect on the early experiences, the 'pure accident' of his climb up Canobolas and the 'ineffectual gropings' of their early daredevil ascents of Notre-Dame and Beachy Head. By comparison, the Alps were exciting and overwhelming in their scale: 'Up to this time I had no conception of the colossal scale of mountain architecture. But here at last was a yardstick with which to whet my curiosity in this new world – adventure, discovery, new horizons – everything followed after this, almost as a matter of course.'

The two boys, so recently from the Australian bush, were introduced to skiing which they quickly mastered and then used to extend their range of climbing possibilities across the lower slopes of the Alps during subsequent visits. Laura Finch, who occasionally travelled with them to Switzerland, continued to insist that they climb with guides and limited their challenges to smaller peaks. It was frustrating, and they occasionally stole away by themselves, but the period spent learning the craft of mountaineering on relatively easy climbs paid dividends in later years when the challenges grew harder.

One of their most important friendships was with a guide named Christian Jossi, famed for having been in the party of climbers who in 1890 had made the first winter ascent of the ominous Eiger. Almost two decades after Jossi's climb, George and Max Finch journeyed to the town of Mürren, built in the shadow of the colossus, to meet the legendary guide who had agreed to take the brothers under his wing. It was a relationship that would shape George's life like few others. 'Old Christian', as George and Max would call him, was a quiet, methodical man who embraced the unbridled spirit of the two Australian boys and fed their passion for mountains while instilling a care and respect for the dangers that would otherwise almost certainly lead to their deaths.

The lessons with Jossi took place on the Grindelwald Glacier where George and Max learned to be wary of seemingly innocuous varieties of snow: it might be packed well enough to be the foundation of a step or it might be loose and dangerous, capable of causing an avalanche. Jossi introduced them to the art of wielding a long-handled axe which could be swung with the minimum of effort to chip steps into hard ice. They spent hours cutting stairways, the steps sloping inwards to allow them to stand safely. It was a skill that had been honed by the pioneers of the mid nineteenth century but had been falling out of favour as climbers increasingly turned to summer ascents when there was less ice to overcome. Thanks to Jossi, ice craft would become a hallmark of George Finch's career. The brothers learned the art of rope safety, too: how to check a slip and hold up a man on the rope, and how to ensure that ropes were kept taut and not looped and tangled. This was a skill that would save their own lives on more than one occasion. They would also be forced to watch, helpless and in horror, as ignorance and haste caused the death of others.

The Strahlegg Pass stood beyond the Grindelwald Glacier at over 11,000 feet, an alien landscape of polished blue-ice walls and pinnacles, crevasses, ice tables and glacial streams from which a climber could see out beyond some of the great mountains of the Alps – the Jungfrau, Eiger, Mönch and Schreckhorn among others. It would become the first exception to Laura's 10,000-foot limit after the brothers had trained with Christian Jossi.

As it had when they'd hiked up the Speer a few years earlier, the balmy late-summer weather suddenly turned and the young men spent nineteen hours in the middle of a snowstorm. Instead of sheltering and waiting out the storm, fearful that they would freeze to death without the right equipment and clothing, George and Max kept moving through the night, stopping only for brief rests and carefully plotting their way by moonlight and compass. They emerged unscathed, revelling in the fact that they had been able to overcome the conditions, and declaring boldly that with a map, compass and a level head, it was possible to tackle mountain storms and even 'enjoy' the experience.

It was also another reminder of the need to equip themselves carefully, not only with the appropriate tools such as ropes and icepicks but with the appropriate clothing: boots large enough to accommodate several pairs of socks and with high toecaps to allow good circulation. Likewise, a woollen sweater worn beneath a windproof jacket made of material such as sailcloth was not only lighter but warmer and more protective than the traditional garb of tweed jackets. Those belonged in a stroll down the high street rather than on a mountainside where they offered feeble protection from the elements and soon became coated in snow, George concluded. Even at this early age the young man could see that convention should be challenged when it made little sense.

* * *

There were a few exceptions to George's distaste for his mother's circle of friends. Although he took no stock in the theories of spiritualism and the occult that many theosophists espoused, he respected the fact that Laura's obsession was an intellectual pursuit that she took seriously, not to mention the fact that among the believers were a number of eminent scientists. Richet was one and the British physicist Sir Oliver Lodge was another. Laura participated in psychical experiments, helped to edit research papers and was credited as a co-author with Richet and Sir Oliver of a book titled *Metaphysical Phenomena: Methods and Observations*.

By 1907, George was getting itchy feet. He had finally completed high school, thanks to the tutors arranged by his mother, and, in spite of his climbing, with grades good enough to enter the

University of Paris, la Sorbonne. But he was ready to give up after two years studying medicine, unfulfilled by a science he regarded as too inexact. George was more interested in the black and white of chemistry and sought Sir Oliver's advice. Should he seek a place at Oxford? No, replied Sir Oliver. Go and study in Zürich.

George didn't need to think twice. It meant he could pursue a growing love of chemistry, be free of his mother's bonds and, most importantly, go climbing every weekend.

5.

A ZEST FOR MOUNTAINS

For most of the year the Limmat River glides gently, almost silently, through the picturesque centre of Zürich. In late spring, however, when the snows in the Glarus Alps that surround the Swiss capital thaw, the flow can become a rush and then a torrent.

This was the case one night in May 1910 when a group of university students were making their way noisily across the Mühlesteg footbridge that crosses the river, heading back to their lodgings around the university after a night of drinking at one of the many bars in the Old Town.

They were singing loudly, their alcohol-fuelled voices ringing off the water that acted like a loudspeaker in the otherwise quiet night. A strolling policeman decided to intervene and strode purposefully toward them, stopping them at the end of the bridge and announcing that they should quieten down for the sake of the law-abiding citizens already in their beds.

It was a reasonable request but one of the student party, described later as large, objected to the directive. Taking the others by surprise, he picked up the officer and hurled him from the bridge into the river below where, unable to swim, the man was swiftly carried away. Acting instinctively, another of the students took off his shoes and jumped over the ornate balustrade in pursuit of the stricken officer. A few assured strokes, learned from a childhood swimming in Sydney Harbour, and George Finch dragged the policeman, who would otherwise have surely drowned, from the ice-cold river.

The other students, minus the assailant who had fled the scene, scrambled down to the riverbank to help bring the pair back to safety. After a few minutes the sodden, shivering officer recovered his authoritative demeanour, first thanking Finch but then demanding the names of the students and that they identify the offender. None could or, more accurately, would volunteer the name of their drunken colleague, and the officer finally gave up and went on his way. The incident was perhaps one of the first demonstrations of Finch's a natural instinct for decisive leadership and was brave almost to the point of foolhardiness, leaping into the dark waters with barely a pause to consider his own safety. A few days later the local constabulary hosted a dinner to toast his bravery.

George Finch was then twenty-two years old, broad shouldered and a touch over six feet tall. Fine-featured like his mother, he was as fair as she was dark, although he also shared her piercing pale-blue eyes – 'glacial', as someone would call them. It wasn't just his physical appearance that commanded a level of respect but his manner: assured and charming for the most part, but with a mind of his own and an abrasiveness that sometimes raised the ire of others. And he did not suffer fools silently.

His entry into Zürich university life hadn't been as easy as he might have hoped. The first problem had been the language. He could now speak French fluently and without a telltale Australian accent, but his courses were taught in German and he'd had to learn the language in little more than six months. For some reason he'd chosen as a tutor a clergyman from the Swiss village of Gais (probably because it was close to an attractive set of mountain peaks) only to find when he arrived in Zürich that he had learned a local dialect that could barely be understood in the city. It took a crash course from another tutor over a matter of weeks to correct things.

His linguistic talents did not go unnoticed among his fellow students at the Eidgenössische Technische Hochschule, otherwise known as ETH (or, in English, the Federal Institute of Technology), when he enrolled in the autumn of 1907. Initial guffaws at the new boy's dialect turned to admiration and he quickly became a class leader. He was a young man who wanted challenges but also expected definitive answers. Medicine had not suited his academic curiosity because it couldn't provide the latter. Besides, he didn't like the dissecting room, perhaps because of his nauseating experience years before in the backstreet restaurant in Paris.

Outside the classroom, he pursued the piano with some zeal. His love of music had been fostered by his mother, a keen harpist as well as singer, from an early age. While studying in Zürich, George sought the advice of the famed Austrian pianist Artur Schnabel, querying whether he was good enough to pursue a career as a concert pianist. The conversation was staccato.

'Tell me truthfully, how good am I?' George asked.

'You are first-rate second-rate,' Schnabel replied.

'I thought so,' said George.

And that was that. George not only abandoned the idea of being a concert pianist but apparently stopped playing the piano almost entirely. He would always retain a love of classical music and would often be seen, even in later life, reading books of music scores.

The perfectionist in him was simply unable to cope with the notion of not being quite good enough. Besides, he was obsessed with climbing mountains and could channel his passion into that endeavour. When Max later moved to Zürich to study, the brothers resumed their affair with intoxicating adventure.

* * *

The Alps were spawned by a clash of continents 300 million years ago, an incremental grind of Africa and Eurasia which crushed and concertinaed the earth's crust, causing the mountain range to rise like a gigantic twisted spine running from the Mediterranean to the Adriatic.

The jagged line of peaks towers almost three miles above sea level in places, forming a 750-mile boundary between languages and cultures across eight nations and evoking stories of brave or foolhardy deeds, from the Carthaginian warlord Hannibal crossing with a herd of elephants, to the French Emperor Napoleon urging 40,000 soldiers across to retake Italy from the Austrians.

Although men had been crossing the mountains via snowy passages and across vast glaciers for thousands of years, it was only since the mid eighteenth century that the summits themselves had become of interest, not because they offered practical riches but because they satisfied the base human desire to conquer. To men like George and Max Finch the Alps were a playground of risk and reward they could not resist.

The pair sought increasing challenges every weekend and every university holiday, often basing themselves for days and even weeks at a time in one of the many mountain cabins set up by Alpine clubs. They tackled new peaks every day, returning to the cabin each night where they nestled under blankets to sleep on musty, straw-filled bunks with only a small stove to warm the room, their spare accommodation only heightening the experience.

Meals were basic but in those surroundings they were feasts. George's favourite was tinned peaches drizzled with thin cream, usually eaten as they sat on a rock ledge, feet dangling into the abyss, or as they gazed over the Alpine spine after they'd conquered yet another peak. The meal was invariably preceded and followed by a cup of tea boiled from snow and the obligatory cigarette.

Laura Finch had long bowed to the inevitable and stopped trying to curtail her sons' adventures. The brothers were free to tackle the highest peak in the Glarus Alps, the Tödi, which stood at almost 11,900 feet. Their only concession to conventional notions of proper mountaineering was to make their first climb during the summer of 1908 – but they returned a few months later to make the same climb in snow.

To George, these were just training climbs, building on the 'scrambling' and gradually more serious ascents he and Max had already successfully undertaken. He was developing much bigger ambitions and was happy to progress carefully and to hone the skills, learned from Christian Jossi, in handling ropes and axes. He also saw great value in planning his climbs, recognising that the use of a map and identifying sensible routes, both before and during the climb, were the difference between success and failure, even life and death.

With Max's agreement, he decided they were ready for the most serious peaks of the Alps: 'Our self-assurance, confidence – call it what you like – seems to have been boundless, for we now considered that our apprenticeship had been sufficiently long to justify us in letting ambitions soar into reality,' he would later write.

Reputation meant little to George at this stage in his climbing career, particularly as he and Max felt as if they had hardly begun. In the summer of 1908, after their success on the relatively straightforward Tödi, they planned a holiday program which was ambitious in its scope and challenge, particularly for two fairly inexperienced men without guides. But it also smacked of a man of meticulous planning, which would become the hallmark of George's later achievements.

They would begin in the Bernese Oberland, in central Switzerland, attempting and conquering the main peaks in order of height, beginning with the lowest of the monsters, the Wetterhorn, at 12,185 feet, before tackling the Eiger (13,020 feet), Mönch (13,474 feet), Jungfrau (13,641 feet) and finally the Finsteraarhorn (14,022 feet).

But that was just the start, and afterwards they made their way on skis, as they might have ridden horses back in the Australian bush, down through the Aletsch Glacier to the Rhône Valley and then up to the village of Zermatt which served as the base for the peaks of the Pennine Alps. First they climbed Dent Blanche (14,294 feet), then ascended the Matterhorn (14,691 feet), the focus of George's hero Edward Whymper's career and one of the deadliest peaks in the Alps.

It wasn't just climbing peaks that attracted the brothers but traversing mountains, which meant climbing by one route and descending by another, thereby crossing them as a traveller might when moving from one region to another. There were three at least that the brothers traversed that summer: Aiguille de la Za, Aiguilles Rouges d'Arolla and Pigne d'Arolla, which all sat near the Swiss border with Italy. Still not satisfied, George and Max headed back to the Glarus region where they repeated their ascents of the main Tödi peaks.

George would rarely keep a diary of his activities but his summary of the 1908 summer gives an indication of his and Max's incredible physical endurance and capabilities. It also indicates their growing fascination with climbing, and the hold it exerted over them, as he concluded in a later reflection:

From its chance nucleus on the hill-top in the Australian
bush, snowball-wise the zest for the mountains grew until

it has actually become an integral part of life itself. The health and happiness that the passion has brought with it are as incalculable as the ways of the 'divinity that shoes our ends' chooses our parents for us and places us in a certain environment.

* * *

The brothers' first target that summer, the Wetterhorn, was not an easy ascent even in midsummer when snow and ice still capped its peak. The mountain, sitting high above the village of Grindelwald, had long been a favourite of artists, and their romantic images drew many climbers.

George and Max decided to bivouac overnight at a hut built on a spectacular overhanging ledge just over halfway to the peak. The huts were basic but provided a sanctuary for the tired and a launching pad for the careful who wanted to ensure they had time to reach the peak via the easier, north-east route, and descend before nightfall – or before the infamous changing weather of the mountains closed in.

Another climbing party of five Germans was also staying overnight at the hut, with the same intention. At 2am the next day, under moon- and lantern light, all seven men set off, George and Max in front and the Germans, roped in two groups, a few minutes behind. Within an hour, the Germans had raced past the two young men who were happy to let them go, preferring to take their time.

They caught up again just before 5am, arriving at a sheltered depression known as the Wettersattel, just as the Germans were tucking into a hearty breakfast before a final push for the summit. George and Max decided to press on after a short pause. It was still dark and a wind had risen which made sitting still uncomfortable.

They left the others and headed upwards, finding the going much easier than anticipated because a snowfall two days earlier had compacted and provided firm footing. George had expected to be cutting steps into ice, but that was only necessary for the final few yards.

Five hours after leaving the hut George and Max reached the highest peak they had ever attempted. They scraped depressions in the snow with their axes and sat contentedly to survey the scene, in no hurry to begin the return journey. The wind had died away to a whisper and the peak was bathed in sunshine, revealing in their full glory the views across the green valley, the village below and, beyond, the peaks of three of their next challenges. It was twenty minutes before two of the Germans arrived, the others having decided against making the final climb.

Their appearance shattered the peace so George and Max began their descent, a few minutes ahead of the German pair who stopped only long enough to take in the view before traipsing after the brothers. George and Max reached the top of a large gully that led to a glacier by which they planned to return to Grindelwald – a different and more difficult route than the ascent. They stopped here, intent on ensuring it was safe to make their way down the slope before setting off.

The three Germans who had not attempted the final ascent were sitting on a ledge nearby, unsure how to proceed. There were signs they had attempted to climb down the gully themselves but had given up and were waiting for their compatriots. As George surveyed the gully for potential problems and tested the snow underfoot, the first German pair arrived. They paused briefly to greet the other three before moving down the slope, taking the lead without discussion, much to George's annoyance. A few minutes later, satisfied that the snow was firm underfoot, he and Max set off, leaving the hesitant German trio still anchored to their ledge.

George was worried, not just about the German pair's apparent thoughtlessness, but because he now seriously doubted that they (let alone the nervous trio) had the skills necessary for such a climb. There was only one way to descend a steep snow-covered slope: with your back to the slope and stepping boldly, like a soldier, driving your heel into the ground with each step to allow your weight to create a sure footing. The Germans were taking short, hesitant steps and one was even reduced to all fours, facing into the slope and trying to descend backwards.

The men had descended about 400 feet when the slope suddenly became far steeper and the surface hard-packed. Even stepping down the slope, as George and Max had been, was no longer possible. Instead, the lead man – in the brothers' case it was George – would have to lean into oblivion, supported by the rope tied to his brother, and wield his axe to cut steps into the compacted snow, creating an ice ladder. It was slow, dangerous work but their only option other than climbing back up.

Below them the two Germans had abandoned the slope and instead moved across to an outcrop of jagged rocks, hoping to clamber down away from the snow. George had assessed that route but dismissed it as too dangerous because the rocks were encased in a glaze of ice, making them treacherous. Step-cutting into the snow might be slower, but it was the only safe way to descend. He called out to the men in their own tongue, expressing his concern. The men stopped, unsure, and sat on the rocks to watch the two Australians.

George and Max kept going, ensuring the rope between them remained tight, as they had been taught by Christian Jossi, so that if one man slipped then the rope wouldn't act like a whip and cause both to fall. It was another concern George had about the Germans.

The rope between them was overly long – he judged it to be sixty feet – and they had struggled to manage it properly.

Moving steadily and securely the brothers soon passed the Germans, who had remained on the rocks. As George turned his attention back to the job at hand, he heard a cry. One of the men had stood up and immediately slipped on the icy rock. He was now sliding down the slope, clawing desperately at the ground to stop himself. George shouted to the second man, warning him to pull in the extra rope to help his friend slow down.

But before he could react the rope went taut and jerked the seated German from his precarious perch, sending him hurtling through the air past his stricken companion. The next few seconds were horrific as he struck an outcrop of rocks, his left arm wrenched from his shoulder socket and his chest crushed by the sharp boulders. The bloodied corpse continued to fall until the rope went taut again, this time pulling the first frightened German from the slope and repeating the horror, his head smashing open on the rocks. The two bodies tumbled in a sickening aerial ballet into the ravine, eventually disappearing into the whiteness below.

The three other Germans above were silent in their terror and despair, while George and Max, who had watched the men fall past them, could only cling to their insecure position on the side of the mountain. Minutes passed before they moved, George finally coaxing his brother to resume the descent. He cut the next step in the snow and moved down in unison with Max, then cut another and another. Then came a cry from above. The Germans were pleading with them to climb back up and get them safely back to the hut. The men were clearly paralysed with fear, the loss of their friends only highlighting their own self-doubt.

Even though they were well down the dangerous section, George and Max had no choice but to climb back and rescue the men whom they roped together and led back to the Dossen Hut where they reported the accident. Although George would later play down the incident, watching the men fall to their deaths would leave a deep psychological scar that would eventually contribute to him quitting his great infatuation.

6.

EVEREST DREAMING

The success of their 1908 summer climbing experience, even taking into account the horrific deaths of the German pair, would only spur the Finch brothers onto grander schemes. The possibilities seemed endless, particularly as George was not interested in mountain scalps so much as challenges of skill and scope involving rock, snow and, most of all, the vagaries of ice.

And the delight of their Alpine adventures fed rather than detracted from George's studies at the ETH where he began to shine not only academically but as a prominent student figure. He joined the Academic Alpine Club of Zürich (AACZ) in 1909, presenting a catalogue of climbs that astounded the club committee, not only because of his youth but because he and Max challenged the notion that English climbers needed the help of local guides to safely negotiate Europe's Alpine playground. To climb independently of guides was the very reason the club had been established in 1896 and George quickly became a favourite among its members.

The brothers returned to Grindelwald in the summer, this time to embrace an endurance challenge of traversing the three peaks of the Wetterhorn massif in a single day – the Wetterhorn, the Mittelhorn and the Rosenhorn. The attempt was launched from the Dossen Hut once more, but this time they were not alone. The brothers had brought with them a seventeen-year-old school friend of Max named Will Sturgess who had never climbed before. It seemed astonishing that George would take such a risk, but such was his self-confidence and lack of fear. In his mind, Sturgess was perfectly safe in his company.

Sturgess, for his part, seemed unperturbed even when a storm kept them inside the hut for two days. Then he slipped twice while crossing a steep snow slope on the first climb, saved by the rope and the fact he was climbing between the brothers. He seemed oblivious to the dangers as he abseiled down vertical cliffs – 'roping down' as it is quaintly called by mountaineers – and scrambled across ridge-tops without hesitation, convinced he was safe with George and Max Finch.

It was typical not only of the utter fearlessness of the brothers and their achievements, but of the sheer joy of their vertical frolics, whether perched on a narrow snowbound ledge cooking a meal, or setting out on a climb at midnight, hoping to catch the dawn from a summit as the morning light spread across the valleys and villages below.

One of the lasting images of this time is a photograph taken of the two brothers sunbaking on the roof of an Alpine hut called the Guggi, set into a bare ledge halfway to the summit of the Jungfrau. The view beyond them, even in the black and white of a shot taken in 1909, is spectacular, but it is the innocence of the moment that is so captivating. It is difficult to tell which figure is George and which is Max, even though they were physically different – George rangy and blond and Max shorter and darker – but both are completely at peace, one sleeping and the other gazing out over the valley.

The photo was taken shortly after midday on July 29 as the young men dozed off a big meal before striking out on an audacious bid of 'boyish enthusiasm' to climb the north face of the Jungfrau, one of the most challenging ice climbs in the Alps. George would describe the mountain as 'an imposing edifice built up of glistening, greenish-white terraces of ice and snow of such purity that it were almost desecration to set human foot upon them'.

It wasn't as though they were unaware of the dangers of their plan, warned as they were by an older climber they'd met at the hut, Dr Andreas Fischer, who was being guided by two famed local guides, cousins Hans and Ulrich Almer. In recounting his adventure some years later, George recalled negotiating an ice pinnacle at the edge of a yawning abyss by hanging from a rope and swinging a metre-long axe to create hand-holds. Dr Fischer watched with growing concern but was calmed by Hans Ulrich, the elder of the two guides, who assured him: 'They are sure-footed like cats, they know how to use a rope, they are quite safe.'

If repeating the guide's words was a rare moment of self-congratulation for George, it was apparent to experienced observers that even at this young age George Finch was supremely confident of his own ability in this most dangerous of pastimes. Although he viewed, and felt, the mountains with at times breathless poetry, George's overpowering sense was one of pragmatism and the desire to pit his puny human strength against overwhelming odds.

The Jungfrau ice challenge – the five great terraces of ice that formed 'a wonderful spiral staircase, as it were, betwixt earth and heaven' – was duly faced and completed. They had set out at 2am under the light of a fullish moon and cloudless sky and stood atop the spectacular peak for the second time by 11am, having climbed almost 8200 feet of ice and snow in just nine hours. It was time to relax, perhaps even doze comfortably under a winter sun for an hour or so, tied to their pickaxes buried beneath the snow in case they slipped or, God forbid, sleepwalked off the top of the mountain. But first a cup of tea.

* * *

While most of his contemporaries were satisfied with their summer sojourns across the peaks of northern Europe, George Finch had already identified a challenge far beyond the view atop the Matterhorn – the Himalayas. As beautiful and difficult as they were, the European Alps paled next to the challenges presented by the behemoths of the Tibetan Plateau – including the ultimate prize, Mount Everest – not just because of their size but because of the likely climbing conditions and their distance from any kind of logistical support. And then there was the political difficulty of getting to the mountain through Tibet, which was closed to foreigners. Although men had dreamed for years of climbing this forbidden monolith, no European had been within 100 miles of her base let alone set foot on Chomolungma (Goddess Mother of the World), as Everest was known in Tibet. That only made it more appealing to the brothers.

It was the chief reason he and Max would target challenges like the north face of the Jungfrau and a few weeks later the first ascent of the north face of Castor in the Pennine Alps, believing that testing their snow and ice craft whenever possible would hold them in good stead for a longer term vision that went far beyond being merely agile on rock, like the army of summer climbers who followed each other up the same safe routes year after year. George regarded that as laziness – a test of nothing but physical strength and endurance requiring none of the pioneering skills of the ice climber who had to carve his own route every time he climbed. Not only could he carve steps in ice walls swinging a pickaxe, but if he had to, as had happened on more than one occasion, George could fashion foot-holds and hand-holds with a pocketknife or even a sharp piece of granite.

As much as the Alps provided the practice ground needed to prepare for the dream of climbing in the Himalayas, there was another aspect of that challenge that was more difficult to replicate – the isolation. In the Alps they were never far from civilisation: the established railway routes and numerous towns filled with hotels and stores; the secure mountain huts with straw-filled bunks and wood stoves for waiting out storms. That would not be the case on the slopes of the great peaks of the subcontinent, most of which could only be reached after many days' march across a bare, harsh landscape in which villages consisted of little more than wind-battered huts inhabited by subsistence farmers.

Seeking a location beyond the comparative comforts of Switzerland, in March 1909 George and Max chose the French-held island of Corsica with its wild barren peaks, reached by a five-hour crossing on a cargo boat from the southern Italian port of Livorno. They had considered tackling the mountains of Norway, the Spanish Sierra Nevada and even the Balkans, but had ruled out each region before chancing across a guidebook about Corsica.

George left Zürich first with a fellow student, Alf Bryn from Norway, who would later write a book about their adventures called *Peaks and Bandits*. Max followed a week later and by the time he arrived in Corsica George and Alf had already organised supplies for a ten-day crossing of the chain of mountains that formed the backbone of the Mediterranean island.

The highest peak, Monte Cinto, stood at just under 9000 feet, which would not rank it in the top 850 peaks of the Alps, yet the Corsican ranges were snow-capped and challenging in their own right, not just the climbs but the access through dense tangles of bushes and undergrowth – a wiry, heath-like combination known as maquis – particularly when tackled carrying tents, sleeping bags, spare clothes, cooking utensils and food on the back of a mule.

The climbing was strenuous and challenging, but the real purpose of the trip was to experience camping each night without the option of retiring to the nearest village hotel. Neither was there a restaurant menu from which to choose, forcing the trio to live off tinned food like sardines and preserves brought out from Switzerland.

They had set off on April 5 and ten days later, with their supplies running low, the trio had tackled most of what the island had to offer. One peak remained, the curved outline of the Paglia Orba, at 8297 feet one of the tallest peaks on the island. But it wasn't the height that drew their attention; rather it was the north-east face, an almost perpendicular wall of dark granite capped by snow.

Most of the peaks on the island had been conquered soon after European climbers began combing the island in the 1870s, but not the north-east face of Paglia Orba. A pair of Austrian climbers had attempted it the previous year but had turned back, and the pioneer of Corsican climbing, a Dr Felix von Cube, had declared it impassable. It was a delicious challenge.

There is film footage of Max, a grim expression on his face that owed so much to his mother's dark good looks, dressed in a loose woollen jumper and broad-brimmed hat, making his way up the first snowbound slope using the handle of his axe as a walking stick. But the footage goes no further, the camera forgotten as the climbers ducked beneath a waterfall and began to tackle the wall, littered with chimneys of rock choked with clumps of snow threatening to slide from their precarious nooks.

By 1pm, after almost five hours of climbing, George, Max and Alf sat, momentarily defeated, on a ledge so flimsy that they couldn't find a belay to secure their ropes. They munched on dry bread and chocolate, contemplating a sheer face that appeared to have no chink but which they needed to climb to reach a broader ledge 300 feet or so above their heads that would leave a clear route to the summit, still 1000 feet away. The tinkling sound of icicles breaking in the warming air shattered the silence, the shards falling past them confirming that the wall they faced was not just vertical but overhanging.

The task seemed hopeless, but before they gave in George asked Alf to photograph the ledge where they sat. The Norwegian crawled along its length to get a better view back toward his friends, then glanced up to spy another ledge, tantalisingly just out of reach. He called to the brothers who joined him and decided to ignore their precarious position to hoist Max onto Alf's shoulders so he could haul himself up to the ledge. It seemed suicidal, balanced as they were on the edge of oblivion, but the young men evidently regarded themselves as indestructible.

If the trio thought the biggest test had been overcome they were wrong, and were now forced to work their way back and forth across the face, climbing a series of precarious rock chimneys connected by narrow, sloping ledges with little room to anchor a safety rope and encrusted with icicles 'clustered together like the pipes of an organ'.

Alf took the lead and, with Max's rope between his teeth, edged across the final ledge while cutting a path through the icicles. George watched, hardly able to breathe, while Max, below Alf, clung with bare hands to the only purchase he could find, an overhanging icicle.

It took fifteen minutes to climb the last chimney, which was infused with an iced waterfall, before Alf reached blindly to loop a rope around a rock at the top to secure them safely as they finally gained the broad ledge spotted a few hours before. They rested a few minutes then scrambled up the last slope, their hands warming on sun-kissed rocks, and stepped out onto the summit as the sun began to set.

A fresh wind made conditions uncomfortably cool, but nothing could detract from the joy of their achievement as they built a cairn of rocks at the highest point, inside which they placed a piece of paper with their names and details of the climb. A piece of rope was looped around a rock placed atop the cairn to alert future climbers.

* * *

George Finch's self-confidence was not misplaced, if judged by the accolades of his contemporaries. Despite their youth, or perhaps because of it, the Finch brothers were already being identified as among the elite climbers in Europe. Aldo Bonacossa, an Italian aristocrat and widely respected climber, was one who heaped praise on George who was still only twenty-one years old. Count Bonacossa was studying in Munich but in the summer of 1909 had taken an overnight train to Zürich to join a group of experienced climbers opening a new mountain hut.

Even among this group of elite mountaineers it was George Finch whom he noticed, as much for his 'exotic' appearance as his climbing ability, as he set himself apart from the others by almost every measure: his style, his clothes, his hair and his heritage. Finch was clearly not one of those English climbers who hired guides to explore the Alps, but as an Australian was 'quite unlike other men', as Bonacossa would recall more than half a century later in an article for the Alpine Club's magazine:

The recognised number-one mountaineer and the most outstanding personality among them by far was George Finch. He was tall and wore his hair long and untamed, quite unlike other men in Switzerland who used to wear their hair cut quite short, and never took off their hat, as we can see in old photographs of mountaineers and guides; this gave him an exotic look. Moreover he came from the Antipodes and as a result was nicknamed 'the Australian'. He was also known to have introduced the anorak to replace the usual heavy jacket, which in hot weather became rather a nuisance.

As part of the opening ceremony the assembled climbers pitted themselves against one another by climbing a fifteen-foot wall at the back of the hut, erected as protection against avalanches from a nearby mountain. One by one, each man hauled himself up by two ropes as quickly as possible. Not all would make it. Bonacossa was one of the first and made easy work of the challenge. He then sat and waited for the others; in particular, for George Finch: 'I kept watching Finch's strenuous efforts to work his way up. In that moment I certainly felt quite important, to have been a match for the famous Finch.'

7.

KING OF HIS DOMAIN

Maxwell Bruce Ingle Finch was destined to live in the shadow of a dominant elder sibling, forever at his feet on or off the slope of a mountain, although it would not become a problem until later in life. For the moment, Max fearlessly accompanied his brother in their all-weather assaults on the mountain ranges of Europe, an even-tempered balance to George's demanding perfectionism It was on one of the rare occasions they were not twinned that the differences between the two men became apparent.

The winter of 1910–11 had been frustrating for the two eager young men aching to test themselves at every opportunity. A run of foul weather had made it impossible to tackle their latest challenge, an ascent of the Tödi on skis. It was a task with some practical purpose, not only for the obvious advantage of quickly traversing flat and downhill sections, such as glacial aprons, but to test the notion that by distributing a climber's weight across the length of a ski it would ease fatigue through thick snow, particularly if seal skin was attached to the underside of the ski, with the animal hair laid toward the front to prevent slippage against the slope. The length of the ski might also lessen the chances of falling into hidden crevasses, the brothers reasoned.

It would be the first days of spring before there was a break in the weather. On the morning of Saturday March 11 the conditions seemed to have cleared enough to make an attempt. Max checked four times with the meteorological office in Zürich before he was convinced that it was safe to plan an assault, although it would have to be without his brother who was busy studying for his final exams at ETH.

From the outset everything went wrong. Two of the four climbers were novices, inadequately outfitted and equipped. Max managed to lead them to their mountaintop goal but it took much longer than expected, climbing through the night and arriving just before dawn. More alarmingly, the weather changed. Clouds broiled below as a mist rolled toward them, bursting through the valleys and gaps between the glacier walls with the pent-up fury of a dam that had broken its walls. In what had seemed like a moment, the beauty had turned into a beast and what should have been a careful descent suddenly became a hurried retreat. It was almost impossible to retrace the route of their ascent. Finding their way by instinct, the climbers at times were forced to their knees to avoid being blown into the now half-hidden crevasses. They had no tents or supplies and were forced to use their skis to dig a trench in which to wait out the storm.

Somehow they made it back after being at the mercy of the mountain and its elements for thirty-five hours. Max escaped with few serious injuries beyond some frostbite and broken teeth but the two novices were in a bad way, with one losing most of his toes from both feet because of tight, ill-fitting boots, and the other losing all but two fingers at either the first or second joint.

* * *

The spring of 1911 was a defining moment in Max Finch's life, as it would be for his older brother, but for different reasons and outcomes. Max returned from his almost disastrous ascent of the Tödi in quiet disgrace, his undoubted climbing talent overshadowed by questions about his risk-taking. It was an inauspicious beginning to his post-school years, given that he had followed his brother to Zürich and would study at the ETH for the next three years, leaving in 1914 in haste as it became obvious that war was about to be declared.

George would never have made the same mistakes: not assessing his novice companions, forgetting to take lamps and cooking equipment, failing to ensure the party wore loose-fitting clothes and waterproof gloves made of sailcloth and lined with wool. Most importantly, he would have carried a barometer to warn of changing weather patterns.

As the recently installed president of the Academic Alpine Club, George had also been placed in a difficult position. If he was to preserve his integrity as a climber, he had little choice but to publicly rebuke his brother's poor judgment. The event would mark the beginning of a change in their personal relationship that would not be obvious to either man for some years.

George's studious efforts that spring, when he had declined to accompany Max to the Tödi, paid off when he was awarded the gold medal as the university's top student for the diploma course in chemical technology. It was a major award and its presentation was an event on the university's academic calendar but there is no hint in the family records that his achievement was celebrated. Certainly, it was a vicarious triumph for both parents, vindicating Laura's decision to stay in Europe and Charles's encouragement of his eldest son's inquisitive nature. Indeed, George had not lost touch with his father, maintaining a steady exchange of letters that would keep the older man aware – and proud – of his son's adventures.

George had already been singled out as a young scientist of promise and was encouraged to take up a position as a research assistant with one of the senior academics, but first there was a summer of climbing to be had, paid for in part by the clandestine sale of the university gold medallion to a local dealer to be melted down for its precious metal content.

As far as George was concerned he would always have the achievement of topping the class and the medal was a more useful award if it provided him with the funds to pay for his climbing. He and Max had been living off an endowment fund provided by their father, earned largely from the efforts of their pioneering grandfather, the late Charles Wray Finch. The money had been carefully salted away, invested in Russian railway bonds that provided the security of government-backed dividends, but they were forbidden from using the funds for equipment, food or train fares as they travelled up and down the Alpine spine of Europe searching for adventure.

Besides, George believed he owed much more to the mountains than a freedom of spirit, as he ventured many years later in a speech in which he reflected on his education:

> Looking back over the years, I see that the learning of my
> school days came too easily. It never occurred to me to
> question the voice of authority by probing into the significance
> of the first principles. In short, my memory was my
> stronghold, with only a modest appeal to reason. Fortunately,
> well before beginning my academic career in Zürich, I already
> had some experience in the, to me, new and strange world
> of mountains. It was then that the desire to survive, inborn
> in all creatures, and anxiety for the welfare of my climbing
> companion impelled me to keep my mind on the work in

hand. So, with the years, my power of mental concentration grew and helped me to deal with the problems of a scientific career.

If George Finch as a youth had indeed ever been unwilling to challenge authority, then he would certainly make up for it as a young man, forever testing boundaries and those who put them in his way.

* * *

George had quickly stamped his authority on the membership of the Academic Alpine Club after becoming president, particularly with his insistence that new members earn their stripes. He wanted eager participants, with or without experience, but they had to have the capacity to climb and not just the enthusiasm. The stone climbing wall at the back of the club hut at Windgällen, which Aldo Bonacossa had scaled back in 1909 when the clubhouse was opened, had become an increasingly difficult testing ground not only for prospective members but experienced climbers. Whenever someone succeeded, George would rearrange the structure to remove a critical hand- or foot-hold to make the climb harder. He, of course, always found a way to the top – the king of his domain.

It was in January of 1911 that a prospective member, a young American named John Crowther Case, arrived in Zürich. His father was an oil company executive who had moved the family to London a few years earlier and the nineteen-year-old now wanted to study civil engineering at ETH. He had joined another university club – the Anglo-American Club – where he had made some friends, some of whom encouraged him to attend an open day at the AACZ clubhouse during the Easter break.

Case had never been climbing but fondly recalled a childhood holiday in Switzerland during which he had been taken on a hike across the top of a small mountain, the Rigi, outside Lucerne. The AACZ clubhouse was situated higher than the Rigi itself, two-thirds of the way up the Gross Windgällen, one of the southern-most mountains in the Glarus Range and about an hour by train south of the city.

There was no shortage of newcomers to the open day, all of whom were eventually led out to the back of the clubhouse where they were encouraged to make an attempt at the wall. Some refused to even try and those who did attempt failed, as George Finch had hoped; after all, this was a test to discover aptitude but also to teach a sense of respect for the terrain.

John Case was the exception on the day, making the top and earning the respect of the president who took him on a testing climb the following day with another student climber, Marcel Kurz. The young man's ability confirmed, George invited Case to join him and Max for part of their summer climbing trip which would include, among a host of others, three of the most dangerous peaks in the Alps: the east wall of Monte Rosa, the Zmutt Ridge of the Matterhorn and the southern flank of Europe's tallest peak, Mont Blanc.

The memories of that summer with the Finch brothers were still fresh more than sixty years later when Case was invited to write for the *Alpine Journal*, the magazine of London's Alpine Club:

On a mountain George gave the impression of being always master of his surroundings. His route-finding and eye for ground were excellent, results of his study of mountain form. On rock, his strength was more apparent than grace of movement. He climbed very fast, going straight from stance to stance, using holds far apart, without pause, rarely hesitating and almost never retracing a step. He seemed able to test each hold without loss of motion for I never saw a weighted one come away under hand or foot. On ice he was superb, cutting steps far apart very fast with a minimum of powerful strokes. On steep ice he liked to cut straight up with his backer-up only a step behind and moving with him. His lead on the Marinelli route on Monte Rosa in the very dry year of 1911 with step-cutting from the Imseng rocks to the ridge of the Grenzgipfel was a perfect example of this technique.

Of the Finch brothers he wrote:

Realising the necessity of acquiring knowledge and skill before they could tackle large peaks on their own, the boys worked long and hard to attain competence in the art of mountaineering and all connected with it: knowledge of weather and its effects on snow and ice, the qualities of different kinds of rocks, the use of the Siegfried map, and the reaction of the climber to cold and altitude. This intellectual attitude struck me forcibly when I first climbed with George and Max as a learner. They formed a perfect team, George the more brilliant and with more nervous energy; Max as a fine mountaineer, remarkable for his steadiness and even temper under all conditions.

It was one of the best insights into the character and ability of George Finch, provided by a man who, as a youth, had put his life into the hands of a near stranger not much older than himself, seemingly without question and based on the premise that George's 'individualism was characteristic and to become president was a mark of the confidence and liking of his peers'.

It had been less than ten years since the teenage George Finch had stood atop Mount Canobolas and wondered at the possibilities of climbing snow-capped mountains across the world. Now, at the age of just twenty-two, he was considered among the best in Europe and a mature, if controversial, leader of others.

8.

THE TYRO COMPANION

It would be in early August 1911, a few days after George's twenty-third birthday, that he and Max organised the challenge of the east face of Monte Rosa, the so-called 'Himalayan face of the Alps': an 8000-foot wall, gleaming white and deadly dangerous – just the sort of challenge that inspired the Finch brothers. George was targeting the Marinelli Couloir, a near-vertical passage named after an Italian climber who thirty years before had been killed in an avalanche with two guides attempting the climb George now proposed with Max, John Case and Franzl Obexer, who had accompanied Max on the gruelling Tödi expedition.

George sat chatting over lunch in the Italian village of Macugnaga with a guide named Alessandro Corsi, the only member of the Marinelli climbing party who survived the avalanche of 1881. There was a buzz around the village, the climb attracting attention because it was by far the hardest route to the summit: long, steep and treacherous, its difficulty compounded for the Finch party by the almost constant sound of avalanches across the 10,000-foot-wide wall of rock, ice and snow, fed by recent unseasonal snowfalls that had left an overload warming in the late summer sunshine.

There seemed no escape from the danger of unstable snow, and finding a route around the gaping crevasses created by moving glacial ice seemed impossible, but George was determined to find a way. John Case watched him closely as he talked to Corsi, all the while making rough sketches and notes to plot a pathway through the vertical minefield. George's aim was to minimise their time cutting ice steps up the couloir, which acted like a collecting point and funnel for the avalanches.

Eventually, George decided to climb almost 800 feet straight up to a point above an outcrop of rocks known as the Imseng Rücken, where the most precarious of the giant seracs, or snow columns, could be seen almost swaying, ready to topple. From there, they would cut steps across the wall to the left, away from the immediate danger of avalanches but into the path of ice cliffs and bergschrunds (crevasses formed by glacial ice), which they would have to negotiate to reach the Grenzgipfel, the highest summit on the Italian side of the border and from where they could access Dufourspitze on the Swiss side, at 15,203 feet the highest of the ten summits that make up the massif known as the Pink Mountain.

The only relatively easy part of the equation was the starting point, a hut positioned about halfway up the mountain at the base of the ice wall. The four climbers, watched by half the village as they left the next afternoon, made the climb to the hut by early evening. As the others settled for the night, George spent the last hours of sunlight standing on a ledge inspecting the route he had sketched from the village below, while trying to ignore the steady stream of wet snow that hissed past, accompanied by the occasional boulder and an ice pinnacle that speared down to shatter like glass into a million pieces: 'The whole wall was literally alive with movement,' he would later write.

When darkness fell he retired to the hut, retrieved the thin, evil-smelling communal blankets that had been aired by the others so they might sleep, and ate a meal over the light of a small spirit stove while scouring a scarcely used visitors book that only confirmed the dangers ahead on a climb that balanced attempts with a 'mortality percentage'.

That night George insisted they check the equipment before leaving, laying out the ropes that would connect them in pairs. He would lead the way to cut steps with his pickaxe while tied to John Case. Max would follow linked to Franzl Obexer whose climbing irons, on inspection, were not only missing teeth but did not fit his boots properly. It meant the steps would have to be cut deeper into the ice wall; this would slow them down, increasing their exposure to avalanches. But the alternative, a likely fall by Obexer, would almost certainly be tragic.

They began in the early hours of the following morning under the light of a bright moon when the lower temperatures were more likely to hold together the unstable snow. Just after 1am they stepped onto the couloir to begin a vertical sprint to clear the danger zone before the 'mad rush' of avalanches that would begin as the morning sun toasted the upper reaches.

The sky was clear, the snow crunching satisfactorily beneath their boots. The slope was 46 degrees as they began, the axe only needed occasionally as they raced to reach the Imseng Rücken where the two ropes were joined to link the pairs. George glanced at his watch – 2.35am – just as the moon disappeared behind the ridges high above their heads, forcing them to resort to candle lanterns. They had climbed almost 1600 feet in a heart-pounding ninety minutes, but from that point the slope steepened sharply, the surface rutted ice and scarred from avalanches.

George began cutting as they climbed: three precise, single-handed swings were required to create each hole deep enough to anchor the front pad of their boots. His way was lit by Case who clung close to his ankles and used the handle of his own axe to hang a lantern. Below them, Max was also cutting to deepen his brother's efforts and accommodate Obexer's faulty climbing irons.

The only sound was the chink of the two axes as they worked steadily, the slope steepening to a point where they had to use hand-holds to steady themselves while cutting steps for their toes. It was precarious work in the dark, suddenly made more serious by the rumbling of an avalanche above, thundering its way down the couloir and across the Imseng Rücken where they had been standing only an hour before.

Many years later Case would describe the climb to a friend, detailing how George led the whole way with him standing close below, his hands placed firmly on George's heels to keep them in each ice step as he cut the next. Max and Obexer did likewise immediately below, the foursome moving together like a linked chain.

The friend remarked:

> When I expressed my amazement at this method of
> protection, John smiled and closed his eyes, squinting so as to
> see more clearly in the past, and said: 'Well, I think we'd have
> had a pretty good chance of holding if anyone had slipped.'
> He then opened his eyes again, and in the clear light of the
> present he laughed at the craziness of it.

Dawn was breaking as they reached the field of crevasses and seracs. It was still too dark to extinguish the lanterns and although the gradient had eased, the way was treacherous as they climbed around, over and under the obstacles that appeared to have been placed specifically to deter them as they traversed the wall. Their progress had been slowed by the step-cutting that was now renewed as they cleared the last serac and began climbing upwards once more, aware of the fast-approaching light that would turn the slopes into a tumbling mess of snow, ice and rocks.

The Grenzgipfel was ahead, but the slope between them and safety had once again steepened to a point where George clung to an icy hand-hold while chipping the next step for his boot. It also meant skirting the edge of the Marinelli Couloir once more and then crossing a ridge beneath the Grenzsattel, a snowy pass connecting the Grenzgipfel and their target, the Dufourspitze. After crossing the path they again resorted to step-cutting their way upwards while groups of onlookers, who were descending from the peak after taking the easier route, stood on the Grenzsattel to watch their progress, like sports fans cheering from the grandstand.

At 6.50am they reached a ledge on the lower reaches of the Grenzgipfel, clear of any danger of avalanches for the first time in almost six hours of climbing. It would take another two hours to reach the peak, the snow and ice giving way to jagged rock, icepicks and crampons replaced by the physical strength needed to haul themselves up a series of six-foot-high ridges and overhangs. Max and Obexer had fallen behind, fatigued by the speed and danger of the ice climb, as George, rejuvenated by the relief of having succeeded, increased the pace. At 9.15am, just over eight hours after leaving the hut, he and John Case collapsed in triumph on the warm rocks of the Dufourspitze. They had completed the ascent several hours faster than any climbers before them.

The record didn't last long, although beating it was a hollow achievement. The next day another group bettered their time by a few minutes – but they hadn't cut a single step, instead using the dozens chipped out the previous day by George Finch.

* * *

George Finch's relations with other climbers were not
always harmonious and he was sometimes regarded as being
overbearing and a difficult climbing companion. He was apt to
be critical of the leadership of others but with few exceptions
his relations with really first-class climbers were excellent.
When in 1911 Val Fynn and Ernesto Martini invited us to
join forces with them on the Zmuttgrat it was interesting
to see how George admired and deferred to these more
experienced climbers and to see their respect for his ability.

This was a prophetic observation by John Case because even though
he wrote it many years after the event, he would not have been
aware of the importance to George Finch's career of this meeting
and climb in mid August of 1911, a few days after George, Max,
Case and Obexer had descended from Monte Rosa and sought the
comfort of a hotel room in Zermatt, a village on the Swiss side of
Monte Rosa and in the shadows of another of the most famous
Alpine peaks, the Matterhorn.

The four had barely walked into the foyer of the Monte Rosa
Hotel before they were greeted by Val Fynn and Ernesto Martini,
two of the older members of the AACZ, who were planning to
climb the Matterhorn in a couple of days via the most difficult
route, the north-west ridge known as the Zmutt.

Valère Alfred Fynn, aged in his early forties, was something of
a maverick, always seeking out the toughest climbing routes rather
than following the crowds, and legendary for once spending the
night sitting on sling ropes as he tried to climb the north-east face
of the mighty Finsteraarhorn. Russian-born and Swiss-educated,
he had run a successful electrical engineering firm in London but
was now taking his creative genius to the United States where he
would develop car engines.

He saw something of himself in George Finch, not only in the young man's desire to tackle the most difficult mountain challenges, but in his meticulous approach to climbing which meant that risk could be tempered by care and skill. Their meeting and the subsequent climb up the Matterhorn would be significant events in George Finch's life, although he couldn't know that at the time. Fynn was not only an admired alpinist but a man of considerable influence where it mattered most – among the senior members of the Alpine Club of London where he would spruik the young man's name to great effect.

George readily agreed to the challenge proposed by Fynn. After all, the Matterhorn had always been one of the main targets of the Finch boys given their worship of Edward Whymper, whose 1865 triumph in finally defeating the great mountain (though via a different route to the one proposed by Fynn and Martini) had ended in the tragic death of four of his seven-man party on the descent. George described the mountain with some passion as he sat writing in his diary in the cosy luxury of the hotel lounge the evening before setting out on the climb:

> Perhaps no other mountain in the Alps, or for that matter
> anywhere in the whole world, can make such an appeal to the
> eye as the Matterhorn. This appeal is not merely one of beauty
> and boldness of form, but also of position. The Matterhorn
> has no neighbours in close proximity to invite comparison; it
> stands utterly alone – a great dark rocky pyramid with sides of
> tremendous steepness, and towering up towards the heavens
> from out of a girdle of glistening seracs and snowfields.

The six men camped overnight at the Schönbühl Hut, a three-hour hike from Zermatt, and were ready at 1am on August 12 for the ten-hour climb which began by traversing the Tiefenmatten Glacier that lay at the foot of the Zmutt Ridge itself. The first part of the climb was a relatively easy scramble as they made their way up broken rocks to a point where there was a deep gap, beyond which stood three giant rocky teeth that could be seen from the village below.

Fynn, the man in charge, called a halt for breakfast on virtually the same spot that the British gentleman climber Albert Mummery had sat with his guides in 1879, contemplating the task of defeating the Zmutt Ridge for the first time. And echoing Mummery's experience, the pre-dawn cold cut through the men like a knife, fed by a wind that whistled from the north and swept across the ridge. It was time to move on, roped in two parties – Fynn, Max and Obexer on one rope and George, Martini and Case on the other – as they edged their way past the teeth.

From here the task grew more difficult. Thunderstorms a few days before had turned a thin layer of new snow into a veneer of ice, making the climb treacherous and forcing the party to traverse a gully that ran to one side of the ridge's backbone. The climb there was steeper and lacked the rocks to anchor a belay, but was free of the ice that might cause a fatal slip.

They tried the ridge again but it was a short-lived attempt, as the slope steepened once more and it became impossible to chip hand-holds into the ice-glazed rocks. Fynn placed the Finch brothers as lead men on the two ropes, putting his faith in their skill as ice men as the two groups carefully negotiated the gully wall, so steep in places that those behind could only see the soles of the boots of the men ahead. To make matters worse, they had to remove their gloves and risk frostbite to get sufficient grip in the tiny fissure hand-holds. It was slow and painful work, but Fynn the cheerleader called out encouragement: 'Take your time. Put your hands and feet down as if the Matterhorn belongs to us.'

Eventually they reached the crest of the Zmutt Ridge, the first place in many hours where they could stop and stand and where welcome sunshine was offset by a bitter, stiffening wind. They ate for a second time but again the meal was rushed because of the cold. It was 8am when they began the last section of the climb up the main ridgeline that might have taken two hours in kinder weather conditions. On this day, however, it would take five hours. They were soon forced once again from the ridge, to ascend cutting steps up and across a wide icy slab with a slope of more than 50 degrees to reach what appeared to be an ice-free ridge, a rocky oasis surrounded by snow and ice.

Fynn had now taken the lead of the second group, following in George's carefully carved steps until he reached halfway across the slope where he stopped and called out a change of plan. He was going to head straight up toward the summit, prepared to cut his way through ice and snow to the top rather than risk a possible avalanche set off by rock that had begun to loosen and fall from above. George nodded but kept his group going across the slope for another 100 feet until he was directly beneath the summit, where he changed direction and followed the older man's lead and headed upwards. It took three hours to work their way slowly to a ledge known as Carrel's Corridor, after the Italian climber Jean-Antoine Carrel, who was Edward Whymper's chief rival in the race to ascend the Matterhorn. From the ledge they made their way back to the main ridge and ascended one last section to the Italian summit.

It was 1pm and the climb under Val Fynn's lead and George Finch's ice skills had taken twelve hours. The triumph was celebrated with a hot lunch, a spirit stove hauled from a knapsack and settled on the narrow peak to boil a kettle of snow for cups of hot tea and drunk as if it were the best champagne. Fynn had brought a tinned plum pudding and Martini produced an Italian salami from his bag which, when combined with the Finch brothers' stash of 'good and solid odds and ends' left over from the Monte Rosa climb, was a veritable mountaintop feast.

The weather was closing in as they finished gorging, a dense cloud mass shutting out the sun and blocking the view across the spine of peaks toward Mont Blanc. It was time to begin their descent, this time via the Italian Ridge to the village of Breuil. With a fog closing in, visibility was reduced to a few yards.

Val Fynn once again took command, shepherding the men into two groups, then taking the rear position on one of the ropes while he encouraged George Finch to take the lead and the responsibility of finding a route down. George later reminisced: 'Acting on Fynn's advice to "go to the edge of the drop" I stepped out carefully towards the brink of the huge precipice that falls away towards Italy. Almost at once I saw before me the bleached strands of a stout rope fixed to a strong pin driven into the rocks.'

One rope led to a second, then a third, and onwards, each pegged firmly by previous parties and intended to guide the way for those who would follow. They descended quickly, hoping to beat what appeared to be an imminent storm, until they reached a steep ice slope, the Linceul, which had to be crossed to reconnect with the main ridgeline. Ahead were four other climbers sitting in the snow. George had seen them a few hours before as he peered over the precipice of the summit. The men had been stranded ever since, unable to cross the slope because none of them knew how to cut steps in ice. They had set out that morning without a guide and followed another group up the mountain, but had been left behind on the descent. George cast his mind back to the awful deaths of the German climbers on the Wetterhorn three years before and grimaced.

As the Fynn party watched, one of the men stood to make another attempt, intending to shuffle out onto the slope and trying to cut foot-holds while being roped and held by one of his companions. It was clear to George and the others that the foolhardy attempt was doomed and the man was likely to fall, perhaps taking one or more of his friends with him.

George shelved his annoyance for the moment and, on Val Fynn's orders, moved past the relieved men onto the slope to create a pathway to safety, reassuring them that he would get them down the mountain. Fynn, Max and Obexer, who were on the second rope, then helped the four men follow in George's carved footprints. Once they'd been deposited on safe ground George unleashed a furious verbal assault on the overwhelmed men. They had no right to be on a mountain as difficult as the Matterhorn, he told them, as unprepared and unskilled as they were. Not only had they placed their own lives in danger but put the safety of others at risk and, in George's mind at least, undermined the cause of the guideless climber.

John Case looked on, astounded: 'George's blistering remarks shocked them into life. He was outspoken in his criticisms of those who undertook climbs beyond their ability through failure to judge the difficulties of a climb or knowledge of their own capacity, and of those who followed others and found themselves in trouble.'

But Case also noticed that George's attitude was much more forgiving to those who were simply less skilful or had made a mistake, even experienced a moment of carelessness. When Case had carried the lantern on the Monte Rosa climb a few days before, it had suddenly slipped from the axe handle where he'd been balancing it. He had managed to reach out and catch the lantern, but the awkward movement on an ice wall would have been dangerous if not for George's steadiness. George had paused, the tense moment clear in his mild admonishment: 'Don't do many things like that, man.'

Leaving the relieved but traumatised men behind, the Fynn party set off down the mountain, arriving at the Hörnli Hut at 6.30pm. It was filled with climbers who were preparing for an assault the next morning, and knowing there were limited beds and that the four men behind them would need a bed for the night, Fynn decided they should push on. They finally reached Breuil at 10pm, twenty-one hours after leaving the Schönbühl Hut.

As they sat devouring a huge meal in the dining room of the *Jomein Hotel*, John Case considered another aspect of George Finch. The man was abrupt at times and quick with his opinions, particularly about faults in others, but there was a deference to those he respected, such as Val Fynn, an unhesitating willingness to help others in distress and a desire to encourage those younger than himself: 'He liked to help and train aspiring young climbers and was very patient with them. I realised that on those first climbs I did with him he was giving me systematic training of a varied nature.' It was something of an understatement considering that George Finch had just led him, a novice, safely over two of the highest mountains and most difficult routes in Europe.

Others, particularly the older gentlemen climbers who had felt the lash of George Finch's tongue, often to their faces, for their laziness, regarded his habit of taking young and inexperienced men, such as John Case, Will Sturgess and numerous others, on difficult climbs as dangerous and irresponsible. George was aware of the criticism and reflected on it some years later, mounting a typically spirited defence:

I have more than once been criticised for taking inexperienced people on difficult and what my critics too readily refer to as hazardous climbs. In reply, I would point out that a difficult enterprise is not necessarily a rash one, though it may well be made out so if one embarks upon it without thorough investigation and detailed planning. If, by the simple inclusion of a beginner in the party, the difficult be transformed into the hazardous, the reflection is on the capability of the leader. Also, years of guideless climbing have taught me, inter alia, that in the mountains one must not take one's responsibilities lightly. Furthermore, the inexperience of the beginner, who is physically sound and no coward, is a much less dangerous drawback to the leader of a party than the argumentative embryo-mountaineer who, after three or even fewer brief summer seasons spent in climbing, often only in a secondary capacity, imagines that the mountains hold no more secrets for him. To the experienced climber who feels that there is still something new for him to learn, I would commend the tyro as a companion – for his puzzled, but often fundamental questioning may suggest a new train of thought or throw fresh light upon what seemed but the obvious and commonplace.

Although he did not know it in the summer of 1911, George's easy acceptance of youth and inexperience would be fully tested in the greatest mountaineering challenge of them all – Mount Everest.

PART II

9.

AN ALCHEMY OF AIR

In 1908 a German chemistry professor named Fritz Haber achieved what had been previously thought impossible: synthesising ammonia – a compound of nitrogen and hydrogen – from the atmosphere. The discovery would remain a closely guarded secret for the next two years while Haber and a team of confidants at the Karlsruhe Institute of Technology worked to turn the 'alchemy of air', as it was dubbed, into more than just a tabletop demonstration.

In March 1910, under pressure to patent his discovery, Haber finally let the cat out of the bag during a public lecture titled 'Making Nitrogen Usable'. The impact was immediate, the scientific world stunned but excited by the implications for agriculture and the potential to revolutionise the production of fertiliser, ending the laborious need to infuse it with ammonia extracted from tons of bird droppings scraped from rocky islands off Peru, Mexico and the West Indies.

The discovery would also, by chance, give young George Finch a flying start to his chosen career. The boy who had struggled with high school mathematics and studied French with a Scottish tutor to eradicate an Australian accent had not only topped his class in one of Europe's most prestigious technical colleges but had now been engaged by one of its most senior academics, Georg Bredig, as a research assistant.

Bredig was a former colleague of Fritz Haber and several years before had been at the forefront of research into the development of catalysts to speed up chemical reactions. Haber now turned to his old friend, drawing him into the ammonia research project in the hope that he could work with Haber's commercial partner, the German chemical giant Badische Anilin- und Soda-Fabrik (BASF), to find an improved catalyst to aid the production of ammonia on an industrial scale.

George Finch suddenly found himself at the cutting edge of what would be regarded as one of the great industrial-scientific breakthroughs of the twentieth century, helping to transform Haber's chemical wizardry into a process that still helps to feed one-third of the world's population. It was a role that not only satisfied George's scientific curiosity but also appealed to both the meticulous side of his nature and his love of a challenge.

The minute details of George's research have been lost in time; the number of people who would lay claim to having a role in the breakthrough combined with his own natural modesty left only the result which saw a significant, if incremental, improvement in the efficiency of iron as a catalyst. His role was clearly of some importance, though, because it brought him to the attention of the BASF management.

The company, until then a manufacturer of industrial dyes, was building its first fertiliser plant in Oppau, a suburb of the southern German city of Ludwigshafen, and promptly hired the young scientist as an assistant manager with responsibility for overseeing the industrial implementation of his own research work. For the next year he worked alongside Carl Bosch, the company's chief scientist, who would be credited with the practical transformation of Haber's discovery and would, like Haber, receive the Nobel Prize in Chemistry.

George Finch's appointment at the BASF factory would be a triumphant beginning to his career, but was not without its problems. He sensed almost immediately an ill feeling toward him by some of the plant staff, unhappy perhaps that an outsider, a foreigner, had been hired over the top of them. He suspected there might be trouble ahead and was proved right one night when he discovered a foreman using a spanner to adjust the pressure in a valve in a way that would have affected the catalytic process.

Furious, he accused the man of sabotage and threatened to report him to the management. The confrontation then turned into a struggle as George tried to wrestle the spanner from the foreman, eventually disarming him and readjusting the valve before chasing the man down and 'giving him a blow that he would remember for a few days'. This was what he recounted to a relative who would later write about the incident as a glowing example of George's unyielding character and his capacity and willingness to stand up for himself in tight situations: 'Thereafter, George told me, he received excellent co-operation but the completion of his mission was most welcome.'

A stint as a researcher at the University of Geneva followed but, by October 1912 and the outbreak of the First Balkan War, mainland Europe was becoming a decidedly uncomfortable place. Military and political alliances were firming – Italy alongside Germany; Britain standing by France – and the threat of a broader conflict began to loom large.

There were many who played down the threat of war but George Finch was convinced it was just a matter of time, given the childish madness of Kaiser Wilhelm II. The disharmony inside the BASF plant only served to underline the growing schism in Europe which meant that he, as an 'Englishman' and no longer living in the political sanctuary of Switzerland, was on the wrong side of the Channel.

London beckoned.

* * *

Fritz Haber's triumphant discovery was a great example of the success of European technical colleges and their expectation that academic staff would not only teach but play an important role in research and pushing the boundaries of science for industrial purposes. Britain, by contrast, had not yet learned that lesson and in the first years of the twentieth century found itself in the midst of a tortured debate in political and educational circles about the need to respond to the evolving demands of industry by boosting practical education in the fields of technical and applied science.

The process of change was compromised by powerful, curmudgeonly establishment voices who could not bear the notion that England, glorious England, with its scientific legacy of Faraday, Newton and Darwin and the like, had fallen behind the Continental types of mainland Europe or, heaven forbid, the United States of America. There were even some in the House of Commons who were dismissive of the idea of improving education for the masses, arguing that Britain should stick to the tried and true system of industrial apprenticeships governed by the great trade guilds that had flourished since mediaeval times.

Eventually, even the most strident opponents of change could not dismiss the groundswell of complaints – not to mention offers of commercial funding – from disillusioned London manufacturers who could not find qualified staff. Instead, they watched promising English graduates choose to study and begin their careers in the classrooms and laboratories of Berlin, Paris and Zürich.

Technical education was a relatively new concept in Britain, where the workforce largely learned skills on the job, but it had become difficult to ignore the success of technical colleges such as the Technische Hochschule Charlottenburg in Berlin and George Finch's alma mater, the Eidgenössische Technische Hochschule, Zürich, as well as American schools such as the Massachusetts Institute of Technology and Columbia University, where staff were increasingly playing the dual role of teachers and researchers. This contrasted sharply with Britain, where science remained essentially a study of pure theory, and colleges concentrated on training science teachers, pushing academic research into the background to the point where it was 'inadequate to the needs of the Empire', as one report commissioned by the Department of Education concluded.

It was only when the bickering ended, and those academics and politicians with reputations to protect were finally convinced that their legacies would remain untarnished, that government approval was given to entertain a more pragmatic approach to science. The Imperial College London was opened in 1907, accommodated within the South Kensington grounds already established by the Royal College of Science, Royal School of Mines and Central Technical College. It would be staffed 'by men of the first rank of their profession' and include subjects ranging from civil, electrical and mechanical engineering to mines and metallurgy and naval architecture. Courses in chemical technology would be added six years later. Even the name of the new college was important, to distinguish the prestige of the existing 'Royal' colleges from the practical but less glamorous contributions to the national economy of the new 'Imperial' school.

The college would be at the forefront of change within the nation's tertiary education milieu, its senior staff no longer viewing academic life as one of 'disinterested scholarship' but willing to engage and respond to the needs of government, commerce, manufacturing and even the military.

It was at this watershed moment, when the untapped mysteries of science met the industrial demands of a new century, that George Finch would find his intellectual home, a world as far from the extreme physical environment of an Alpine ascent as he could get, his ropes and axes, sailcloth jackets and nailed boots replaced by Bunsen burners and tweezers, white lab coats and soft leather shoes.

* * *

It would be overstating George Finch's arrival in London in 1912 to call it a 'return', given that his visit as a teenager had been fleeting. He was now aged twenty-four, an Australian-born and European-educated man who conversed mostly in German, wore his hair long when in the mountains and, by reputation, was prone to challenging conventional thinking and overbearing authority, often in face-to-face confrontations. It was too late for him to go back to Sydney; the lure of the mountains of Europe and the excitement of his new world of science were too great to contemplate finding a place in his childhood home even though he was, and would remain for many years, an outsider searching for an identity of his own.

At least London offered opportunity. There was plenty of work for a chemist as England geared up toward a possible confrontation with Germany. George was in no hurry but was quickly offered a job as a research chemist with the Royal Arsenal at Woolwich under Sir Robert Robertson, the director of explosives research and later the head of the Government Chemical Laboratory. Again, it would be a short tenure for George – four months – although not because of an ill fit so much as an opportunity he could not resist.

In July 1913 he applied to join the staff at the Imperial College as part of its expansion into chemical technology. George would sign on as a demonstrator in the Fuel and Refractory Fuels section, running a course on explosives for the princely sum of £150 per year. Although the pay was significantly less than what he might earn in the commercial world, it seemed that George had already made up his mind that the freedom to explore the challenges of science provided by the academic world was more important than the financial rewards offered by private enterprise.

The pay might have been meagre, equivalent to £15,000 nowadays, but when added to the annual stipend paid by the family investment in Russian railways it would ensure he had few money worries. It was the financial fillip he needed to pay for his Alpine exploits.

* * *

Often it is a quirk of fate that sometimes creates an opportunity. In George Finch's case, fate delivered a professional relationship that would help define the second half of his life. But it might never have happened.

George Finch's new boss, Professor William Arthur Bone, had bought a ticket to sail on the maiden voyage of the SS *Titanic* to New York in April 1912 but cancelled at the last minute because his travelling companion had fallen ill. At the time, the senior academic at Leeds University had been travelling to London once a week to give a lecture on chemical technology as part of the mainstream chemistry course at the Imperial College. It was a natural area for expansion and in 1913 he was asked to join the staff permanently and create a new department.

George Finch would be one of his first appointments. Bone interviewed him in mid July and ordered him to return one month later at 10am. Detecting the importance of following the order exactly, George was outside Bone's door at exactly 10am on the appointed day, but there was no answer to his smart rap so he wandered the grounds for an hour, knocking again at 11am and then at noon when the door finally opened and Bone appeared, an angry look on his face.

'And who may you be?' he demanded.

'I'm George Finch, your new staff member,' George replied, confused.

'Didn't I tell you to be here at ten o'clock,' Bone replied, his face reddening. 'It's now noon.'

George might have cowered before the onslaught. Instead he bristled at the injustice: 'Not only was I here at ten o'clock but I also knocked at eleven and now twelve.'

Bone glared, silent for a moment, and then burst into laughter: 'Come in, come in, young man. Thank heaven for someone who can stand up for himself.'

It would be the first of many 'sword-crossings', as Finch would later write, and the beginning of a professional relationship, mutual respect and friendship that was as important as any in his life. William Bone was cantankerous and eccentric, but brilliant and fastidious when it came to pursuing his work, not unlike George Finch who was keenly aware of Bone's personal shortcomings and argued passionately that they were outweighed by his integrity.

Over time, Bone's abrasiveness undoubtedly also helped George to realise and curb his own tendency to rub people up the wrong way, although he would always maintain a reserve and an air of authority that was felt by those around him, students and colleagues alike.

Typical of Bone's decisions was his insistence, when the chemical technology buildings were being constructed on the college grounds, that they be spare and functional, almost shed-like, because he believed the money would be better spent on what was being done by staff and students inside them than on architectural flourishes. The buildings would stand at the back of the college grounds in 'ugly isolation', as one former student would remark when Bone retired in 1936; a collection of huts that had an air of mystery and foreboding and which sometimes erupted in unexplained explosions. The teachers to be found inside were often as eccentric in their own ways as the head of the department.

When Bone died in 1938 it was George Finch who wrote his obituary for the Royal Society, reflecting many of his own feelings when he summed up his mentor's career:

> To create something new is the born artist's real desire
> whether he be a poet, painter, musician or scientist and into
> the creation of a new department of fuel technology at the
> Imperial College, Bone threw himself with whole-hearted
> vigour. Whither his urge for self-expression bore him the
> years have amply shown. Under his inspired leadership rose a
> research school of worldwide renown.

George Finch would be a central component of that success.

10.

THE UPSTART

The Field magazine was founded in 1853 with the objective of being an influential journal for the rising upper-middle class of Victorian England, a 'sporting, farming, and a sort of high-life-in-London paper with a summary of all that is going on', as it was described by its founder, the sports writer and novelist-cum-publisher Robert Smith Surtees.

Mountaineering featured strongly in its pages, particularly during the second half of the nineteenth century as the peaks of the European Alps were gradually conquered by moneyed English gentlemen climbers who were the natural readership of the magazine and enjoyed reading of each other's triumphs, invariably guided though they were.

But times were changing and as the summer climbing season of 1913 approached, the magazine editors decided to ask George Finch, one of the most prominent of Europe's young alpinists, to write an opinion piece about the new wave of mountaineers who were dismissing the wisdom of their elders and assailing dangerous peaks without guides. The practice had provoked a hostile response from many of the establishment climbers who accused the young climbers of being careless and suicidal, even wicked and immoral.

George did not mince his words in the article, published in the middle of June, lambasting the 'intolerant exclusiveness of older men' and ridiculing their climbing as 'walking uphill':

> A man who climbs consistently with guides may be a great
> mountaineer but he need be nothing more than a good walker
> to 'climb' any peak in the Alps. The man who has to depend
> on his own skill, strength and nerve must have the craft at his
> finger-ends. The guided mountaineer need only follow patiently
> in the footsteps of a guide. He may and often does climb for years
> without the power to lead up easy rocks, to cut steps in ice, or find
> a route up an easy snow route. In the early days mountaineering,
> because of its expense, was almost exclusively the luxury of
> men who had made a position in life. It was controlled by men
> to whom years had brought prudence, men who looked with
> suspicion on enterprise beyond traditional limits.

George had not finished, writing a blistering critique of the qualifications for membership of the august Alpine Club on Savile Row, dismissing them as 'a list which proves nothing more than a possession of a good wind and a long purse'. By contrast he cited clubs like the Academic Alpine Club Zürich, from which he had stepped down as president but remained a member, that refused admission unless the applicants had proven themselves able to 'lead up first class peaks'. European clubs, he added acidly, used funds to build mountain huts and secure cheap railway tickets for climbers rather than providing libraries, plush armchairs and wait staff.

> It is no longer the monopoly of rich Englishmen. The younger
> men are taking up the sport and gradually coming to the
> front. The development of guideless climbing has brought

the Alps within reach of young men with limited means. For good or evil, guideless parties composed of young Englishmen are becoming more and more common. The attitude of the older climbers is changing. The spirit that saw the Alps a preserve for moneyed and middle-aged Englishmen is dead.

Although his name did not appear as the author of the article, it was clear that George Finch was the young upstart responsible. Its publication would be met with stony silence from the establishment, but their memories were long and George would pay a price for his impertinence. The only saving grace, in the eyes of 'those moneyed and middle-aged Englishmen' was an oblique reference in the penultimate sentence to two unnamed, senior English mountaineering figures: 'Many young climbers owe their introduction to the sport to a great Cambridge mountaineer and good work either on the mountainside or in the written record of exploration never fails to find generous recognition from those who now control the *Alpine Journal*.'

Geoffrey Winthrop Young was the great Cambridge mountaineer and Percy Farrar the editor of the *Alpine Journal*, mouthpiece of the Alpine Club of which Farrar would become president. Both men would prove invaluable allies for George Finch some years later when the now silent but clearly angry establishment voices attempted to thwart his mountaineering career.

* * *

Even though the Alps had been traversed by men with serious intent for more than half a century and peaks of any significance had been climbed and climbed again, there were still challenges that remained unconquered: routes mainly, formidable faces of formidable mountains that dared men to try to ascend, spider-like, to their summits. Some accepted the dare and most failed, even falling to their deaths. Most would choose an alternative, safer route, preferring the thrill of reaching the top to the fear and thrill of climbing what appeared to be impossible.

George Finch was firmly in the group intent on seeking out the more difficult, and therefore lonely, routes rather than following the throng up well-worn paths and camping in overcrowded huts like the Grünhorn and Fridolin. He dreaded having to listen to what he regarded as the inane conversations of the types who had incurred the wrath of his slashing pen in *The Field* article; men intent on 'pouring unstinted abuse upon those who dared indulge in the new form of [guideless] mountaineering'.

In September 1913, during a final summer climb before beginning his new job at the Imperial College, George and his friend Guy Forster went searching for one of these impossible routes. George had known Forster, the son of a well-to-do Wiltshire family, since they were both students in Zürich. They were the same age and despite their different backgrounds had quickly become firm friends, bonded by similar life experiences, including having eccentric mothers, although it took some years for George to persuade Forster to join him on a climb.

Forster was now an enthusiastic convert and had been an almost frenetic climber over the springs and summers of 1912 and 1913. He and George had planned to climb in the Mont Blanc range, but heavy snowfalls had made it impossible so they switched their attention to the northern end of the main Alps chain and a mountain named Bifertenstock, after the mighty glacier which separated it from one of George's favourite peaks, the Tödi.

The mountain itself was not particularly high, at 11,217 feet barely within the highest two hundred Alpine peaks, and had been conquered from the south, but the western ridge, so far, had resisted any attempt to climb it. In fact, there had been no attempt for more than three decades as the challenge drifted from view, perhaps because the mountain was at the northern extremity of the spine.

It was a day's climb up the relatively easy first half of the mountain. Now, as he and Forster stood at the base of the ridge assessing the bleak wall, George was awestruck, later writing that it looked as if it had been fashioned for the Titans:

> … belted, as it were, from head to foot with girdle upon girdle
> of bronze-coloured rock besprinkled with the crystal of snow
> and ice, unique not only in its appearance but in that west
> ridge, which rears itself up … towards the summit in a series
> of huge, precipitous, even overhanging buttresses. It had never
> suffered the imprint of human foot.

The reason George believed that he and Forster might stand a chance of scaling the fortress-like ridge was the recent introduction of a simple tool that would revolutionise mountain climbing. The legendary Tyrolean mountain guide and blacksmith Hans Fiechtl had developed the piton, a metal spike that could be driven into a seam or crack of a sheer rockface to anchor a rope. Combined with a metal loop that could be clipped to the piton called a carabiner, it made it possible to climb the previously impossible.

It was an innovation that embodied George's belief that progress and change should be embraced, including in the form of new and better equipment that enabled climbers to tackle new challenges rather than tread the same, worn path. He and Max had previously felt the wrath of older climbers when they dared try something new, like in the summer of 1911 when George began experimenting with a shorter axe handle to make step-cutting easier using only one hand. The next year he and Max began using silk and cotton ropes that were lighter and yet stronger than traditional hemp. Most controversial of all was the introduction of the piton, which helped climbers pin themselves to sheer rockfaces. George would sometimes return from a climb chanting loudly, 'Blessed be the piton,' in defiance of older disapproving onlookers.

George and Forster would tackle the Bifertenstock wall in two phases on separate days. The first day was devoted to finding a route up the first of the buttresses, a giddy precipice that fell away more than 3000 feet to the glacier below. Wearing rope-soled canvas shoes rather than heavy boots, George had no choice but to inch his way onto the face while Forster slowly played out a rope he hoped would hold if his companion slipped on the exposed rocks.

George had edged out almost thirty feet before he spied a narrow fissure above his head, a chimney through which he might be able to squeeze to begin moving upwards. It was an agonising, inch-by-inch climb, the rope around his chest slackening slightly as he gasped from the effort, but he eventually reached another ledge less than a foot wide on which he balanced while Forster made his way up from below.

The ledge on which he stood with his shoulders flat to the rockface was so tiny that at the moment his companion reached out to grab it and haul himself up, George was forced to start climbing up a second chimney. It meant they were now defenceless: if one slipped, they would both fall to their deaths. With no respite and no way back to the bottom of the ridge, George was struggling physically.

It was here that the piton was invaluable. Noticing a seam in the otherwise impregnable wall, George wedged himself into a gap and, using a rock, tapped the steel peg into the crack, threading the heavy rope through the carabiner and testing the anchor point with a sharp tug before putting his full weight on the rope. It held, and they were safe as he contemplated the next move.

But their difficulties were far from over as George continued to use pitons to secure their path, roping and unroping as he moved slowly up the now overhanging wall. As he gained another ledge, George attempted to clear the ground beneath his feet only for the surface to crumble and fall, not only leaving him balanced precariously on the shattered remains but causing the rock fragments to strike Forster, who was climbing directly below. The force knocked the Englishman from his hold on the cliff face and he swung helplessly in space. George had to summon all his strength to hold the rope, but the pitons stayed fast and prevented them both from falling.

The gash in Forster's head was still pumping out blood, spattering his coat and drenching his thick handlebar moustache, when they finally reached the lip of the first buttress, hauling themselves to safety to stand and howl like wolves in triumph. The duo eventually retreated down the face, leaving the path to the top, which they would complete three days later, now easily accessible, thanks to the trail of pitons that had already saved their lives.

* * *

By Easter 1914 George had settled comfortably into academic life but couldn't resist another climbing stint in Switzerland. On April 9 he boarded a train at Charing Cross bound for Zürich where Max was finishing his studies at ETH before following his brother's lead and heading for London.

George hadn't warned Max that he was coming, the decision an impetuous one made in a moment of exuberance and affection. His arrival the next day was a pleasant surprise to his younger brother and a welcome distraction from study. Max needed little persuasion to close his books and within a few hours they had packed and left for a week's skiing across the mid peaks of the Bernese Oberland.

They had been here before, back in 1908, then aged nineteen and sixteen, just as they had begun to break free of the shackles imposed by their worried mother, and had made their first major cross-country winter ski trip through the glacier regions. It had been a thrilling adventure, often beneath cloudless skies that seemed to shimmer and change in colour as they lay on their backs, relaxing after a climb, and let their eyes roam from the yellowish-green near the horizon to the pale blue that thickened to a dense hue overhead.

But there were also dangers in the Oberland, like the fish-shaped clouds that appeared in the early afternoon and warned of gusting winds that could quickly turn into what George would describe as the 'ruthless, deadly force of the elements let loose in winter' that whipped and shredded and blasted everything into submission. And it wasn't just the ever-changing weather that posed problems, but surface perils like snow shields, avalanches and especially crevasses concealed beneath the winter snowfall, invisible to all but the most experienced eye that could discern the slight hollowing as the snow compacted and sagged above the hidden chasm.

It was on this first trip that George and Max had experienced the terror of a hidden winter crevasse. In the relative calm of an afternoon, a friend with whom they were climbing suddenly disappeared as a snow bridge collapsed beneath his skis. George, skiing behind, was almost catapulted into the giant crevasse which had opened up beneath their feet. The trapped man swung helplessly, the rope attached to the three men his only lifeline. It had taken two hours for George and Max to haul him free of this frigid potential grave.

Worse had followed a few days later when George and Max were on their way back down from the mountains. The brothers were on their own, having ignored the advice of other climbers who worried about an approaching storm and suggested they wait it out in an overcrowded mountain hut. Bravado prevailed and the duo waved goodbye and skied off confidently into the grey mist.

All had gone well at first and they made good time until the storm hit, even then only slowing rather than stopping, intent as they were to be proved right. A few hours later, having battled through the worst of the weather and with safety in sight, George became buried in an avalanche.

It had come without warning, in a rush of wind from above as they passed beneath the foot of the mighty Eiger. Max, skiing behind, watched in horror as his brother disappeared in a cloud of snow dust, the rope that connected them the only indication of where he might be lying beneath the deluge. Thankfully, George had the presence of mind to keep his arms above his head and move them in a swimming motion as if he was back in Sydney Harbour, creating an air pocket that gave Max the time to find his brother and dig him out. But it had been a close call and left them both shaken.

Now they were returning six years later as seasoned, even celebrated, alpinists, aged just twenty-five and twenty-two respectively, with a trust in each other that was as unbreakable as it was instinctive. This trip was not a meticulously planned expedition with a goal of conquering a series of difficult summits but was a fun excursion, driven by George's sudden desire to enjoy the company of his younger brother, probably underpinned by a growing belief that war was inevitable and the future was too difficult to predict.

They based themselves in the Konkordia Hut set above a sea of glacial ice. They would explore in a different direction each day, skiing 'in a sheer riot of exhilaration down toward the Jungfraujoch', 'humbly pottering across the Konkordia Platz' and 'whizzing down on the Aletsch Glacier'.

There were climbs too, summits like the Weissnollen, Ebnefluh and the Fiescherhorn which they explored with ease, the perfect climbing conditions making most of it child's play. They might as well have been climbing in midsummer, the rocks so warm they lay basking for hours, and yet there was no green amid the perpetual snow and ice of the Oberland. Neither was there any sign of humanity (save the hut) to spoil the silence, the nearest village at least six hours away.

They revelled in their week of solitude, so much so that George did not even use his camera, a Folding Pocket Kodak No. 3 which he'd bought in the summer of 1911 when they had taken the American John Case to the top of the Matterhorn and climbed with Val Fynn. He would assiduously document most other trips he made, capturing the contrast between the glorious crystal serenity and the shuddering violence of avalanches cascading down 2000-foot cliffs.

In the library of negatives that he would leave behind there are scenes of soaring majesty and the terror of gale force winds threatening to tear men from snowy ledges and toss them to their deaths. Some show men improbably balanced on sheer rockfaces while others record tense moments as they prod with axe handles to test for hidden crevasses. Others fix on the grubby, grinning faces of friends triumphant atop stone spires and there is even a shot of Guy Forster, blood-spattered but defiant, after the rock fall on the Bifertenstock.

But the brothers' audacity and skill is perhaps best captured in a triptych of images taken at the end of the 1911 summer. The brothers were descending Mont Blanc, at ease with the hard work done for the day. They reached a wide saddle known as Col Maudit where they paused, studying the possible routes and deciding to tackle a steep but short ice slope which appeared to lead directly to a gentle snowfield below. George began cutting steps but soon realised there was another obstacle in their path that had been hidden from above – a large crevasse gaped between them and the snowfield, with no obvious way across.

It was too late to climb back up and find an alternative. The gap in front of them was about 16 feet across at its narrowest point and could be negotiated if they could find a way to secure a rope and lower themselves past the hole. But there were no rocks around to which they could belay a rope and the ice was too packed to bury an axe handle and create an anchor point. The skies were darkening quickly and there seemed to be no option other than to leap and hope the steep angle would be enough to carry them across the gap, as George later recalled:

> Leaving my axe and climbing irons with Max I screwed up my courage and leapt wildly out into space, to strike with my feet into the deep, soft snow below the bergschrund with such force that I was almost submerged and snow found its way into my clothing in a most disconcerting fashion. Then came Max's turn. He first threw down the axes, climbing irons and other paraphernalia. Then, while I trained the camera on him, he jumped and landed with such a thud that he likewise was almost buried in the powdery snow. After a rest and a meal to soothe our shattered nerves, we gathered up our belongings and commenced stamping down towards Mont Blanc de Tacul.

George's description was typically understated but the photos still exist more than a century later and show not only the drama of the moment but also the skill of George as a photographer. The first of the images is of Max, head down and pensive, ropes hanging uselessly by his side as he considers the jump that his brother has just made successfully. The third shows the relief on his face; he's wedged chest-deep in snow at the base of the crevasse, but alive.

But it is the middle photo that is the most stunning, the blurred but distinct image of Max in mid-air, arms outstretched as he plunges down a slope close to 70 degrees, the Alpine spine of Switzerland stretching into the distance behind him. It would have been difficult enough to capture with a modern camera let alone with the foldout bellows model George carried in a coat pocket while balanced on an icy slope.

There is a difference between the photography of mountains and mountain photography, he would write some years later. Photography of mountains is taken by those who see them from afar – from roads and trains, valleys and pathways – which means the photograph itself is the chief object. Mountain photography, by contrast, is incidental to the main activity – climbing mountains.

Photos did, however, keep memories 'fresh and true for all time, enabling us to retain a faithful picture of the many striking incidents, the wonderful surroundings and the fellow actors who have played with us in the great game'.

By *us* George probably meant *I*, although he might have meant the Brothers Finch. They certainly felt almost inseparable during the week on the glaciers of the Oberland where the camera was not needed to record a wonderful sibling relationship, a friendship and a bond created by experience that George could not have envisaged at the top of Mount Canobolas. George would indeed describe the week with Max as glorious, but when he looked back on it in later years it must have been with sadness, because they would never climb together again.

11.

A JILTED HERO

As a young child Alicia Gladys Fisher was nicknamed Betty, most probably because her mother was named Alicia too. Whatever the reason, the name Betty would be a constant in a long life riddled with numerous identity crises.

Betty Fisher's father, Frederick, was a barrister from a wealthy Manchester family who took his wife and daughter south soon after Betty was born in 1893, partly for health reasons but also to pursue better career opportunities. The Fishers settled in the pretty seaside town of Margate, and six years later little Alicia was belatedly christened in the local church. Despite the splashing of holy water she remained Betty. By 1901, the family was living the well-to-do life with two maids in a house a few streets back from the beach.

But life can change suddenly and with far-reaching consequences. The household was torn apart just two years later when the marriage of Frederick and Alicia Fisher ended. Betty would tell people that her father had died suddenly, but official records suggest that he was very much alive, and that the couple had separated. Either way, the family was split up, the house sold, the servants dismissed and Betty, then aged almost ten, was farmed out to be raised by relatives while her parents went their separate ways. There were no divorce proceedings so custody was never discussed. Instead, Betty was abandoned.

Frederick moved back north and died aged fifty. His estranged wife wandered, searching for a new life and never settling for long enough to establish a secure home for her daughter, whom she saw rarely. Once doted-upon, Betty Fisher was now alone, unwanted as she recalled bitterly in later years, with the most influential family member being an uncle named Bill, married to a woman whose name she had forgotten: 'I never really had a home as a child. My father died when I was nine, my mother married again and I was brought up by an uncle.'

After Frederick Fisher's death, Alicia quickly remarried and in 1911 reappeared with her new husband, a stockbroker named Conran Smith, to reclaim her now seventeen-year-old daughter. By early April the trio was living in the village of Limpsfield on the southern outskirts of London. But the reunion with her mother lasted only long enough for Betty to be sent away even further, this time to Paris where she spent a year with a French family to be 'finished'.

Betty dreamed of being an actress, inspired as an impressionable teenager when she accompanied her uncle to an opening night performance at a West End theatre. She pored over magazines featuring actors and actresses, dreaming of a glamorous life on the stage and it all seemed possible when she met a theatre agent one night at a party who invited her to audition. The next day she headed off down the street in her best dress only to be stopped by Uncle Bill who was having none of it. Little did she know that her own son would one day achieve what she could only dream of.

It was not surprising then that Betty Fisher, the young adult, was always seeking the attention and affection she had lost so early in life and so desperately craved. If she could not be an actress then she could still behave as she thought one would behave, batting her eyelashes and coquettishly tossing her pretty mane of ash-blonde hair. She was constantly surrounded by men who couldn't see, or more likely didn't care, that hers was a mask to hide uncertainties and an emotional fragility. When war was declared in August 1914, the mask became permanently fixed.

'I was living on the Isle of Wight and at an age when you go to a lot of dances,' she recalled in 1977, aged eighty-four. 'I had lived a sheltered life and had no idea or thought about anything outside my limited, shallow circle. Suddenly the war came and everything changed radically forever. At first we thought it would all be over by Christmas but in 1915 men were dying by the thousands. You do mad things, and my first marriage was the sort of thing a young girl of my background and temperament did. No one knew what was going to happen and we all went mad. Boys were going off to the Front and they were dead within a week.'

* * *

It was very unlike George Finch to be rash, but these were different times. He had barely cemented his place on the staff at the Imperial College when the world was upended by the assassination of the heir to the throne of Austria–Hungary, Archduke Franz Ferdinand. Britain entered the war on August 4 – George's twenty-sixth birthday.

He resumed teaching at the Imperial College in early September after the summer break, but felt uncomfortable sitting on the sidelines. If there was one area where he and William Bone differed in their views it was the subject of war. Bone was a pacifist, only willing to participate in research on behalf of the military on two conditions: that his students and staff were excused from active service as their work was of national significance, and that they not be involved in any research work associated with poisonous gas.

George Finch felt otherwise about the need to fight and in late September 1914, along with five of his students, he applied for a temporary commission. The enlistment papers described the 26-year-old as 'pure European' and living at the Royal College of Science in West Kensington. They noted his preferences to be in either the cavalry or an artillery unit, but he would eventually serve on the frontline in neither. An accompanying medical report was brief and positive – six feet tall, of medium build, with good hearing, vision and teeth. The final conclusion – 'fit' – was something of an understatement.

Second Lieutenant Finch was assigned to the Royal Field Artillery and spent the next few months as a riding instructor at Woolwich before being sent to Portsmouth. George hated both places and by January 1915 was bored and frustrated, stuck in barracks and wanting desperately to either see some action or, more importantly, for the war to be over so he could return to the spartan laboratories of the Imperial College and his climbing holidays in the mountains of Europe.

It was at an officers' dance some time in the spring of 1915 that George Finch met Betty Fisher. It was the first indication that he had an interest in anything beyond outdoor adventure or chemistry, let alone in the fairer sex, but he was obviously smitten. Years later Betty was still effusive about George, describing him as 'a remarkably handsome man, brilliant, tough and exceptionally brave', although even in the first flush of love she'd noticed there was something distant about him – 'indifferent to comfort', as she put it.

Despite their obvious differences, George and Betty quickly fell for one another and were married in a rush at the Registry Office in Portsmouth on June 16, 1915. The union, like many of the time, was a hasty, ill-considered product of war and almost certainly doomed. A century later the marriage certificate remains a revealing document about their mindset and misgivings: there's Betty's longing for the late barrister father whom she listed as being alive and a 'man of independent means' and George's frustrations and irreverent sense of humour, giving his address as 'No Man's Land, Fort Spithead', in rebellious reference to the historic floating seaports moored off the coast of Portsmouth.

Still, he was respectful enough to write to his father, Charles, about the marriage, but only after he and Betty had returned from the honeymoon. He had very little to say about his new bride:

> My dear father,
>
> I have some quite startling news for you – I was married last week quietly by special licence to Miss Fisher to whom I have been engaged but a comparatively short time. We spent our honeymoon – three days was all I could get – in London. My wife is staying at Southsea [a suburb of Portsmouth] and will remain there until I get my marching orders, which I hope will not be long now.

* * *

Little remains of George Finch's war records. Like the records of so many men who served in the Great War, the handwritten file which detailed his service was destroyed during a German bombing raid over London during World War II. But one thin file survived, an intriguing collection of documents tucked away in a manila folder at the National Archives in Kew, among them his pink enlistment papers and the green notice issued on the day in May 1919, almost five years later, when he was demobbed. But the surviving document of most interest is a copy of the letter he wrote to Marcel Kurz, his climbing friend from ETH days, on January 9,

1915. In it George describes his frustrations at being in Portsmouth in the damp cold of an English winter:

> Dear Marcel,
>
> Many thanks for your welcome card [thanks also to the fool of a censor who let it pass!]. Lord! What a dull life in this godforsaken hole, and I've got to stay here till the spring. The powers that be imagine that I can't take the cold in France. At the end of March I shall probably go across with a 9.2 inch Haubtize – at present however the beastly thing is not yet ready. Just think, I have not seen snow this whole winter. Heaven knows when I shall see it again. Next summer will certainly be no good. Last week I had two days' leave. Of course I rushed straight to London, saw Farrar [and] Max too, who by the way looks jolly well and will soon be over there. In the nights I raced about like mad & danced in all the nightclubs and now I am back again as dull as usual. I have been promoted and have my second star as a Lieutenant. I caught a spy [an Englishman who turned out to be an awful fool and not at all pleasant], and I fired upon two disobedient steamers – that is the sum total of my activities on Long Curtain battery. How is the AACZ? Remember me to everybody – Theo, Jeanne, Kalamer, Egger, Miescher, Heller & Phuty [I should like a letter from him]. And how is Mantel, and where?
>
> Love and good luck to you and the AACZ.
> Yours
> Geo Finch Lt. RGA

The letter was not posted to Kurz, at least not initially. It was stopped by army censors at the Portsmouth base who were shocked first by the fact that George had written it not in English but in German and, secondly, that he had discussed weapons. (The *haubtize* was a howitzer, a short-barrelled cross between a gun and a mortar.) There are several memos on the file that reveal the concern his superiors felt about what was an innocent letter, penned for a Swiss man who spoke German by a friend who had studied at tertiary level for three years in the language. Instead it was read as a possible missive written by a double agent.

The first memo was written by a senior officer at Portsmouth who wanted the letter translated into English. A second memo was written by a 'concerned' officer further up the chain of command: 'The writer knows German unusually well. Attached is a copy of the letter. Perhaps the War Office should see the letter.' By January 21 the translation was on the desk of the Officer Commanding-in-Chief of Southern Command, based in Salisbury. Finch's letter had been marked with red lines drawn under phrases that caused concern: the howitzer, his criticism of the censors, 'my activities on Long Curtain Battery' (part of Portsmouth's sea defence system) and references to the AACZ (the Academic Alpine Club of Zürich).

It was here that common sense finally prevailed and the investigation was dropped. George was cleared and the letter sent to Marcel Kurz. It reveals much about the character of George Ingle Finch, as he now referred to himself more often than not to distinguish himself from other branches of the family, including his flippant disdain for officialdom. And George's downplaying of having captured a spy was typical of his pragmatic personality as well as demonstrating a genuine modesty, just as his description of the howitzer as *beastly* demonstrated his disdain for violence. Mostly, the letter highlighted his love of the mountains and his respect and affection for his climbing colleagues, contradicting those who would claim that he had difficulty making and keeping friends.

* * *

George had installed his new bride in a small house at Southsea, not far from the Portsmouth barracks, and waited impatiently. He had expected to be in France by March but it would be late November, sixteen months into the conflict, before he got his orders and embarked, not for Europe, but the Middle East. By the time George left England there were already signs of strain in his relationship with Betty. She was used to the attention of men and found it hard to give up what she called 'the feeling of euphoria and living in the moment, the gaiety before the international storm'. Her husband was simply not interested in what she called her 'social swing', meaning her circle of friends and their frivolity.

There had been tension even on their brief honeymoon during which George accused his bride of 'flirting rather heavily with other men', something he did not tell his father. Betty couldn't deny it – after all, it was her habit – instead spitting back angrily with taunts that she had married him for his money and position. Distraught and realising that he had made a mistake, George had spent the next few months trying to engender in Betty what he would later call 'something akin to loyalty'. She made promises, but even as he left for the Front, perhaps never to return, George remained unconvinced of his wife's constancy and feared the worst.

The one saving grace, he thought, was that Phyllis, the wife of his friend Major Fred Powys Sketchley, would be moving into the house with her two children while her own husband was away, fighting at Gallipoli. Betty would have the company of a woman she liked and might be forced to behave herself. After all, Phyllis and her sister Molly Campbell had been witnesses at their wedding six months earlier.

Instead, he had inadvertently let a fox into the hen house, or at least someone to open the front door for the fox. Six weeks later, in early January 1916, Phyllis had a visitor – her younger brother, Wentworth Campbell. Campbell was variously called 'Jock' or 'Bertie', depending on the company and the situation. He was a career soldier in a family whose military legacy stretched back to the eighteenth century; he had been educated at Sandhurst and then joined the Black Watch, the famed Scottish infantry regiment. In January 1914 he had transferred his commission to the Poona Horse and when war was declared was stationed in India. But men were needed in Europe and after extended leave he would be joining others in France, at the Somme.

Jock had spent a few weeks in London and was making a fleeting visit to Portsmouth to see his sisters, Phyllis and Molly, then heading back to the city for some last-minute fun before shipping out to the Front. Instead he stayed in Portsmouth for ten days, seduced by a wanton Betty Finch who had already forgotten her promises to George, as she reflected more than fifty years later: 'Jock was a darling and I fell madly in love with him, but he was far too kind and gentle with me. I treated him very badly but for a time we were very happy. I needed a stronger, less kind man. George was certainly that, but my marriage to George was a terrible mistake. We were just temperamentally unsuited.'

* * *

George Finch would be in for several surprises when he arrived in Alexandria in December 1915. The first was meeting up with Guy Forster, who had been serving in France and was now bound for the trenches of Gallipoli. George was expecting to follow him as a gunner in the Royal Garrison Artillery, so the two friends spent a few days together near the seaside at Sidi Bishr, relishing what might be the last days of their lives and filling the void of fear with discussion about post-war strategies.

It was as if the apocalypse they were about to face had torn a ragged hole in their suits of youthful invincibility. Before the war they had set out to climb higher and harder than anyone else, refusing to yield even to the forces of Mother Nature. Their post-war pact was the opposite, flushed with the fears of mortality. If they survived, George and Forster would climb only for fun, never climb more than two days in a row and would withdraw to 'lesser mountains' if the weather worsened.

They parted after a week, when Forster sailed for the Dardanelles with the Royal Engineers, but George would not follow. Instead, he was transferred to the Royal Army Ordnance Corps as a support expert and sent to a new frontline in the Balkans. About the time that Jock Campbell was bedding his wife back in Portsmouth, George was acclimatising to the heat and dust of Macedonia.

A joint French and British campaign had begun there the previous year, supposedly to help Serbia stave off aggressive manoeuvres from a combined German, Austro-Hungarian and Bulgarian army. But by the time the French and British arrived the Serbian troops had already crumbled and retreated to the ancient city of Salonika. Despite this, the decision was taken for the new troops to remain and protect what was regarded as a strategic position.

George Finch would make his name here, not so much as a warrior but as a man of science. He had been promoted to captain and drafted to join the Ordnance Division where his skills as a chemist were needed, both to be innovative and build new explosive devices but also, more importantly, to maintain, repair and test the army's stock of shells and bombs. A history of the Division penned after the war showed that he had made a significant contribution: 'The Ordnance was fortunate to possess such a distinguished man of science.'

George revelled in the environment, as harsh as it was with soaring temperatures during the day and the cold of a desert at night. The mountains were not snow-capped but brown and hard, the winds screamed and the marshes in the flatlands were full of malaria-carrying mosquitoes. But George Finch was in his element in the open air with all its challenges, and he was keen to make an impression. The opportunity soon presented itself when his superiors came to him with a problem.

It was the summer of 1916 when it was discovered that thousands of shells, most of which had been stacked inside camouflaged bunkers carved into the rocky hillsides to hide them from enemy aircraft raids, had leaked in the extreme heat. The oozing amatol, a highly explosive mixture of TNT and ammonium nitrate inside the shells had soaked the fuses, which meant that almost all of the army's stock was unusable and would leave the frontline exposed to an increasingly aggressive enemy.

There seemed little chance of getting new supplies shipped across the Mediterranean from Egypt, so George was given the job of trying to salvage the ammunition. It was a dangerous task, working with unstable explosives, and made worse because most of the positions were strung out across rugged mountain passes between Albania and the mouth of the River Struma in Greece. Access roads, at times, were impassable by vehicle.

Over the next few months, Finch and his team were able to clean 60,000 shells of the leaked material and fill the cavities with a molten paraffin mixture before replacing the fuses. He did not escape unharmed, though; one eye was injured in an explosion and he would use a monocle in later years. In the opinion of his commanders, George Finch was a war hero.

* * *

In December 1916, a year after leaving Portsmouth, word reached George that his wife was seriously ill. There had been infrequent correspondence between them since he'd left, but now George was spurred into action. After his heroics in rescuing the armaments stock, compassionate leave was assured and he was back in London by the end of January 1917.

There was a shock waiting for him when he got down to Portsmouth; not only was Betty in fine health, contrary to what he had been told, but she was nursing a four-month-old baby. The message had been a ruse to hide controversial news. He had not even known that she was pregnant. Frederick George Peter Ingle Finch had been born on September 28, 1916, more than nine months after George had left for Egypt. Surely he could not be the father. So who was?

Betty crumbled and revealed her affair with Jock Campbell, insisting that the relationship had now ended. Initially fraught, George gradually came to terms with the situation and even agreed to let the boy share his name, registering his birth a few days later and naming himself as the father: 'She implored my forgiveness,' he later wrote to a friend. 'I still loved her after a fashion. My feelings towards Peter were none other than those of intense pity. For his innocent sake, for the sake of my own people and name I forgave my wife. I gave Peter my name as if he were my son.'

But George hid the truth from his family, writing to his mother: 'My son was born on the 28th of September last. His name is Peter. He is a splendid boy and you will be awfully proud of him.' He also wrote a letter to the young boy, which was addressed 'To my son' and explained his feelings for him. Sadly, Peter was never made aware of its existence.

But George also wanted retribution. Instead of staying in Portsmouth with his wife for the rest of his leave, he set out for France to track down and confront Jock Campbell. Just how he managed this and where he found Campbell is uncertain but he would write about the confrontation a year later: 'I had a further ten days leave in France, which I employed looking for Campbell. I found him, thrashed him into unconsciousness but unfortunately (so I thought then and for a long time afterwards) did not kill him. I narrowly avoided having to face a court martial.'

George did not return to Salonika immediately. In his private records there is a map of France with his scribbled handwriting on the front cover: *Finch 1917*. Inside he had drawn an arrow to the town of Breteuil and in red ink vigorously circled the area west of another town, Crèvecoeur-le-Grand, labelling the whole area with a capital 'F', which might refer to the battlefront.

The only other clue to his war-time travels was a conversation he would have more than half a century later during which he reminisced with a young relative about the happy experience of mingling with Australian and Canadian soldiers in France in 1917 around the time of the Battle of Vimy Ridge, part of a major Allied offensive in April 1917, soon after the United States formally entered the war.

The memory was clearly quite powerful, although he did not go into detail other than noting a confrontation with a senior officer who chided him for having mud on his uniform. He reckoned the officer wouldn't have known 'where the hell' he'd been, but he didn't make it clear if he'd risked a charge of insubordination by voicing the opinion, or whether it was merely a mental response.

Soon afterwards George headed back to Salonika and, for a time, felt he had been able to salvage his marriage. Betty wrote regularly for the next few months, raising his hopes that they had a future together and might eventually have more children. It was a hope to cling to as the war continued into its fourth year but the letters eventually trailed off and George feared the worst. He asked a friend back in Portsmouth to check on Betty and he quickly confirmed that Jock Campbell had reappeared and the two had begun seeing one another again. Despite the beating he had received at the hands of George Finch, Campbell was staying in his house and in his bed. It was the end of the marriage as far as George was concerned although he would have to establish proof of the affair before he could begin divorce proceedings.

12.

PLEASURE AND PAIN

A young German fighter pilot named Rudolf von Eschwege was cutting a swathe through the British Royal Flying Corps along the Macedonian Front through late 1916 and most of 1917. The 'Richthofen of the Balkans', as the 22-year-old was known because of his Red Baron-like success, had shot down more than twenty British planes, and won a dogfight with the English ace Gilbert WM Green, whose wingman was shot down.

The dominance of the German, played out above the disputed Front and in plain sight of both armies, was having an impact on troop morale. He had to be stopped, particularly when he began seeking new targets and turned his attention to manned observation balloons. The sausage-shaped inflatables were sent aloft on cables well behind Allied lines, beyond the range of enemy gunfire and protected by their own anti-aircraft guns, to gather information about the battlefield ahead.

The Eagle of the Aegean Sea (another of von Eschwege's nicknames) was so skilful and elusive that he would simply fly across the Front, keeping the sun behind him so that he was difficult to spot, then dive unseen from the heavens in surprise attacks that forced observers to leap from their baskets and parachute to safety as their hydrogen-filled balloons erupted in flames and fluttered to the ground like dead leaves. Such was his aerial dominance that on one occasion von Eschwege even shot down a British Sopwith Camel sent to protect a balloon. Something had to be done and it was George Finch who came up with the solution.

Direct confrontation had failed so George laid a trap for the increasingly confident pilot, hoping to use his own arrogance against him. On November 21, 1917, the Allies sent an observation balloon aloft near the inland city of Orljak. It was floated to 3200 feet, higher than usual, so it could be easily seen from the German side of the battlefront. In the basket beneath the balloon was a dummy soldier as well as 550 pounds (250 kilograms) of explosives and a detonator connected to a concealed wire taped to one of the ropes that anchored the balloon to the ground where George had rigged a trigger switch.

The bait had been set, and was quickly taken. A German scout plane soon spotted the balloon and not long afterwards Rudi appeared in his powerful twin-gunned Albatros fighter. The young German made a beeline for the balloon, firing specially made incendiary bullets as he closed in. On the ground below, George watched and waited patiently until the pilot, still firing, came close to the balloon. He then triggered the explosives.

A group of Bulgarian soldiers manning a German observation post some miles away had gathered to watch their champion through binoculars. Their translated report gave a colourful description of the attack as it unfolded:

Now appeared the German ... he rushed like an eagle on its prey. He shot well. Had his incendiary ammunition fired? Now he was within a few yards of the balloon – now the aircraft lifted its head again – now it flew just over the balloon – and now the envelope was in flames. Hurrah! But it was different than usual: the balloon blazed into a powerful pillar of fire. Slowly the burning scraps of shell tumbled to the ground. The soldiers roared and cheered. But an officer felt a foreboding that made his heart tremble. 'Where was Eschwege?' Yes – thank heavens! – he had come through safely. His plane came out of the smoke – then, oh, woe! – it bent over its left wing – now it slipped off to the side – and then it turned over, the heavy motor dragging it down, and crashed down to earth. Horrible! It was not possible that Eschwege should be no more! The cheers gave way to a wailing grief. 'Eschwege dead! Our Eschwege dead!' We cannot believe it!

George Finch, man of science, was once again a hero.

* * *

In a conflict that would become known as the Doctors' War because twice as many men were casualties of illness as of fighting, it seemed inevitable that after three years in Macedonia George Finch would be among those who would succumb. Not long after his triumph against von Eschwege, George became one of the 160,000 men in the Balkans who would fall to malaria, a disease fed by the swamps that lined much of the Front and passed on by the clouds of mosquitoes that swarmed above the mud.

The illness would not only have a profound effect on George's health for the rest of his life but would also stand in the way of some of his most important mountaineering opportunities. He lay for weeks on a camp bed in an overcrowded makeshift tent hospital where hygiene was almost impossible to maintain and the only known treatment was doses of quinine, which saved many lives but caused side effects such as bleeding under the skin, the loss of sight and hearing, chest pain and blackwater fever. It was there as he convalesced for several months that George met a young woman who would take his mind off the disloyalty of Betty Fisher.

Her name was Gladys May. Her father, Robert, was a shipping merchant, and the family – Robert, his wife, Maud, Maud's mother, Gladys and her much younger brother – lived in a sizeable house in a prosperous suburb and employed two servants. In her teenage years Gladys attended boarding school.

When war broke out Gladys joined the Volunteer Aid Detachment of the Red Cross where she trained as a nurse before being sent to Cairo as the disasters of Gallipoli began to unfold. In 1916 she was transferred to Salonika and, as the war entered its fourth year, she found the love that she hoped would last beyond the fighting.

George hoped so too. Gladys was the antithesis of Betty Fisher; a strong and practical woman with a quiet personality in contrast to his wife's flittering ways. They were qualities he admired under normal circumstances but with the backdrop of war and illness she must have seemed an angel. He began to call her Eve – his temptress and saviour – as the relationship developed beyond that of nurse and patient into a close friendship. Soon they were lovers. George told Gladys about his wife and her infidelity, but he avoided any mention of Peter.

In September 1918 he was back in England after being invalided out of Salonika, convalescing in the town of Lewes and reading all six volumes of Gibbon's *Decline and Fall of the Roman Empire*. Perhaps inspired by his reading he wrote to Gladys in October, confessing his 'misery'. He wanted them to marry without secrets: 'Listen, you shall know all that matters now. I could tell you nothing of this before, simply because I did not feel sure of you. Darling, for years I have hidden my misery from you and all the world with the most cheerful lies I could sum up. But now when I feel you love me as I love you, you are going to be told everything.'

The letter then detailed the sequence of events leading up to his return to London to discover that his wife had borne a son with another man, and his decision to give Peter his name and try to save the marriage before discovering that Betty and Jock had resumed their illicit affair.

> In 1917, I was more or less certain that my wife had gone off
> the rails again. It was then that I found out that Campbell
> and my wife had lived together in my house in November
> 1916, just after Peter's birth. But as I had already condoned
> this by living with my wife in February, and as other proofs
> I had were not valid enough to stand up to court, it had
> to wait until I found letters of absolute proof. Before the
> absolute proof, my wife's object in refusing to divorce me
> was: to remain my wife, have a good time and do what she
> liked until I should slip and give her a chance to divorce me.
> I have now procured legal proof. What I want is to be free of
> my wife. I want Peter who bears my name now. He is rather
> a dear little fellow. I cannot bring myself to letting his life
> be utterly ruined through the faults of others of which he is
> innocent.

A month later, as the church bells across England rang out joyfully to declare the end of the Great War, George wrote to Gladys again. He still intended taking custody of the boy who shared his name but not his blood, although it was clear that his future wife wanted children of her own and was not interested in taking care of someone else's child, particularly when he wasn't her future husband's real son.

George, reluctantly, gave in: 'In all fairness to you, and the dream baby we are going to have, you and yours must come first. Peter will not live with us, for my mother, who knows nothing of the truth about him, is going to bring him up in the company of my younger brother Antoine, who is fourteen.'

It was a decision he would regret.

In a letter to his mother, George revealed a hard-nosed streak, softened to some degree by a concern for young Peter: 'I told Betty that I intended taking proceedings. She fell in quite merrily with the idea until her hearing that it would naturally involve losing all touch with my son. She grovelled. Well she may continue to do so. I cannot take Peter away from her yet. That worries me for he is over two years old and active in mind and body beyond his years.'

George began divorce proceedings on January 3, 1919. His sworn affidavit contained what he said was proof 'that the said Alicia Gladys Ingle Finch has frequently committed adultery with William Dallas Campbell'. They had been together for eight nights in April 1918 at the Moorlands Hotel in Surrey, then again in early May at the South Western Hotel in Southampton. There was no need to list any further transgressions.

* * *

The imminent divorce of George Finch and Betty Fisher had descended into an ugly game of hide-and-seek by the early months of 1919. Betty, advised by her angry husband that he planned to take Peter from her, frequently moved house, sometimes shifting hundreds of miles at a time, to thwart any attempt George might make before the case came to court.

It was clearly the jilted man's intention to take Peter from her, so confident was he of his legal grounds in a society that had only just given women the right to vote and was still some years away from allowing them the choice to initiate divorce proceedings. His determination was detailed in a statement delivered to the court which showed the time he'd spent trying to find her and the trouble she had taken to avoid a confrontation. It listed several addresses in Southsea, Haslemere, Maidenhead and Brighton to which he'd tracked his estranged wife over several months, adding she had been 'at divers other places'.

He eventually ran her to ground in the Sussex market town of Lewes, the same town in which he had earlier been convalescing, turning up one day in March 1919 with his sister, Dorothy, and taking Peter who, they would claim, was being fed champagne in a room full of drunken soldiers. It is not clear where Betty was at the time, although years later all she recalled was that Peter had 'disappeared' from the garden. She did not deny the presence of the soldiers.

Betty's only hope for contact with her son was Laura Finch, who did not approve of George's actions and believed Peter belonged with his mother, no matter how 'loose' she may have been. A few months after she began caring for Peter, Laura sent Betty a series of photographs of the young boy with a note in which she described the break-up of the marriage and the treatment of Peter as a 'sorrow' in her life. It prompted a heart-rending reply in which Betty described the photos as 'pleasure and pain':

> I worship my son every moment of his small life. I try not
> to think of Peter more than I can help because that way
> leads to madness. But there are still times when the longings
> to have him are well nigh more than I can bear. I am not
> seeking sympathy and I intend to rebuild my own life with
> the priceless possession of loyal friends. I hope you believe

that I am sorry to have been the indirect cause of sorrow in your life.

But George Finch, filled with misgivings about his own upbringing by an errant mother, was not about to change his mind, particularly with the expectations and pressures of a new relationship in the background. As far as he was concerned, Betty Fisher was not fit to raise the child and he expected his mother's support on this. Laura Finch, under the impression that Peter was her 'blood' grandson, would eventually yield to her oldest son.

Betty's bravado was punctured as the reality of her loss set in. Pleas for Peter's return had fallen on deaf ears and her grief would eventually be replaced by a hardened determination to forget about Peter and begin again.

There was one more twist. At the time Peter was taken from her, Betty was pregnant again. Given the acrimony between them, and even though he might have been in England on leave in the final months of the war, it is hard to imagine that George, in the throes of an angry divorce, was the father of a child conceived some time in the autumn of 1918. Yet the birth certificate, registered two months after the birth of the boy, Michael Roscoe, on June 17, 1919, named him as such. A telltale sign as to its lack of authenticity might be the misuse of the name Ingle as part of a hyphenated surname. Nonetheless, more than ninety years later Michael's descendants still carry the hyphenated surname and introduce themselves as George's great-grandchildren.

Michael Ingle-Finch would always believe that his father was George Finch and not Jock Campbell, with whom he lived, along with his mother, for the first eight years of his life. He would remember Jock fondly as the man who played a fatherly role, teaching him to ride and hunt while they lived in the lap of luxury in India.

But when Betty and Jock's marriage ended so too did the relationship. Michael would never see Jock again, although someone was paying his mother an allowance that meant he could be schooled at Harrow before joining the Hampshire Flying School from where he was recruited into the RAF, becoming a hero during World War II. Michael Ingle-Finch was an ace pilot, flying Hurricanes during the Battle of Britain, and was among the first to fly the next generation fighter, the Typhoon. He was awarded the Distinguished Flying Cross (with bar) in 1943 and rose to the rank of Wing Commander. After the war he continued to have an association with the aviation industry, as a test pilot and teacher. He died in 2002 aged eighty-one, never having met the man he believed was his father.

In all likelihood, George Finch never even knew Michael existed.

13.

THE LAST FRONTIER

The Alpine Club of London had been rudderless, at least in a formal sense, during the early years of the Great War. Between 1914 and 1917 there was no president and only minimal activity by its committee, mainly to manage the premises at No. 23 Savile Row in the centre of the city. These had remained open, the comfortable lounge and library filled most days with elderly members. But, as with society in general, the energy and drive of its youth had been stripped away, many younger members never returning from the mud of the Somme and the myriad other sites of mass death.

It was a far cry from the glory days of the mid nineteenth century when the world's first mountaineering club had been created to harness the interest and enthusiasm of the so-called golden age of climbing, when the imposing phalanx of Europe's Alpine peaks had been conquered, one by one. The club had hummed with activity and stories of the triumphs and tragedies of men in Norfolk tweed jackets and nailed boots who, carrying only rope and pickaxes, pitted themselves against extremes of weather and terrain. The club was devoted not just to the physical challenge of mountaineering but to the recording of climbs and expeditions in volumes of beautiful and gallant prose.

But half a century later all the main peaks had been conquered and the search for fresh challenges had been reduced to finding new climbing routes to ascend the same mountains. Now, as the war years churned on, it was those same old men who'd been part of the golden age who mostly sat in the club, their unread books lining the walls, and the club magazine, the *Alpine Journal*, forced to fill its pages by retelling old stories, as the Bernese Oberland, Graian Alps and Pennines were largely inaccessible while Europe remained in the darkness of turmoil.

John Percy Farrar edited the journal during these trying times. Born within days of the club's formation in 1857, he had become its most prominent figure, not only keeping the journal alive, but in 1917 assuming the presidency and breathing new life into the club by creating excitement about what might happen in mountaineering when the war was finally over.

He was the right man for a difficult time, a decorated soldier during the Boer War with an engaging personality and an impressive climbing record. He was credited with four first ridge ascents, including the north ridge of the Wetterhorn, in a career that would eventually tally more than three hundred expeditions across Europe, South Africa, Japan and Canada.

On February 15, 1918, in a typically expansive letter to one of the main contributors to the *Alpine Journal*, the Swiss-based American writer Henry Montagnier, Farrar revealed there were influential men, particularly in the rival Royal Geographical Society, who were considering new climbing frontiers outside Europe now that the war seemed, at last, to be coming to an end: 'There are rumours flying about that there is to be a big mountaineering expedition to Everest directly after the war, but I do not know what truth there is in it. Possibly it arises through the death in action of General Rawling who, you remember, made a very adventurous journey down the Brahmaputra.'

Farrar was right on both counts. Brigadier-General Cecil Rawling, a larger-than-life figure whose career represented everything that the British establishment regarded as romantic and heroic, had been killed in action at Passchendaele the previous October. A man of adventure in the Victorian mould, he had explored the foothills surrounding Everest in 1904 when part of a British expedition to survey the mountains of Tibet and had even considered attempting to climb Everest, had it not been forbidden by the Tibetans. His death had sparked renewed interest in the ambition of reaching the roof of the world.

Rawling had been a prominent member of the Royal Geographical Society, and it was probably at the society's premises in Kensington where Farrar, who was a member of both clubs, had heard the rumours, although it would be another ten months before a letter was drafted by the society to the Secretary of State for India to ask for leave to submit requests to the Tibetan government to mount an Everest campaign.

The letter's contents revealed the complexity of the challenge of tackling a peak that no European had even seen in its entirety, given the access restrictions. It had been mapped in 1841 by the Surveyor-General of India, Sir George Everest; observed on the horizon through a theodolite from huge towers erected to complete the great survey of India, and its height determined from calculations made more than 100 miles from its base. The best guess was that it would take two or three years to prepare, not only mapping the mountain and its geography and surrounds, and improving climbing equipment, but also pondering the question of oxygen and specifically 'the construction of an oxygen helmet to enrich the attenuated air and thus minimise the distress hitherto produced by physical exertion at altitudes above 22,000 feet'.

Everest was a challenge British alpinists had been eyeing at least since 1885 when the surgeon and mountaineer Clinton Dent, in his book *Above the Snow Line,* concluded: 'I do not for a moment say that it would be wise to ascend Mount Everest, but I believe most firmly that it is humanly possible to do so.'

But it would take time and diplomacy to open the Tibetan borders and the issue had been put aside until the war wound to its bloody end, the celebrations had died and the reality of the decimation of society had set in. By 1919 it seemed here was the opportunity the British establishment had been longing for. Everest was the early twentieth century's final frontier. Man had been to the extremities of the earth in every direction except *up*, including to the North and South Poles, and this was the chance for an Englishman – Britain had been beaten to the Poles – to be the first to conquer the highest summit and stand on the roof of the world. In the post-war years Britain was struggling to find a pathway to economic and social recovery and the conquest of Everest would provide a much-needed fillip, particularly as they controlled India, the only known way of access.

In March 1919 the idea was raised publicly when Captain John Noel, a soldier, adventurer and photographer, addressed a packed meeting of the Royal Geographical Society to speak about his adventures in the Himalayas. Disguised as a local in the forbidden land, he had got within fifty miles of Mount Everest in 1913 and glimpsed the top 1000 feet of the monolith through the haze of biting winds before being forced to retreat, but not before photographing the mountain for the first time – a 'glittering spire of rock fluted with snow'.

Noel insisted it was time that an attempt on the summit was made, if not by a British climber then someone else: 'It cannot be long before the culminating summit of the world is visited, and its ridges, valleys and glaciers are mapped and photographed. This would perhaps have already been done, as we know, but for the war.'

The speech was a set-up, the brainchild of the Royal Geographical Society president Sir Francis Younghusband, who wanted to inject some urgency into a plan that seemed to have been languishing for years. He had been agitating for some diplomatic action for some time and on the back of the enthusiastic response that night he arranged another mission in India to negotiate with the Tibetan government. Others like Percy Farrar immediately began discussing possible climbers, and a week later he mentioned the challenge again in a letter to Montagnier:

> I shall strongly support the inclusion in the party of the two brothers Finch [George and Max]. They are at present gunners, but I believe we could easily get them seconded. I know them both very well and they are, in my opinion, two of the best mountaineers we have ever seen and much more likely to carry out a job of this kind than other men I know, whether a guide or a mountaineer of any nationality. They are both under thirty and the very men for the job. You might casually sound Kurz out as to his opinion of the two Finch brothers. I think you would find he would not wish for better comrades.

Marcel Kurz was the man to whom George Finch had written in January 1915 when he raised the suspicions of his superiors by mentioning howitzers in the same breath as his Swiss mountaineering friends in the Academic Alpine Club of Zürich.

He had also mentioned visiting Farrar (at the offices of the Farrar family's mining company in East London beneath London Wall).

The Farrar–Finch friendship appeared a strange one, at least on the surface. Farrar was more than twice the age of Finch and very much a part of the British climbing establishment that the younger man despised. The pair had met several times during the summer climbing seasons, often at the Monte Rosa Hotel in Zermatt. They had been introduced by Val Fynn, a close friend of Farrar who had been impressed with the boys during their climb in 1911.

There was another, compelling, connection between them. Farrar's only son, John, was twenty-seven when he was killed in action in April 1915. He was the same age as George Finch and, in his grief, the older man clearly saw the daredevil climber as a son of sorts and a kindred soul.

Finch felt the same warmth and admiration for Farrar. Even before the war when he wrote his controversial appraisal of British climbers in his article for *The Field*, George had found praise for a few individuals, including Farrar, and it was obvious that he regarded the older man as something of a saviour of modern mountaineering.

Farrar was also not blind to the shortcomings of his fellow Alpine Club members, and acutely aware that many of them, as pointed out so robustly by Finch, were not mountain climbers in the strict sense but gentlemen rich enough to pay guides to ease their way. He was also embarrassed that only British climbers were being considered for the Everest expedition and wondered why the Royal Geographical Society didn't seek out the best possible team. After all, the task was monumental and would not be decided in the homeland of the climbers. In any case, the climbs in Europe were higher and tougher than those in Britain. French, Swiss and even Italian climbers should be considered, he believed.

The way forward was the young, he argued in another letter to Montagnier, written in May 1919, in which he revealed that he had sounded out George about taking up the Everest challenge: 'As to the Himalayan business, nothing more has been done. I saw young George Finch who is about to be demobilised, and I think he would be quite willing to go. If he and his brother Max and young Kurz cannot do the job then we have nobody who can.'

The expertise of Marcel Kurz was well known to members of both the Alpine Club and the Royal Geographical Society, but the fact he was Swiss, not British, would make him the first of Farrar's preferred trio to be ruled out if an expedition was ever mounted, as Farrar pointed out to Montagnier in another letter, marked 'Confidential': 'Apparently the Geographical people are very intent on this Himalayan expedition, if it comes off, being purely British. Moreover, I understood from [fellow Alpine Club member Douglas] Freshfield that Kurz had made an unacceptable proposition.'

Farrar had begun discussing Everest with George Finch just as George was orchestrating the removal of Peter from Betty Fisher. The possibility of being chosen in the climbing party to tackle Mount Everest, as theoretical as it was at the time, must have been on his mind when he decided to shunt Peter off to his mother in Paris. How could he take responsibility for a child – someone else's child at that – when he would be attempting the greatest adventure of his life? And he knew that Gladys May did not wish to take care of him.

By August 1919 official moves were under way, seeking permission from Tibetan authorities for Britain to mount an expedition to the Himalayas. Behind the scenes, George Finch was submitting his own plans to Farrar for the makeup of a possible climbing party and suggesting strategies for including Marcel

Kurz, particularly as it was going to be impossible to find enough 'good Englishmen' with sufficient skills to make the attempt. Farrar agreed with him, at least privately, but held out little hope of convincing the committee of the Royal Geographical Society, which effectively controlled all aspects of the proposed expedition.

14.

THE LOST BOY

George may have been struggling to find support for his suggestions concerning the Everest expedition, but he had no trouble winning over a divorce court magistrate. It had taken ten months since his application to get a hearing, by which time he had been demobbed with the rank of captain and was back working as a lecturer at the Imperial College, and living in Kensington. More significantly, he had been made a military Member of the British Empire (MBE) 'for services in connection with the war in Salonika'. King George V would pin the medal on his chest during an investiture ceremony at Buckingham Palace in December 1919.

It only added to his credibility before the court, although none was needed. The hearing was swift, uneventful and like most cases of the period it was uncontested, allowing Mr Justice McCardie to find that George Finch had 'sufficiently proved the contents of the said petition' and decree that the marriage was dissolved because Betty Finch was an adulteress. Jock Campbell, the adulterer, was ordered to pay court and legal costs of £126.

But it was the final few words of the judgment – 'that the child, Frederick George Peter Ingle Finch, remain in custody of the petitioner' – that would prove the most important and far-reaching. George Finch would take custody of a child whom he believed

131

was not his and whom he had no intention of taking care of in the future.

Peter Finch, then aged four, was already ensconced in the French home of his grandmother. In his dismissal of Betty as a woman incapable of being a decent mother, George was repeating the pattern of disharmony that had affected his own teenage life, but had little option but to leave Peter in a house with an eccentric woman in late middle age and his teenaged half-brother, Antoine, who was studying to be a concert pianist.

Peter had stayed with George's sister, Dorothy, during the divorce proceedings as she roamed the English countryside working as a post-war nurse, trying to put aside the grief of losing her fiancé in the fighting, but the young boy would remember none of this nomadic existence. It was as if his memory only began when he walked through the doors of the Villa la Fleurette.

Laura Finch had long ago moved from central Paris when her grandson arrived on her doorstep. The funds from Charles Finch, which continued to flow despite their long estrangement, would no longer afford a grand apartment and she had found a villa in Vaucresson, an avant-garde commune near the Seine on the far western fringe of the French capital.

Despite the strangeness of his surroundings, or perhaps because of them, Peter would regard the years with Grandma Laura as happy ones, particularly given his ultimate career as a gifted but tragic Hollywood actor.

The villa was a crumbling, mottled white and pinky-brown stone building with a big garden filled with cypress trees, lilac bushes, hedges and ivy-covered walls. It was a playground of imagination, always full of wonderfully strange people who attended what became known as Soirées Chez Laura: artists experimenting with Dadaism and Surrealism and musicians, intellectuals and poets;

people like the American dancer Isadora Duncan whom Peter remembered dancing semi-naked while his grandmother played the harp dressed in a Grecian tunic and gold headband. The legendary Russian dancer Vaslav Nijinsky was another visitor, a quiet and withdrawn man until the music began when he would leap around the room like a grasshopper. Next door lived an artist who painted animals and kept a tiger in his studio.

But Laura was perhaps the most colourful of them all, a demanding yet delightful fairy queen dressed in gold lamé who fostered and inspired Peter's creative spirit: 'She was the most exotic, marvellous woman I can ever remember and even more of an eccentric egotist than I am,' he later told his close friend, the actress Enid Lorimer. 'I must have learned great deal from her subconsciously as an actor and I'm very grateful to George for sending me to her and that I lived with her as long as I did.'

In another interview he was equally effusive about his grandmother, who often brought him out to show his skills as a mimic in front of her friends. He revelled in the attention: 'She taught me to explore the frontiers of experience. She encouraged me to explore new places, to meet new people. I was a ready pupil.'

But the attention Peter would silently crave was that of the man he believed was his father. All the young boy knew was what his grandmother told him: that his parents had divorced, his mother had married another man and his father was climbing mountains in India. It was true, but avoided answering *why* he had been left in Paris and *why* he never saw either parent. Although George kept tabs on the boy through Laura, he never travelled to Paris. The letter titled 'To my son' was either never posted or Laura simply forgot to give it to the boy. A stub noting the title inside the notebook from which the letter was torn is all that remains of it.

Betty Fisher would eventually marry Jock Campbell in 1922 and accompany him to India (with her other son, Michael, who also bore George's name) when Campbell was appointed regent to a young maharajah after the boy-king's father had been killed, apparently squashed by an elephant. Any plans the couple may have had to retrieve young Peter had long since disappeared and she never made any attempt to contact him.

Despite the neglect of his mother and George, who had so righteously petitioned for his custody, Peter would have a happy and carefree existence in Vaucresson until the autumn of 1925 when Laura, in her late fifties and becoming increasingly eccentric, decided to travel to India to attend the 50th International Convention of Theosophists held in the city of Madras. She, Peter and Dorothy left France in December and would not return.

It was in India, amid her obsession with spiritualism, that Laura lost control of her precocious nine-year-old grandson who one day simply wandered off with a Buddhist monk and was found three days later, sitting in a dimly lit room, wearing a yellow robe and with his head shaved. He declared he was a *chela* – a disciple.

Laura decided she could no longer be responsible for the boy she still believed was the biological offspring of her oldest son, but rather than demand that George either take Peter back or return him to Betty she entrusted his care to two Australian delegates at the convention. Captain Dick Balfour-Clarke and a former Anglican bishop named CW Leadbeater agreed to take Peter back with them to Sydney, where the plan was that he would be handed to Dorothy Finch, who had carried on to Sydney and was now living and working in rural New South Wales.

George knew nothing of the Australian plan. He had remained in contact over the years, and knew that his mother had left for India, but had presumed they would return to Paris after the conference. His interest in Peter, while not completely abandoned, had been pushed aside by a new relationship and children.

* * *

Peter arrived in Australia with the two men in the summer of 1926, a thin, frightened boy in a cut-down white suit with a pith helmet on his shaved head. He had no passport, a cheque in his pocket for £12 and a letter addressed to a group of theosophists who lived in a large house known as the Manor in the suburb of Mosman, where the society would make its Australian headquarters. The letter read, in part: 'If my daughter Dorothy won't look after him then please will you take Peter.'

The cheque was a monthly fee to look after her grandson but it was the only one Laura would ever send. She never went back to Paris to live, instead settling in the city of Darjeeling in northern India. In 1938, in her seventies, she wrote to Peter: 'Remember your grandmother of thirteen years ago?' she asked, adding that she was happy he had found a foot-hold on the slippery path of life through his happy nature and intelligence. He did not reply and never saw her again.

In Australia, Peter had struck more family troubles. Dorothy thought she had made it clear that she could not take Peter so the boy had to stay in Mosman, now totally alone: taken from his mother and biological father, farmed out by his legal father, cared for and then discarded by his grandmother and unwanted by his aunt. Other children who were living at the Manor would later talk of a happy, imaginative boy who told amazing stories, including that his grandmother had sold him to an Arabian slave market from which he had escaped. Behind the stories and laughter, however, it was a different story. For a start, Peter couldn't read or write English. Enid Lorimer taught him by reciting Shakespeare to him and later recalled finding him on a verandah mimicking her delivery.

Peter would stay in Mosman for seven months until his grandfather, Charles Finch, turned up one day bearing papers to prove his identity and their relationship. The old man, now eighty-seven, was angry that he had been thrust back into the dysfunctional family, blaming his irresponsible wife to whom he was still paying a stipend despite not having seen her since he left Paris in 1903.

He was also bearing a letter from his son, George, who had given his father power of attorney over the boy he still claimed as his own. George was angry that Peter had not been returned to Paris after the conference and appalled that he had then been abandoned in Sydney. The letter read in part: 'I was most distressed to hear that my mother had sent him to a theosophical school. Had I known she intended doing that I should not have given her control of the boy. She knows, or should know quite well, that I completely abominate anything to do with spiritualism, theosophy or any form of charlatanism.'

But, like everyone else in the family, Charles had no intention of taking responsibility for the boy. At eighty-seven he was simply too old. Instead, Peter was sent to live with Charles's younger brother, a 73-year-old retired banker named Edward, who lived with his thirty-something spinster daughter, Betty, who could serve as a mother figure. It was all very confusing for the boy. The carefree magic of his grandmother and her friends was gone, replaced by the strict regime of a well-meaning but socially conservative household. Chores replaced creativity and there were regular beatings with a riding crop from a woman who'd had motherhood forced upon her and couldn't cope.

Peter attended a public school and wore a uniform, yet another costume change that only highlighted the sense that he didn't quite fit anywhere, and wasn't wanted by anyone. The one relationship he cherished was with his grandfather, whom he visited regularly. It was like a re-run of George Finch's childhood, with the elderly man encouraging the young boy to learn to swim below Greenwich Point and offering him the freedom of his library, although Peter would recall his angry reaction one day when his grandfather found him rifling through papers in his study 'trying to find out who I was'.

He 'escaped' when he left school at sixteen and was offered a job as a copy boy with the Sydney *Sun* newspaper by its editor, who lived near Edward and Betty and felt sorry for a boy he considered to be an orphan. Peter's journey into the city each day would open the door to the world of theatre. Within a year he had moved out of Edward's house to live, carefree, in the bohemian vibe of Kings Cross. His acting career, once begun, took him to London in 1947 and, ultimately, fame and a posthumous Oscar in Hollywood.

* * *

It would take almost three decades but Peter Finch would eventually be reunited with his mother when he moved from Sydney to London.

There are two versions of the reunion. Betty would say it was Peter who tracked her down. She remembered his phone call: 'Hello, I'm your son Peter. Would it embarrass you if I came back into your life again?'

Peter's version was the other way around. He told his second wife, the actress Yolande Turner, that it was during the run of a play called *Daphne Laureola* in London, in which he had his first big success, that he took a phone call backstage one night from a woman he assumed was yet another admirer.

'Hello, my name is Betty Staveley-Hill,' the woman began. 'Are you Peter Finch?'

'Yes I am,' he replied, a little impatiently.

'Peter, I think you are my son.'

The statement shocked him: 'What? I thought you were dead.'

Betty was living in a cottage in Cornwall. Her marriage to Jock Campbell had ended in divorce in 1928 when she and Michael, Peter's half-brother, moved back to England. Two years later she would marry the much younger Alexander Staveley-Hill, a former soldier whom she had met in India. The marriage would produce a third child, a daughter named Flavia, in 1934, but it would end as badly as her first two marriages.

Betty, still glamorous at fifty-six, was waiting on the platform with Flavia when Peter arrived by train a few days later. 'Call me Betty,' she said, thrusting out a gloved hand before commenting that he hadn't cleaned his shoes properly. The conversation was at first stilted, both steering well clear of the past, but relaxed as the night wore on and Michael arrived. The two men ended up getting drunk at the local pub, their camaraderie clear and lasting.

Mother and son would stay in touch, although it would take months before Peter finally built up the courage to demand answers. Betty wasn't going to ask for forgiveness: 'When you are as old as I am and have made as many mistakes as I have then you can ask me that question.' She had no choice but to relinquish Peter, she correctly insisted, as the legal system would always back a wronged husband over an adulterous wife. She had tried at various times to get him back but to no avail, and eventually she gave up.

It would be another thirteen years before Peter met Jock Campbell. Peter would tell friends that Jock confirmed that he was his biological father and that the two men had liked each other. But Irene Campbell, Jock's wife of forty years (after Betty) and mother of his three other children, insisted that her husband had never accepted paternity. He and Peter had met only once, in 1962 over tea, she said, but there had been no correspondence before or since, and Peter had not visited them in Scotland as he claimed.

It was typical of Peter, who often resorted to imaginative fiction to sweeten an otherwise sour story, frequently joking about his double heritage, even to those who knew him best, like Enid Lorimer: 'Peter had a deep-rooted fear of not knowing who he was, of belonging nowhere, always in transit, rootless, defending himself by attunising and with the romantic fantasy of acting every second of his life.'

In some ways Peter's private life would mirror George Finch's, the man he had believed was his father and whom he would eventually meet again. He married three times and had four children, and even named his one son after his Australian grandfather, Charles. Yet he made the same sad choices about fatherhood as George. Peter's children would grow up feeling abandoned.

In a coda, young Charles Finch was with his mother, Yolande, when she travelled to Scotland in the late 1960s to confront Jock Campbell.

'My sister, Samantha, and I sat in a small room in front of a big fire having tea. I remember Jock telling me that he definitely was *not* my grandfather, and that is what I believe.'

15.

'YOU'VE SENT ME TO HEAVEN'

Somewhere between the granting of the decree nisi in his divorce from Betty Fisher in March 1920 and the arrival in September of the decree absolute that opened the door for their planned marriage, George Finch fell out of love with the angelic nurse he had nicknamed Eve.

Perhaps it was the removal of the backdrop of war that changed things; the realisation that the woman whom he had needed so much during his illness in Salonika was not the partner he wanted for the adventurous life that lay ahead. As cruel as it would appear, George seemed to have concluded that they were different – and incompatible – people in peacetime. It was a common enough end to a war-time relationship.

But there was a complication. Gladys May was pregnant and this time there seemed little doubt that the child was George's; it had been conceived in the middle of July 1920, a few days before he took leave from the Imperial College and headed back to his beloved Alps for six weeks of climbing. George hadn't been to the Alps since the summer of 1914 and would have been thinking of little else but the challenge and joy of scaling the peaks that had been out of his reach for five years.

He would not have known that he had left his girlfriend 'in the family way', even though there had been so much talk between them about marriage and having children. It was only after he returned to England at the end of August, flushed with the success of a trip that included ascending the Matterhorn, Mont Blanc and another dozen or so peaks, that Gladys's condition was obvious.

George must have already had misgivings about the relationship, although he made no mention of his doubts as he settled back into the life of a university lecturer and wondered what to do. He could not in all consciousness avoid the civil ceremony that would make the arrival of a child, and its mother, socially legitimate. After all, he had already taken one drastic parental decision, cutting a young boy off from his birth parents, and even though that situation had not been of his own making he would have to live with the consequences of his decision.

Whatever his reasons for leaving, George Finch was clearly the party at fault this time. His decision to marry Gladys and give her the legitimacy of being a wife and married mother did not stretch to being a man of his word, to holding to his earlier promise to love her and raise the 'dream baby' they'd spoken of a year before. George Finch, so deeply wounded by the disloyalty and infidelities of his first love, Betty, knowingly if naively chose to wreak similar pain on a young and vulnerable woman he believed he had once loved.

They wed on a leaden November day at the Kensington Registry Office, Gladys's condition impossible to hide even under her modest dress, although the registry official and two witnesses, a married couple who knew the bride, were the only ones there to notice. As with his first marriage, George had insisted on a swift civil ceremony, although for different reasons. Unbeknown to his new wife and contrary to the vows he took that day, George had no intention of making the union last. Just three weeks after the ceremony he moved out of the house they had rented in the town of Witney, west of Oxford, leaving a note rather than face personal explanation for his unfathomable actions.

Gladys waited a week before writing him a brief, entreating letter on December 5, which perhaps suggests that he had admitted to adultery, which she was willing to forgive or simply that she would excuse his running off, provided he come back to her.

> My dearest Geof,
>
> I am heartbroken at the way you have treated me and the letter you wrote me after you went away last week has crushed me, and means more than you can possibly realise. I entreat you to return to me and live with me as your wife, letting all that has passed be forgotten. Whatever you have done I am only too willing to forget if you will only come back. Do let me hear at once from you. Ever still your loving wife. G

The diminutive 'Geof' mimicked the manner in which her now errant husband affectionately signed his correspondence – a shortened version of Geo Finch. The letter was addressed to his rooms in South Kensington, a pleasant stroll across Hyde Park to the Imperial College. George replied immediately but gave Gladys no hope, coldly signing his note as Geo I Finch. The magic had gone:

> My dear Gladys,
>
> I have received your letter of the 5th inst. When I left you I also wrote explaining my reasons for going. I regret to say that nothing will induce me to return and nothing you may say or do would cause me to deviate in any way

whatsoever from the course I have taken. I am sorry for
having caused you pain. I shall continue your allowance with
the note of £100 a year.

Gladys did not include among the court papers her husband's letter explaining his reasons for leaving her, and they would remain a matter of conjecture. The financial offering he made was more than he could afford, but it would go some way toward salving a guilty conscience. George was almost broke, his modest savings in the form of the family endowment gone because of a now worthless investment in the Trans-Siberian Railway. The investment had been promoted heavily in France and England before the war, encouraged as Russia built a transport artery to feed its economic expansion. But the dream died with the collapse of the Russian economy during the Bolshevik Revolution in 1917 and with it the savings of many Western families like the Finches.

But Gladys wasn't after money. She wanted her husband back, refusing to accept that he could simply walk away from not only a marriage but also their unborn child. She promptly lodged a petition through the courts, demanding that a judge order him to return to the marital home. Her petition laid out the sequence of events – his sudden disappearance and cold dismissal – but made no mention of George's reasons for leaving or her pregnancy, concluding: 'As my husband has not returned to or sent for me I desire therefore to obtain from this Honorable Court a decree of restitution of conjugal rights.'

* * *

In the last days of 1920 word reached London that the Tibetan spiritual and political leader, the Dalai Lama, had acceded to the diplomatic pleadings of the British India Office and agreed to open the country's borders to offer safe passage for an expedition to attempt to climb Mount Everest. The proposal was announced in *The Times* on January 11, 1921 and made clear just how difficult the challenge would be:

Sir Francis Younghusband, President of the Royal Geographical Society, announced at a meeting of the Society last night that the political obstacles to the proposed attempt to climb Mount Everest have been removed, that a preliminary reconnaissance will be made of the ground this year, and that the actual attempt on the summit will follow in 1922. Such an expedition, said the President, must be essentially a great adventure: 'High risks will have to be run, and severe hardships endured – risks from icy slopes and rocky precipices, and such avalanches as buried Mummery's party on Nanga Parbat twenty-six years ago; and hardships from intense cold, terrific winds, and blinding snowstorms. In addition, there will be the unknown factor of the capacity of a human being to stand great exertion at a height more than 4000 ft higher than man has as yet ascended any mountain. The expedition will also be in the highest degree scientific. We may take it as certain that the summit will never be reached unless we have first explored with the greatest care all the approaches to it through country at present entirely unknown; and then examined, mapped, and photographed the mountain itself in fullest detail. In the present year the Alpine Club and the Royal Geographical Society propose to organise a reconnaissance party to acquire this geographical knowledge. Next year we will send to Tibet a climbing party to apply it in a great effort to reach the summit. We hope that the reconnaissance party may cross into Tibet when the passes open, about the end of May'.

A fortnight later a joint committee of the Royal Geographical Society and the Alpine Club was formed to plan and fund the mission as well as select the reconnaissance party, as Younghusband explained to *The Times*:

> Climbing Mount Everest was a matter which interested both the Royal Geographical Society and the Alpine Club. It interested the former because the Society will not admit that there is any spot on the earth's surface on which man should not at least try to set his foot. And it interested the latter because climbing mountains is their especial province. It was decided, therefore, to make the Expedition a joint effort of the two societies. And this was the more desirable because the Geographical Society had greater facilities for organising exploring expeditions, while the Alpine Club had better means of choosing the personnel.

The Alpine Club nominated its new president Professor Norman Collie, along with Percy Farrar and Charles Meade as representatives on the new Everest Committee. Collie was a chemist who had been on the first Himalayan expedition with Mummery in 1895, an intriguing character who was said to be the inspiration behind Arthur Conan Doyle's Sherlock Holmes character. Meade had also climbed in the Himalayas, although he had not set eyes on Everest.

The Royal Geographical Society representatives would be Younghusband, Colonel M Jacks, who was the chief of the geographical section general staff, and the society's treasurer, Edward Somers-Cocks. None had any mountaineering experience although Younghusband had spent time in Tibet where he had led the controversial British military 'expedition' in 1904 during which an estimated 700 monks and villagers were mowed down by machine-gun fire while trying to block the British advance with revolvers and swords in what became known as the Massacre of Chumik Shenko.

There were two other members of the Everest Committee. Both organisations nominated their club secretaries, Captain John Eaton for the Alpine Club and Mr Arthur Hinks for the Royal Geographical Society, and it was here that the real political sway would lie, as Hinks, with the imprimatur of Younghusband, quickly assumed the dominant role, which he would not relinquish for the next two decades.

Events began to move quickly. The meteorological window of opportunity was narrow, particularly as no one had ever set foot on the mountain. Nothing was known of its dangers, beyond the obvious, and there was little time to choose the team let alone to do any meaningful work on the equipment that would have to carry the party into the unknown.

Some appointments were made immediately by necessity, although not without controversy. Brigadier-General Charles Granville Bruce, a bear of a man and a career soldier who had been on Mummery's Himalayan expedition in 1892 and had also ventured to the Himalayas in 1907 appeared the obvious choice to lead the new expedition, but his age (he was fifty-five) and ill health counted against him. Instead, the 39-year-old adventurer, soldier and writer Colonel Charles Howard-Bury, who had made the initial approach to the Tibetan government seeking access to the mountain, was offered the position. It was a brave choice – youth over the establishment candidate – and inspired by his strong diplomatic links with the Indian government as well as the Tibetans. Howard-Bury had immersed himself in the region, its culture and its languages, even once staining his skin with walnut juice to travel safely through Tibet in the guise of a local, as John Noel had done.

But youth was overlooked in other appointments, most notably with the strange selection of the Scotsman Harold Raeburn to co-ordinate the climbers. Raeburn, who had been in the Himalayas the previous year, was a hard, stoic man with a grip of iron and a temperament to match, but at almost fifty-six years of age it was unlikely that he would get far up the mountain. But the Everest Committee, led by an insistent Hinks, was trapped by its desire to choose only British men, despite the obvious merits of European climbers like Marcel Kurz (who was also a noted cartographer), as pointed out a year earlier by George Finch and Percy Farrar.

At fifty-three, Scotsman Alexander Kellas was yet another ageing participant, although he seemed to be a necessary addition, not only for his considerable climbing expertise but also for his theories about oxygen at altitude. Kellas, short, slight and bespectacled, looked like the academic he was and yet he was also an intrepid mountaineer who had been one of the first to tackle the Himalayan peaks in the early years of the twentieth century, having made eight summer sojourns in the Indian provinces of Kashmir and Sikkim by 1916, often climbing alone except for local porters. In 1911 he reached the top of Mount Pauhunri which measured 23,386 feet, an achievement that only a few years before had been thought impossible because of the thin oxygen levels at extreme altitudes. Besides, Kellas was already in India. He had been there since June 1920 conducting a series of experiments on the practicalities of carrying oxygen bottles up Mount Kamet. His conclusion was that the weight of the bottles offset any advantage that oxygen might give the mountaineer.

Alexander 'Sandy' Wollaston, chosen as the expedition doctor, was forty-six and another of Hinks's choices, although age was perhaps not as important for a medic as for the men who would undertake most of the climbing in the party. He was Cambridge-educated but had largely eschewed medicine for adventure as a botanist, ornithologist, climber and incessant explorer throughout Africa, Japan, Lapland and Papua New Guinea.

There was no controversy about the selection of the men who would accompany the climbers to study and map the landscape. Alexander Heron, Henry Morshead and Edward Wheeler were all plucked from the ranks of the Geological Survey of India. Heron was a 37-year-old Scottish geologist as quiet and worthy as his career, twenty-three years of which were spent completing a geological survey of the state of Rajasthan. Morshead had joined the Survey of India in 1906 at the age of twenty-four and never left except for the years of the Great War during which he attained the rank of major, fought at the Battle of the Somme and was awarded a Distinguished Service Order. He was climbing Mount Kamet with Alexander Kellas when invited to join the expedition. Wheeler was a 31-year-old Canadian who had climbed in England and the Pyrenees, but mainly in his homeland. He had fought with a British regiment during the war and had been awarded a Military Cross as well as winning membership in the French Legion of Honour, which was probably why his birthplace was ignored.

George Finch was interviewed by the selection committee on February 9, 1921, aware that his candidacy was controversial despite his spectacular climbing record. It was not only the manner of his mountaineering exploits, unguided as they were, but his background and, above all, his prickly relationship with the establishment that might stand in his way. His 1913 appraisal of English mountaineering published in *The Field* had come back to bite him; the older committee men who had been his target had long memories.

Arthur Hinks, in particular, could not stand George Finch and didn't hide the fact. It was surprising in some ways as both were men of science – Hinks was approaching fifty years of age, a brilliant Cambridge astronomer credited with determining the mass of the moon and the distance of the earth to the sun – but George stood for everything that Hinks disliked: he was a long-haired upstart colonial who had been educated on the Continent rather than at Oxbridge, a modern-thinking man (Hinks even hated the telephone) who dared challenge social norms and held scant regard for his elders and presumed betters. Hinks, who had never climbed higher than his chair, as writer Wade Davis later observed, was a fleshy, humourless and bitter man who had taken the Royal Geographical Society post after resigning from Cambridge because he had been overlooked for a senior position in favour of a younger scientist.

Whatever his reasons, Hinks set about trying to kill off George Finch's candidacy by character assassination, even writing to George Leigh Mallory, the most promising English alpinist of his day and the obvious favourite to lead the climbing party, asking if he was prepared to share a tent with Finch. Mallory, to his credit, replied that he didn't care who he slept with provided they reached the summit of Everest.

Mallory had no doubt about George Finch's skills and was clearly content to climb with him. They had met in Wales in 1912 during a weekend climbing event at Pen-y-Pass beneath Snowdon. Two years later, as editor of the Climber's Club journal, he had published George's account of climbing a difficult route up the Aiguille du Dru, a peak of the Mont Blanc massif in the French Alps. They had also climbed together during the summer of 1920 when both were part of a group that had ascended the Matterhorn.

Francis Younghusband also argued against Finch behind closed doors, as did Charles Bruce who, although smarting from not being chosen to go on the expedition, still had a powerful voice within the Alpine Club committee. He felt that he was among the targets of Finch's antagonism toward the older 'gentlemen climbers' and agreed with Hinks that Finch would be a disruptive influence, even though there was no evidence he had ever caused friction or been incompatible in any climbing party of which he'd been a member.

Younghusband revealed the level of angst about George Finch in his 1926 book *The Epic of Mount Everest*, although without naming him:

> As a mountaineer this other was all that could be desired;
> but he had the characteristics which several members of the
> committee who knew him thought would cause friction and
> irritation to the party and destroy the cohesion which is vitally
> necessary in an Everest Expedition. At high altitudes it is
> well known that men become irritable. And at the altitudes of
> Mount Everest they might find it wholly impossible to contain
> their irritation; and an uncongenial member might break up
> the party.

George's champion inside the committee was Percy Farrar, supported enthusiastically by Geoffrey Winthrop Young who had been the second man praised by George in his 1913 article. Winthrop Young was not on the committee that made the final decision, but he was an influential figure, admired not only for his own pre-war climbing exploits but for his insistence on continuing to climb, having lost a leg in the war, with an artificial limb. He was also the man who had persuaded an initially reluctant Mallory to accept the Everest challenge and was in no doubt of George's skills, even including a chapter about George's Corsican adventures with Max and Alf Bryn in his book *Mountain Craft*, which had just been published. Finch, he declared, was the pre-eminent 'snow and ice man' of his generation and the perfect foil for Mallory whose own strength was climbing on rock.

For once Arthur Hinks would not get his own way. On February 16 the committee met and decided on the final composition of the team. When they emerged some hours later, the two Georges had been appointed the designated climbers for the mission. The men were very different: George Mallory, aged almost thirty-five, was a member of the establishment, a Cambridge graduate and the son of a clergyman, flamboyant and naturally gifted as a climber, and was once described breathlessly by the writer Lytton Strachey as 'six foot high, with the body of an athlete by Praxiteles, and a face – oh incredible – the mystery of a Botticelli, the refinement and delicacy of a Chinese print, the youth and piquancy of an imaginable English boy'. By contrast the younger George Finch, though an equally fine physical specimen and natural climber, was an outsider in terms of birth and education and a man of detail and intensity who did not crave acceptance, only respect for his achievements.

But for all their differences, the two men were similar in two important aspects that would prove significant in their destiny on one of the great modern adventures. Both were working men who struggled financially in a world where most participants were wealthy aristocrats with little empathy for their kind, and both had an unflinching confidence in their own abilities.

Their individual responses to being chosen for the expedition were also starkly contrasting. Mallory was invited to lunch with Younghusband on February 17, and the Royal Geographical Society president later wrote of the conversation: 'When the invitation was made he [Mallory] accepted it without visible emotion. He had the self-confidence of assured position as a climber. He had neither exaggerated modesty nor pushful self-assertiveness. He was conscious of his own powers and of the position he had won by his own exertions.'

George Finch was also invited to the president's office, although not for lunch: 'He was a tall, well-made athletic man with a determined look about him,' Younghusband later reflected. 'His keenness was evident from the first moment. For a few seconds he seemed unable to speak from the intensity of emotion that was surging within him. Then he said, "Sir Francis, you've sent me to heaven."'

16.

'DEAR MISS JOHNSTON'

A fortnight after being selected to make the first attempt to climb the highest mountain in the world, George Finch was brought back to earth with a thud. The magistrate who had heard Gladys Finch's conjugal rights case issued an order on March 2 directing him to return home to his heavily pregnant wife who was now just five weeks from giving birth. Despite her condition, or perhaps because of the public embarrassment it might cause him, Gladys personally served George with the document on March 3 as he walked down Prince Consort Road on his way to work.

But if she was hoping the confrontation would frighten her estranged husband into acquiescence, then Gladys was wrong. It merely hardened his stance and the situation quickly descended into farce. Intent on forcing a divorce through the courts, he set up a bogus liaison with a fictitious woman, booking into Room 477 of the Strand Palace Hotel in central London on Tuesday, March 15, for two nights.

It was a common tactic at the time by those seeking a divorce. The newspapers frequently carried court reports of men being 'caught' at hotels like the Strand Palace, but the trysts were almost always bogus, set up to satisfy tightly worded divorce laws. Chambermaids happy to make a little extra money were sometimes paid to pose as the love interest or provide 'eyewitness' statements that the illicit couple had been sighted together and so create a body of evidence that adultery had been committed.

Gladys bowed to the inevitable and filed for divorce on March 19. Three weeks later, as she prepared to enter a North London maternity hospital, her lawyer lodged a petition that cited the Strand Hotel 'meeting' as proof of adultery 'with a woman whose name is unknown to your petitioner'.

The lawyer was the only person in court for the hearing on April 8 that would last only a few minutes. Magistrates were generally willing to shuffle the unhappy couples quickly through court if the paperwork was convincing, although in this case Mr Justice Barnson didn't even bother to call for an independent witness or ask how a heavily pregnant woman knew her husband was in a city hotel with another woman. Neither did he check the petition, which did not nominate the Strand Palace as the venue but a non-existent hotel called the Shand Palace. It was presumably a typographical error by a legal secretary but it only confirmed the sad nature of the relationship and its farcical ending.

Two days later, on April 10, Bryan Robert Finch was born. His parents would still be officially married until the decree absolute came through, but he would grow up with only one of them – a mother who would never recover from the disappointment of being abandoned. In the space of six years George Finch had married twice, divorced twice and been named on birth certificates as the father of three young boys he either did not believe were his, did not want and was most probably not even aware of.

Bryan was the second of these options. He would never meet his father but still acknowledged his paternal heritage by adding the name Ingle to official records when he married in 1950, perhaps because George, a man capable of simply cutting off his feelings continued to at least provide some financial support for Gladys.

Bryan and his wife, Margaret, settled in the Dorset town of Poole, raised two children and ran a successful motorcycle business for many years. Bryan died in 1994 after marrying a second time. According to those who knew him, he never spoke about George. Neither did his mother, although Gladys kept and treasured the letters he'd sent her during and after the Great War. She never remarried and died, as Gladys Ingle Finch, in 1971 at the age of seventy-six.

George was despondent about the turn of events with Gladys, riven with guilt and turning to drink for the first and only time in his life. It was in this period of personal darkness that he met and fell in love with a young Scotswoman named Agnes Isobel Johnston, from Coldingham, Berwickshire, on the Scottish Borders.

Agnes was one of four children whose father, a gentleman farmer named Archibald, had died from peritonitis when she was six years old. There were some assets – a modest amount of money and two small farms – but Agnes's mother, Margaret, would see little of it as she struggled to raise her son and three daughters in a small house not far from the family lands controlled by her older brother. Despite the financial difficulties, Agnes (who hated her name and as a child reversed the letters to call herself Senga) put herself through Edinburgh University and gained an English degree before taking a job in London with the Foreign Office.

It was not in Whitehall that she met George Finch, but at the Imperial College, the day in December 1920 that she applied for a job there as a secretary. George was immediately smitten when he met her by chance as she waited to be interviewed, taken by her forthright manner and neatly clipped diction offset by a disarming Scottish beauty and a head of wild curls, for which he would later call her Bubbles.

The first formal indication of the relationship between them is a handful of letters George wrote and that Agnes kept among her personal mementoes. The first was dated January 2, 1921, in which George addressed 'Dear Miss Johnston' and invited her to visit him, adding that he had arrived late at the famous Brompton Oratory that morning but had caught the tail end of the service. He had attended, even though he wasn't Catholic, to hear the music: 'It was Beethoven and beautiful,' he commented, before signing formally as George Ingle Finch.

Less than three weeks later he wrote again, but the tone and language had changed dramatically. 'Miss Johnston' had become 'Beloved' and a polite invitation to dinner was now 'a desire for such utter abandonment':

> Beloved, I want to write to you just a brief note before I go
> out. My one, I love you as best I know and with a desire
> for such utter abandonment and sinking of hopes, dreams
> and all else of self in just you & your happiness that both
> our aims & lives may be one. That is all I have to hold out
> to you, to keep as you will. My beloved dream child, your
> friendship is all to me. May God bless you and keep you. I
> love you. Geof

Anyone reading the letter would have questioned whether it could have been written by a man who was regarded by those who knew him well as pragmatic, steely and even aloof, but as sure-footed as he was on an icy mountain slope, George Finch was foundering, his emotions precariously balanced between the regret and remorse over Gladys and the baby and his sense of giddy excitement about the new relationship. He had fallen head over heels again, although this time he couldn't bring himself to tell the woman he loved that he was already married and that the wife he intended divorcing was pregnant. It was a secret that he would keep for the rest of his life.

* * *

In the midst of his self-made personal quagmire, George was trying to prepare for a journey that could either be the triumph of his life or end it. Thanks largely to Percy Farrar and Geoffrey Winthrop Young he was on the expedition team, and due to leave in early April, just as Gladys was going to hospital to give birth.

The selection of Mallory and Finch as the specialist climbers had been announced succinctly in *The Times* on February 22 by Younghusband: 'As members of the expedition on whom we will have to depend for reaching the highest point we have selected two younger men who have made names for themselves by their efficiency in climbing the Alps – Mr GL Mallory and Captain George Finch. Our party for the reconnaissance is thus complete.'

There was also recognition back in Australia, although its significance was either missed or ignored by the city papers in Sydney and Melbourne. Only the *Leader* newspaper in George's old home town ran a front-page story headed 'Mount Everest expedition – Orange boy's share', which included excerpts from a letter George had written to his father detailing his selection and the travel plans which would get the party to the foot of the mountain by late July: 'Then the stupendous task will commence,' he wrote in acknowledgment of the difficulties that lay ahead.

George had said the same thing, only with more detail, at a meeting of expedition team members in early March. The reconnaissance mission had two purposes: firstly, its stated intent to map the area and establish a route to the mountain; but also to make an attempt at the peak if the opportunity arose. The get-together at the

Royal Geographical Society rooms on March 7 was full of bravado, self-congratulation and promises of discovering dozens of new plant and animal species as well as undertaking studies on the effects of altitude on the climbers. Finch was more circumspect, warning of the dangers and hazards they faced and insisting that even the journeys to the North and South Poles could not be compared with what lay ahead. The last part of the climb, where temperatures could be 60 degrees Celsius below zero and they would be exposed to potentially dangerous levels of ultraviolet light, would require 'a concentrated effort and strain such as no expedition has ever demanded. Every one of us will have to call up all we ever knew about snow conditions.'

It was George Finch at his most precise, a fearless explorer who tempered his adventurous spirit with the pragmatic vision of a scientist. This unique combination should have made him the most valuable member of the team and the first chosen, rather than the most distrusted and the one the others would have liked to dump.

George had only one fear, not of death, which he and the others had faced every day for the more than four years of the Great War, but of the impact on others of his possible death, and, in particular, on his two children, Peter and Gladys's unborn son. In private, George pleaded with Percy Farrar to help make provision for them in case he did not return from Everest. Farrar agreed and went to the committee asking that they insure George's life for £5000 at a premium cost of £75. The request was denied. The risk was his alone.

There was one last hurdle for the designated climbers. Mallory and Finch had to pass a medical exam conducted by two doctors chosen by the expedition doctor, Sandy Wollaston. It seemed a belated bureaucratic requirement, with less than four weeks before their departure, and should have been a mere formality. On Thursday March 17, the same day he was supposedly in the arms of a woman at the Strand Palace Hotel, George Finch was examined by Dr H Graeme Anderson who operated from rooms at 75 Harley Street in Paddington, less than a mile from George's flat in Sussex Street, South Kensington. Anderson was a former RAF officer who two years earlier had written one of the first books to document the effects on the human body of being at high altitude, *The Medical and Surgical Aspects of Aviation*.

The following day George went back to the same rooms to submit to a second examination, this time by Anderson's partner, Dr FE Larkins, a physician and pediatrician who, it had been decided, was sufficiently qualified to provide a second, independent opinion. In reality, it was an appointment of convenience rather than rigour.

The examinations were over quickly and George went home without a care, believing he would be passed without question. That night he wrote to Arthur Hinks, telling him that he had arranged adjoining berths – Numbers 45 and 46 – for himself and George Mallory aboard the SS *Sardinia* which was sailing for India on April 8, the same day his divorce from Gladys May was due to be granted and two days before his child was due to be born. It was an escape on many counts.

But there was a cruel twist in store for him. Far from passing him as fit, both doctors cleared Mallory with flying colours but questioned George's physical condition and wondered if he was capable of making the trip to Everest. The two handwritten documents were brief and would be questioned for years, first for their competence and secondly as to whether Finch's selection had been deliberately sabotaged.

Anderson's report was a few short sentences that began positively enough with the assessment that George could hold his breath for almost a minute, which was regarded as 'good'. From there the report was almost entirely negative: 'Sallow. Nutrition poor. Spare. Flabby. Pupils react. Knee jerks present. Cerebration active. Mentality good – a determined type. But his physical condition at present is poor. No varicose veins, no hernias. No haemorrhoids. Movement of all joints full and free.'

Larkins produced a different type of report, which detailed George's physique and noted his pulse, blood pressure, nervous system, hearing, sight, ear, nose and throat. There were no noticeable abnormalities other than the fact that George Finch had a lot of teeth missing, which was quite normal at the time. But Larkins, seemingly copying his colleague's language, concluded that he had a 'sallow complexion and poor nutrition', ending with this assessment: 'This man is not at the moment fit. He has been losing weight. His urine reduces Fehling. He is slightly anaemic and his mouth is very deficient in teeth. He may improve considerably with training.'

There was silence for the next four days until Arthur Hinks received an urgent, staccato letter from Wollaston, which read:

> Medical report of climbers has only just reached me. It was delayed by the marriage of one of the consultants. Mallory – excellent in every way. Finch – described as 'not fit at present'. I enclose reports of both physician and surgeon. This is very serious and I am strongly of the opinion that a substitute should be found, if possible. It is of course conceivable that he may become fit by training, but there is a risk of failure. The two medical people knew nothing more of these two young men than their names at the time of their examination.

Hinks moved swiftly. Rather than questioning the report or seeking George's response, he took the result as the opportunity he needed to get rid of the man he heartily disliked. Over the next week there was a flurry of letters between committee members as Hinks directed traffic and hurriedly arranged a replacement, 48-year-old Arthur

Ling who was president of the Scottish Mountaineering Club. Finch was outraged, accusing members of the committee such as Hinks and Bruce of colluding to exclude him and the doctors of being bought off. It was an extraordinary explosion in such circles but did little to force a rethink, even though Mallory threatened to pull out.

He had initially been supportive of Finch's selection, telling his mentor Winthrop Young in a letter that 'Finch and I have been getting on well enough and I am pleased by the feeling that he is competent. His scientific knowledge will be useful and has already borne fruit in discussions about equipment.'

Likewise, his first response to the medical report was disappointment that Finch wouldn't be going and a growing worry about the quality of any replacement. He wrote to Hinks on March 27:

> Since receiving your letter telling me that Finch is not coming with the expedition to Mount Everest I have been thinking very seriously about my own position. We ought to have another man who should be chosen not so much for his expert skill but simply for his power of endurance. I have all along regarded the party as barely strong enough for a venture of this kind with the enormous demand it is certain to make on both nerve and physique. I wanted to have Finch because we shouldn't be strong enough without him. You will understand that I must look after myself in this matter. I am a married man, and I can't go into it bald-headed.

The proposed selection of Ling only hardened Mallory's concern, and he told Hinks that the party was now seriously weak, even if there was no intention to 'push to the top'. The expedition was in jeopardy but there was no turning back on the Finch decision as far as Hinks was concerned. He had to save face, convincing Ling to decline the invitation and then placating Mallory by agreeing to his request for an old school friend named Guy Bullock to be drafted in as the replacement. Satisfied, Mallory then rewrote history, claiming he had always harboured doubts about George:

> Finch always seemed rather a gamble. He didn't look fit and I had no confidence in his stamina. I feel sorry for Finch. The medical exam ought to have been arranged at a much earlier stage. But he forfeits any sympathy by his behaviour. We shall be weaker on ice and in general mountaineering resources without him; but we shall probably be stronger in pure physique and much stronger in morale.

Percy Farrar was deeply worried about the calibre of the expedition party and its safety. Even before the negative medical reports on his young protégé, he had warned Francis Younghusband that if either Mallory or Finch were forced to drop out he feared there would be no climbers capable of taking their places, adding, 'I speak probably with an unrivalled knowledge of the capacity of every British climber, and a good many foreign climbers of the day.'

Now Finch had been ruled out, he argued that the committee should consider abandoning any notion of a major assault on Everest and instead concentrate on exploration and wait another year until the best climbing team could be assembled. His chief worry was how the party would cope in snow conditions without a team member like Finch, 'who has as wide a knowledge of the condition of winter and summer snows as any man ... and if there is insufficient knowledge in the party of such conditions then there is going to be an accident'.

They would prove sadly prophetic words.

* * *

For all the criticism levelled at George Finch for being abrasive, he quickly put aside his personal disappointment at being dropped and continued to help work on improving the expedition's equipment. In particular, he had offered to use his scientific skills to experiment on ways to improve the small camping stoves the men would need to cook simple meals during the long trek to the base of Everest and as they scaled the mountain and established the tented camp sites at various heights, which would be essential to survival, not just on the ascent but also on the way down.

The Primus stove had been devised in the 1890s, designed to act like a grounded blowtorch, but sturdy and rugged enough to operate in adverse weather conditions. It had been used successfully in the Alps and on expeditions to the North and South Poles, but at the higher reaches of the Himalayas it weakened and spluttered in the thin oxygen and could not be used at all above 20,000 feet, barely two-thirds the height of Everest.

George reconstructed the burner to use a mixture of benzene and kerosene in the lower camps and a newly created chemical compound in tablet form called Meta, an aldehyde which bonds carbon, oxygen and hydrogen, in the virtually oxygen-free heights up to 30,000 feet. On March 25 he travelled to Oxford University to test the adapted stove with Professor Georges Dreyer, a Shanghai-born Danish scientist who, in 1907, had been appointed the university's first professor of pathology. Dreyer had constructed a large steel pressure chamber in his laboratory, the first of its kind in Britain, in which he had conducted research in an effort to help pilots combat the effects of hypoxia during the Great War.

By pumping air out of the chamber Dreyer was able to reduce the pressure to mimic oxygen levels at 40,000 feet above sea level, well above the height of Everest, but he needed someone inside the tank to light the stove. George Finch seemed the obvious choice, although the structure of the experiment meant he would have to stay sealed inside the oxygen-free tank for two hours.

The solution was to provide George with oxygen through a flexible rubber hose: 'The biggest surprise was that I suffered barely any discomfort,' he wrote later. 'I remained fresh, strong and awake, as though being in a normal everyday atmosphere.' Not only had the reconfigured stove worked perfectly, but George was now convinced that climbing Mount Everest was possible if there was some way to provide climbers with oxygen. The problem was how to carry it up a mountain.

Dreyer guessed George's thoughts and asked if there were plans to take oxygen on the 1921 expedition. George shook his head. No. The equipment used by Kellas five years earlier to carry oxygen up Mount Kamet was too heavy to justify its use; the heavy steel containers had been a hindrance rather than a help. Anyway, the present expedition was a reconnaissance mission, with no stated plans to make an attempt on the summit.

Dreyer persisted: 'I do not think you will get up without oxygen, but if you succeed you may not get down again. And I can prove it.'

George agreed to stay in Oxford overnight and go back into the steel chamber the next day to be exposed to oxygen levels akin to the levels at 22,000 feet and then to be tested for reflexes, blood pressure and composition, physical condition and psychological function.

George would also undergo a proper fitness test, something that the Harley Street doctors, Anderson and Larkins, had not included in their examinations. And the test would be at the simulated altitude of the Everest challenge. First Dreyer, who agreed to use the experiment to assess George's fitness, set the chamber at 23,000 feet before George, carrying a 35-pound (16-kilogram) load on his back, did a series of twenty step-ups on a chair, first with one foot and then with the other at a rate judged to be similar to a fast climbing pace. His normal heart rate was 68 beats per minute, but in this high-altitude environment, albeit artificial, it was 104 beats per minute, rising to 140 beats per minute immediately after the exercise.

The chamber was then depressurised to mimic 30,000 feet, above Everest's height of 29,029 feet, and George was given oxygen through the flexible hose before doing the same step-up test. By comparison, his heart rates were 77 beats per minute at rest and 100 beats per minute after the exercise. The result was remarkable, and clearly showed that Finch could function better at the higher altitude with artificial oxygen than at the lower height without it.

There was a witness to the experiment. An Alpine Club member, Percy Unna, had been drafted to help because of his background in engineering. He later wrote about his observations when George was without artificial oxygen at the equivalent of 22,000 feet: 'The hands and face lose their red colour and become bluish. The subject tends to become incapable of taking exercise … The symptoms, of which the subject is unaware, of the approach of unconsciousness are mental confusion and a tendency to quarrel, while the blueness becomes more apparent.' By comparison, he said of the second experiment with oxygen: 'Those taking oxygen retain the red colour in face and hands and the normal colour in their blood. Nor do they exhibit the other symptoms.'

Percy Farrar had also travelled to Oxford for the first day of experiments to watch the Primus stove tests. He reported to Hinks, insisting that Finch's ability to talk and take notes 'in the most natural manner' while inside the chamber, with and without artificial oxygen, was proof that the medical reports should be ignored and Finch should be reinstated to the expedition team: 'This is the weakling whom we have flung out,' he noted sarcastically.

But the letter fell on deaf ears, as Hinks made very clear in a missive written to George Mallory on the same day as he received Farrar's letter: 'I don't think Farrar is the only authority. We have seen enough of him at the committee to learn that he frequently talks at random and when he differs on almost every point from Collie and Meade, who have both much Himalayan experience, I do not myself feel that Farrar is the best judge.'

The promised medical report by Dreyer on George Finch arrived in a four-page letter to Farrar on March 28. It was barely a week since the examinations by Anderson and Larkins, yet gave completely the opposite assessment of George Finch's capacity: 'Captain Finch is slightly underweight at present but otherwise his physique is excellent,' Dreyer wrote, before becoming more expansive:

> He [Finch] has an unusually large vital capacity. This indicates a high degree of physical fitness, and he should therefore be able to stand great exertion at high altitudes better than most persons. Furthermore, the tests in the low-pressure chamber proved that Captain Finch possesses quite unusual powers of resistance to the effects of high altitudes. Among the large number of picked, healthy, athletic young men which we have examined, more than 1000 in all, we have not come across a single case where the subject possessed the resisting power to the same degree.

There was still time to reverse the decision and send Finch and Mallory together when the *Sardinia* sailed on April 8. Farrar continued to press for Finch's reinstatement but even Dreyer's report would not sway Hinks and Younghusband, so Mallory sailed by himself, now with the choice of two cabins in which to sleep.

The murmurs of a conspiracy grew when Howard-Bury published the official version of events – *Mount Everest, the Reconnaissance 1921* – the following year, relegating the controversy to a few inaccurate words: 'Unfortunately, Captain Finch was for the time indisposed and his place at the last moment had to be taken.'

In his own account, written some years later, George would also play down the incident for the sake of diplomacy, commenting only that he 'became unable to participate in this first expedition at the very last moment'.

As he retreated to his laboratory, George was already looking to the future. The reconnaissance expedition couldn't possibly make it to the top of Everest, he'd decided. Dreyer's experiments at Oxford had convinced him of that. There would be another attempt, probably the next year, and he wanted to be ready for it. As he wrote a few years later: 'I had been completely converted to Professor Dreyer's viewpoint, the problem of climbing Mount Everest was now changing within me into the problem of how a lightweight and easy to transport apparatus for our goals could be constructed.'

17.

THE THRESHOLD OF ENDEAVOUR

In early July 1921, a few days after the Imperial College campus closed for the European summer, George Finch headed for Switzerland. He longed for the solitude of the Alps to soothe his soul, unable to bear staying at home in London to wait for news of the Everest reconnaissance mission. It was not that he did not care or that he wished the others ill – quite the contrary – but the indignity of his rejection was too raw and he felt the need to prove to himself that Hinks, Younghusband and others against him on the committee were wrong and that his selection should have stood.

He also needed the support of a close friend to steer his mind in a positive direction, a mate like the redoubtable Guy Forster with whom he had made the pact to enjoy climbing while they sat on the seafront in Alexandria in January 1916. Forster was in Ireland tending to a family dispute created by his inheritance of a large estate (which would also mean changing his surname to Smith-Barry), but he promised to be in Switzerland by the end of the month. In the meantime George would ease his way back into climbing, although he believed it was a mental rather than physical attunement he needed: 'In spite of a sedentary occupation, wholly unrelieved of any form of sport, I am always ready to start climbing by climbing and not by indulging in a ramble.'

By July 31 Forster had still not arrived and George was getting impatient, his annoyance heightened by Percy Farrar, of all people, who was in Grindelwald, about fifty miles north but refusing to climb, as George complained in a letter to Agnes Johnston: 'Farrar's an infernal nuisance hanging about the hotels ... I am so fed up wasting this glorious weather doing nothing.'

On the bright side George had met four other climbers, Englishmen Stephen Courtauld and Edmund Oliver, and two Swiss guides, the brothers Alfred and Adolf Aufdenblatten. Courtauld, a wealthy philanthropist who would become George's close friend, invited George to join them and they'd been on 'a rattling good climb' over the Col Tournanche, which crosses the Swiss–Italian border between the Dent d'Hérens and the Matterhorn, before descending into the Italian town of Breuil. It was the boost, mentally and physically, that he needed.

The next morning the others left to catch a train east to Courmayeur from where they planned to make an ascent of the south face of Mont Blanc, a difficult route that was rarely attempted and had been completed but a handful of times. George was eager to join them but first had to return to Zermatt across the mountains on foot to check on Forster's whereabouts and retrieve his luggage. He would then take a train via Milan back across the border to Courmayeur.

He had two options: either to take the Theodul Pass, a snowbound eight-mile track carved between two mountains – the Matterhorn and the Breithorn – or to take a higher pass, the Furg Joch, which ran beside the eastern ridge of the Matterhorn. As soon as he had mailed a letter to Agnes he planned to set off – alone:

I hope to land up there in time for dinner tonight. Am
feeling awfully fit & managed yesterday's climb without
the least effort. I love you, dear one. Write soon and give
me all your news. The fields here are thick with a thousand
different flowers. St George thrives!

My love,

Prof

Agnes would not have been concerned about his welfare because
she would not have received the letter until a week or so after he
had arrived in Zermatt, but his trek had not been as smooth as
George had imagined. He had never made the Furg Joch crossing
before, let alone by himself, and conditions meant it took him
almost five hours to reach the top of the main ridgeline, only to
find that the descent to Zermatt was full of cliffs and ice slopes that
were impossible to tackle alone.

Luckily he found a slope further along the ridge that was
passable, although he had to negotiate a giant bergschrund, which
required more than an hour of carefully cutting steps into the ice
before he could cross and make his way into the town. He arrived
in the evening, exhausted, only to be confronted by the very people
he was seeking to escape.

He lamented the experience in a second letter to Agnes:
'Zermatt is filled with non-climbing trippers and crowds of hoary-
headed Alpine Club has-beens who seem to delight in discouraging
would-be climbers as much as possible – a beastly atmosphere!'

Worse still, he was challenged by a pair of those same hoary
heads about his perhaps rash decision to cross the Furg Joch
alone. His typically heated response to them risked far-reaching
consequences, given he was hoping to be chosen for the 1922
expedition to Everest, a possibility he conceded in his third missive

to Agnes in as many days, this one decorated with pressed sprigs of the white mountain flower, edelweiss:

> The 1st August is a Swiss national day, hence the uni-colour bouquet of edelweiss. Next year we'll hunt for real live ones together. There will be no Himalayas for me – I was rude to two most important old boys of the AC who said I should not have come over the Furg Joch alone. I wound up by asking one of them point blank if he measured my capacity as a climber by his view. If it wasn't for my promise to you I think I would have started off right away to traverse the Matterhorn alone, just to spite them.

But George was not just planning his mountaineering future. Before leaving for Europe he had proposed marriage to Agnes, and she'd happily accepted. There was no need to ask for permission from her father who had died some years before, but he was worried about how he had broken the news to her mother in a letter: 'I would far rather have told her personally [and] I'm afraid now that my letter was very formal. Will you put that right for me? It was strangely difficult to write of our love to a third person. I am counting the time to the New Year.'

In spite of his engagement to Agnes 'Bubbles' Johnston, George's life was, in reality, at a crossroads. There was the mess of misfortune and misjudgment that included two broken marriages and at least two children who were now without a father, along with the loss of his financial lifeline – the endowment from his father – which had vanished with the Russian revolution of 1917. The couple would be forced to rely solely on his modest income from teaching.

And now his mountaineering aspirations had been stymied unfairly too.

To add to this was George's faltering relationship with his brother Max, who had fallen in love and married soon after the war. His wife was a professional pianist and the daughter of a Serbian diplomat, and by 1921 the young couple was living in the village of Frascati, near Rome. They were about to have their first and only child, a boy they would call Edward.

But the imminent birth was not the main reason that George had not asked his brother to meet him in the Alps that season. It was far more complicated and, sadly, permanent. The last time the brothers had climbed together was in April 1914 when both knew war was coming and they'd spent a joyful week skiing and climbing in the Bernese Oberland. It had never occurred to either that it would be their final climb, and even though both had come through the war unscathed, things had changed.

The loss of the family endowment had hit Max harder than his older brother. Although far from financially secure, George had already established his career as an academic before the Great War. Max, by contrast, had barely completed his degree and there had been no time for him to even get a job, let alone consolidate a career. And despite appearances, his wife had no access to funds, which meant there was simply no money to be spent frolicking in the Alps. The most significant block, however, was his wife's vehement opposition to a pastime she feared would kill her husband and leave her as a widow with a young child.

It was an attitude that would all but end the relationship between the brothers even when Max later moved his family to London and worked in the banking industry. The bond had been broken and they simply lost contact, their lives drifting in separate directions.

Many years later a family member asked George about the rift. Instead of upsetting him, the subject seemed to invoke pleasant memories. It was clear that the old man, then in his late seventies, was enjoying reminiscing about his youth and the uncanny abilities of his brother. He recalled the pair's ability to negotiate difficult terrain without speaking, seemingly just sensing the other's movement and needs. So why hadn't they spoken in more than four decades? Wouldn't he like to see his brother again, the relative asked.

George didn't answer immediately and the conversation moved on, but he would revisit the subject a few days later. Their bond – the difference between life and death so many times in the Alps – had been broken by the fact that they no longer needed one another. He felt certain that Max would feel the same way; after all, there had been no attempt by either of them to make contact in the years since. There had been a relationship of glorious youth when they were inseparable and invincible. Now they were just old men. Sadly, George would not be aware that his younger brother died before him, in Brighton in 1966.

* * *

Percy Farrar may have been reluctant to drag his 64-year-old body up an Alpine peak alongside George Finch in the summer of 1921 but he was quick to point out his young charge's accomplishment in climbing the southern flank of Mont Blanc in a letter to Arthur Hinks when he returned to London in mid August: 'Our invalid Finch took part in the biggest climb done in the Alps this summer,' he wrote sarcastically.

It was a pointed remark that rankled Hinks who did not reply, not just because it was yet more evidence of his mistake but because of his worry about the reconnaissance mission, which was still circling the base of Everest and would not make an attempt for another month, far too late, as the monsoon season approached.

Hinks had desperately wanted immediate success, making it clear to Mallory and Raeburn before they left that although it was officially a reconnaissance mission they had his permission, indeed his strong encouragement, to make a serious attempt for the summit if the opportunity arose – 'full liberty to go as high as possible'. Howard-Bury was also told that the 'first objective is to ascend the mountain and all other activities are to be made subordinate'.

But that was now improbable. There had been delays from the start when the stores were held up at the Calcutta docks and then had to be sent by rail north to the town of Darjeeling, where the team of nine white men waited with one hundred mules, forty coolies, four cooks and two interpreters. They had finally set off from Darjeeling on May 18 on a 300-mile march to the base of a mountain that Europeans had only glimpsed from afar.

The difficulties on the trek began almost immediately, the trail alternately plunging and then rising hundreds of feet at a time through steamy tropical forests in a roller-coaster of the spectacular – scarlet hibiscus, mauve solanum and rainbows of orchids, rhododendrons, primulas and magnolias – mixed with unrelenting heat and deluges of rain that turned the track to mud. Within days the mules began waning; some were left behind and others died from exhaustion. The men, too, struggled, mostly with stomach complaints. Kellas, in particular, had looked exhausted when he'd arrived in Darjeeling only two days before they were due to leave.

They crossed the state of Sikkim, heading toward the Tibetan Plateau and beyond to the Himalayas, their snow peaks visible in the distance through the subtropical foliage. The route took them through the Tista Valley and over a mountain pass known as the Jelep La, which connects India and Tibet, and on into the Chumbi Valley.

Howard-Bury telegraphed the Royal Geographical Society when the expedition party crossed the border into Tibet. The message, sent from Darjeeling after being relayed by a 'native runner', was received in London four days later, just in time for Sir Francis Younghusband to announce the achievement, to rapturous applause, at the society's anniversary dinner.

But behind the self-congratulations there were serious concerns. On May 29, eleven days after setting out from Darjeeling and less than halfway to the mountain they still could not see, the men reached the village of Phari, built almost 14,500 feet above sea level on the dry, stony, windswept plain of the Tibetan Plateau. Trees did not grow here, let alone the jungle they had travelled through a week earlier.

The bleak surroundings and the grime and poverty of the village with its starving populace only emphasised the party's own problems. More than half the mules had to be replaced with horses, donkeys, oxen and yaks, and four of the nine men were ill – Wollaston, Wheeler, Raeburn and Kellas.

Mallory wrote of his despair in a letter to his wife, Ruth:

> I suppose no one who could judge us fairly as a party
> would give much for our chances of getting up Mount
> Everest. The hardships such as they have been so far
> have not left us scathedless. Dr Kellas arrived in Phari
> suffering from enteritis and though he is somewhat better
> now he has been carried from there on some form of
> litter. Wheeler has constantly been suffering more or less
> from indigestion and has been sufficiently bad these past
> two days to make it a real difficulty to come on. Raeburn
> seems frail. All have been more or less upset inside at
> different times.

Mallory's words showed the sheer logistical problem of the assault. Everest was like no other mountain, not just because of its size but because it was so inaccessible, hidden like a shy child at the back of the classroom and only revealed when the others stepped away. George Finch had recognised the problems back in 1909 when he and Max had travelled to Corsica to test themselves in a hostile environment. As he wrote: 'For the Himalayas we judged that ... mistakes or omissions would not easily be rectified after one had left one's base, usually the last outpost of civilisation.'

There had also been ructions inside the team. Mallory, who appeared to have embraced the role of gentleman, suddenly found he didn't much like the attitude of a man like Howard-Bury and found it difficult to hide his contempt for the expedition leader's arrogance – 'too much the landlord with not only Tory prejudices, but a highly developed sense of hate and contempt for other sorts of people than his own'. To add to the discomfort, Harold Raeburn's abrasiveness was alienating the others. So much for George Finch being a 'morale' problem.

* * *

```
From Colonel Howard-Bury
    Pharljong, Tibet, June 7, via Simla,
June 8 (delayed).
    I deeply regret to report the death
of Dr AM Kellas, of the Mount Everest
Expedition, at Kampa Dzong, on June 5,
from sudden heart failure.
```

On reflection they would all agree that Alexander Kellas should not have even begun the expedition. He was the last to arrive in

Darjeeling, clearly exhausted and already ill. Within a matter of days he was being carried and, although he rallied on occasions, his death was inevitable. It was another sign of just how unprepared and poorly resourced the mission was, and when Harold Raeburn, the climbing co-ordinator, was carried back to Darjeeling two days later with dysentery, it threatened to unravel.

Back in London, Hinks and Younghusband issued a statement that mourned the death of Kellas but vowed to carry on regardless, concluding: 'The expedition will proceed, relying for its success on the same undaunted spirit which had always animated Dr Kellas and which in men nearly thirty years younger, like Mallory and Bullock, Morshead and Wheeler, will, the committee are confident, carry out the expedition through to its end.'

On the morning of Kellas's funeral (he would be buried on a stony hillside, the grave facing three peaks in the distance that he'd previously climbed – Pauhunri, Kangchenjhau and Chomiomo), George Mallory and Guy Bullock rose early and quietly left the camp to climb a steep hillside on top of which sat an ancient fortress, although they were not interested in the architecture.

The two men climbed about 1000 feet before the object of their scramble came into view – Everest: 'There was no mistaking the two great peaks in the west; that to the left must be Makalu, grey, severe and yet distinctly graceful, and the other away to the right – who could doubt its identity? It was a prodigious white fang excrescent from the jaw of the world.' Everest was still more than one hundred miles away, behind another range of mountains that had to be crossed, but at least their goal could now be seen.

The mission, in its darkest hour, was saved in a sense by the tragedy of Kellas's death and Raeburn's illness because it elevated Mallory to the head of the climbing party. It was a leadership role that he grabbed eagerly, and even though Raeburn would recover and rejoin the party, Mallory had become the head, heart and hope of the mission to conquer Mount Everest.

There was another salvation at this critical moment. As the party crossed the Gyankar Range and drew closer to its goal the group split in all directions, with Morshead and Wheeler leading smaller groups as they surveyed and mapped 12,000 square miles while Wollaston collected flora and fauna specimens and Heron conducted geological investigations.

Howard-Bury, now cut off from Mallory's climbing group, led Wheeler and Heron west as far as Nagpa La, the ancient trading route that linked Tibet and Nepal, while Morshead and Wollaston crossed the Nepal border into Tibet at the holy village of Lapchi and continued exploring to the north.

The enforced separation ironically preserved the expedition's unity. Mallory and Bullock set off with sixteen sherpas and porters to reach the southern end of the Rongbuk Valley, then pushed on to the Rongbuk Glacier where they pitched their base camp at 16,400 feet. It was higher than the summit of Europe's biggest mountain, Mont Blanc, and yet they had not even reached the base of Everest which they could now see clearly, from closer than any European had ever been.

In the first few days of July, after a week of acclimatising to the altitude and as George Finch headed to Switzerland, Mallory and five sherpas traversed the glacier to reach the base of the mountain's North Col, the point where climbers would begin their ascent of the north ridge toward the summit. It would be almost three months, their progress interrupted by the monsoon, before Mallory and Bullock climbed the col, reaching 23,622 feet where they were forced back by high winds. By September 26, with gale force winds now driving across the ridge, Howard-Bury abandoned the upper camps and ordered the party back to

Darjeeling where they arrived a month later. The reconnaissance mission was over.

On November 16, a few days after being reunited with his wife in Marseilles, Mallory wrote to Arthur Hinks to confirm that he would be available to return to Everest in 1922 if, as expected, an expedition was mounted. But he added a prophetic warning: 'We must remember that the highest of mountains is capable of severity, a severity so awful and so fatal that the wiser sort of men do well to think and tremble even on the threshold of their high endeavour.'

* * *

George Mallory was bothered by something other than death – money. Unlike most of his companions who came from wealthy backgrounds, he was a working man, a teacher like George Finch, although not at the tertiary level but at the swank Charterhouse School in Surrey. Mallory had initially turned down the offer to join the reconnaissance mission because of the financial burden it would place on his family, and it played on his mind even as he sheltered against the squalling rain and ripping winds on the lower slopes of Everest, as he wrote to Arthur Hinks on August 21:

> I needn't conceal the fact that having given up my job last
> April I owe it to my family to make some money this winter
> and I should like to earn something by lecturing about
> Everest. But for the convenience of making arrangements I
> am willing to lecture on any terms which may be considered
> just by the committee – either as their servant at so much
> per lecture or as a contracting party under the auspices of
> some lecturing firm and paying so much of what I receive to

the committee. The position as I see it from a business point of view is, simply, that I have something to offer which no one else can give.

It took Hinks more than a month to reply, writing back on September 30 with the cautious approval of an administrator with his own interests at heart: 'I do not doubt that some arrangements equally advantageous to you and to the funds for next year can be reached … would you be prepared to lecture on the Continent and in America?'

The right to earn an income from lecturing would also become a critical issue for George Finch.

PART III

18.

PROSPECTS OF SUCCESS

The Queen's Hall, a gilded West End amphitheatre with walls painted 'belly of mouse', was packed on the night of December 20, 1921. Every one of the 2500 seats was taken and hundreds more people stood at the back of the room to witness the public return of the eight surviving Everest heroes from the reconnaissance mission.

Prince Albert, the Duke of York and second in line to the throne, was on hand to hear the expedition leader Colonel Howard-Bury describe how the climbers had persisted through appalling weather conditions to find a possible route up the mountain via the North Col, and Sir Francis Younghusband wax lyrical about the fruits of the mission: the seeds of rare primulas, gentians and rhododendrons brought back by Wollaston and already planted at Kew Gardens and Edinburgh; the extensive mapping by Morshead and Wheeler; and Heron's account of the geology of one of the last unexplored regions on earth. Even the cost of the trip had been a success, the expenditure of £4000 having already been recovered by selling rights to the story to newspapers.

But the crowd had only come to hear one man – George Mallory – and they only wanted to know one thing – was it possible to climb Mount Everest?

The Times reported his reply the next morning, delivered from a stage decorated with aquariums of goldfish to a room full of expectant men in dinner jackets and women in furs, most of whom could never imagine the grime of a six-month expedition in the wilderness, let alone the life and death exertion of a mountain ascent.

Mallory spoke from the head and heart:

> We have not had a single convincing argument to solve that
> problem. I felt, somehow, when we reached the North Col
> that the task was not impossible; but that may only have been
> a delusion based on the appearance of the mountain from
> that point. It looks much smaller than it is. I believe it to
> be possible at all events, for unladen mountaineers to reach
> 26,000 feet, and if they can go up so far without exhaustion,
> I fancy the last 3000 feet will not prove so very much more
> tiring as to exclude the possibility of reaching the summit. But
> in asserting this bare possibility, I am very far from a sanguine
> estimate as to the prospects of success. Before we parted I put
> this question to [his climbing partner] Bullock: 'What are the
> chances that a given party will get up in a given year?' After
> considered reflection he replied: 'Fifty to one against.' That
> answer expressed my own feelings.

George Finch listened carefully as he sat in the front row in a group of invited guests, including three men who were about to become his companions in one of the most dangerous adventures ever undertaken. Neither Brigadier-General Charles Granville Bruce nor Lieutenant-Colonel Edward Lisle 'Bill' Strutt could be described as friendly toward George. Both were the epitome of the elite he detested: General Bruce the son of Lord Aberdare and Colonel Strutt the grandson of Lord Belper.

Although clearly struggling with his health, Bruce had already been appointed to lead the 1922 British Mount Everest expedition after Howard-Bury agreed to stand aside. Strutt, a career soldier approaching fifty years of age who had climbed mostly in the northern Alps, was second in command and would lead the climbers headed by the two Georges – Mallory and Finch.

On the surface it was a recipe for disaster, considering both men's intolerance for anything new. Strutt, in particular, deplored the use of climbing tools like crampons and pitons, let alone canned oxygen. Like Hinks, he and Bruce dismissed the argument that using oxygen was akin to wearing clothes and boots designed for the mountains, eating nutritious food and sleeping in wind- and rain-proofed tents. Their attitude made no sense given that these same men were content to let 'coolies' carry their equipment and employed guides to show the way.

The third man was Howard Somervell, a 31-year-old doctor and later a missionary who had been born into a wealthy family but did not have the arrogance that often came with money. He had registered more than 350 climbs in Great Britain before tackling the Alps where, on a six-week vacation, he climbed thirty peaks. Importantly for George, he was a man of science who would prove a rare ally in the coming battle over the use of oxygen.

George had known for almost six weeks that despite his run-in with the older Alpine Club members back in Italy during the summer, he was likely to be selected as a climber. A carefully worded letter from Hinks had arrived on November 10. It began: 'I am instructed by the Mount Everest Committee to say that they would like to be able to consider the possibility of inviting you to join the Mount Everest Expedition which will leave London on 2 March 1922 and be in the field until the end of September.'

Hinks wanted to avoid the farce of the March medical report by clearing George's candidacy before making a decision, and despite the controversy that assessment had caused he insisted that George be tested by one of the doctors who just eight months earlier had come to the conclusion that the mountaineer was not fit to climb. Dr Graeme, the altitude specialist, either was not available or had decided against being involved again. Instead, it was left to the physician and pediatrician Dr Larkins. After a terse exchange of letters, George went back to Larkins's Harley Street surgery on November 19.

The appointment was brief and within a few hours Larkins reported to Hinks: 'I have re-examined GI Finch today. He is now absolutely fit and has lost his glycosuria. In my first report on him I stated that I thought all he needed was to get into training.' Larkins had clearly been stung by the earlier row and wanted it known that his assessment had been misinterpreted or, worse, misrepresented by others with possibly dubious agendas.

But the attempts to undermine George Finch hadn't finished. Behind the scenes there was more evidence of sabotage. Just as the previous year Hinks had written to Mallory hoping he would object to George's selection, Younghusband was now busy stirring up disharmony by writing to Strutt and Norman Collie, the Alpine Club president and Everest Committee member, asking if they wanted George on the team.

It is not known what allegations he made against George because copies of these letters were not, unlike most of his correspondence, kept in official records. The worst that could be said of George Finch was that he could be abrasive and was a man who, at times, expected others to simply take him at his word. But that was also true of Hinks, Younghusband and Bruce, as it was of Howard-Bury and Strutt.

And George had not even met most of the other members of the expedition, let alone annoyed them to the extent that they wanted him off the team. His crime was simply that he had the audacity to disagree with, challenge and defy the establishment who believed themselves untouchable. Of that he was certainly guilty and would continue to pay a high price for.

But for the moment at least, George was safe, as both Strutt and Collie had said yes to his inclusion. Strutt cited George's exemplary war service record as a reason to support the selection and his belief that Finch was the climber most likely to reach the summit of Everest:

> Personally, although my acquaintance with Finch is slight I have no objections to his inclusion. He served at the same time as I in the British Salonika Force, did good work and was popular with his unit. I think that Charlie Bruce and I should be able to manage him. At the same time if the other members dislike him, which I fear is the case, it rather alters the situation. However, in reply to your question I should like Finch to go. He is the one man that I would back to reach the summit, and we should always remember that!

Collie also cleared the way for George's selection:

> I am willing to accept the view that Bruce and Strutt should be able to manage Finch. Last year I was most anxious to safeguard Col Howard-Bury but the situation is different now, and as Bruce and Strutt both say they don't mind his going, I cannot object any further. Of course I know that as a climber he is as good a man as we can get. I have never heard anything about Finch's matrimonial arrangements. All I know is the opinion of the people who worked with him at Woolwich and at South Kensington.

Collie appeared to be admitting that the reason George had been excluded the previous year was not on medical grounds but because of a perception that he would make life difficult for Howard-Bury. The committee, it seemed, was prepared to sacrifice his climbing ability to ensure they chose an expedition leader with the capacity to unify his team. As it turned out, it was Howard-Bury who was the problem during the reconnaissance expedition, with Mallory, in particular, regarding him as a pompous ass.

The other disturbing aspect of Collie's reply was the revelation that Younghusband and Hinks were fishing for potentially scandalous information about George's personal life – his marriages – that might give them new reason to exclude him.

Unable to forge a division between George and the other men, Younghusband and Hinks reluctantly let his selection stand. On December 1 George was called to a meeting with Younghusband in his office at the Royal Geographical Society in Kensington Gore. He scrawled a note at the bottom of the invitation: 'Saw Sir Francis 11.30am who tendered me an invitation to join the expedition for Everest.'

George was brimming with enthusiasm about the adventure ahead, as he wrote to Farrar the next day: 'I am seeing Mallory on Saturday and hope to get numerous tips from him. Re food, at ordinary altitudes where the cold is not excessive, almost anything suits me (except prunes) but at higher altitudes I can dispose of quantities of raw fat-smoked ham. But perhaps I should come round some time next week and see your provision list.'

* * *

As usual, George's messy personal life seemed intertwined with momentous events in his career. On December 12, the same day he informed Hinks that the Imperial College had granted him six months' leave on half pay (£20 per week), the final decree was issued in his divorce from Gladys May. He was now free to marry Agnes Johnston.

The flurry of correspondence continued as plans for the expedition proceeded. The committee offered to pay the cost of the climbers getting to Darjeeling if they were not able to afford the ticket and would even contribute £100 per man toward the cost of their equipment, including clothes, boots and climbing equipment, but the rest they would have to find themselves.

On December 15, in a letter to George formally offering an expedition position, Hinks enclosed an undertaking that had to be signed by George, and the other climbers, acknowledging the authority of Charles Bruce as the expedition leader and pledging to avoid contact with the media, publishing photographs and articles and delivering public lectures 'without the sanction of the Mount Everest Committee'.

George was content to sign the document because the request seemed reasonable, particularly as the Royal Geographical Society and the Alpine Club needed to find ways of raising funds to cover costs, such as selling rights to various newspapers, charging for public lectures after the party returned, hopefully triumphant, and even producing a film and a book.

But he was perturbed by a rebuke from Hinks over a story that had appeared in the *Illustrated London News* in March, a few weeks after Francis Younghusband had publicly announced George Finch was a member of the reconnaissance team. The two-page profile, according to Hinks, had 'created an unfavourable impression' when he then had to remove Finch from the team after receiving the controversial medical reports. But rather than acknowledging the obvious – that it was Younghusband's announcement that had sparked the media interest – he blamed George or an 'injudicious friend' hoping to make money by selling a photograph of him to the magazine. The missive ended with a warning: 'I am sure you will do your utmost to put a stop to anything of the kind.'

It was typically antagonistic – the tense relationship highlighted by Hinks's addressing his letter to 'Mr Finch' rather than using the more friendly 'Finch' – but George held his tongue, promising: 'I will be careful that as far as lies in my power, no pictures of myself shall appear in the Press.'

Besides, there was a far more important issue at stake, although neither would realise it at the time. The committee had decided to send an official photographer, Captain John Noel, with the expedition, and George wanted to know if that meant that the photographs he planned to take, and the sketches and paintings he might want to make, would remain his property. Hinks wrote a lengthy reply, assuring him that the photographs would indeed remain his property, but were not to be published without the consent of the committee, concluding:

> I am sure you will find that these provisions are both necessary for the proper conduct of the expedition and that they will not be used by the Mount Everest Committee in any oppressive way. It is however necessary that the committee should, for a certain time, control all the results of the expedition and treat them all as official.

And there lay the important words – 'for a certain time'.

* * *

There would be thirteen men on the expedition, with George Mallory and Henry Morshead the only members of the reconnaissance mission who would return to the mountain in 1922. Along with George Finch, they would be three of the six designated climbers. The others were Howard Somervell, Edward Norton and Arthur Wakefield.

Major Edward 'Teddy' Norton had a mountaineering pedigree, his grandfather Alfred Wills being among the first to climb the Wetterhorn and a foundation member of the Alpine Club (although he was probably best known as the presiding judge in the 1895 trial of Oscar Wilde for acts of gross indecency). Teddy had been educated at the Charterhouse School before embarking on a military career. He first learned to climb while staying at the family chalet in the French Alpine region of Haute-Savoie, and was a renowned linguist and bird lover.

Dr Arthur Wakefield was a boyhood friend of Geoffrey Winthrop Young, George's supporter, and, like him, the privileged son of a wealthy family. As young men the two had attended Trinity College together. Wakefield had climbed in Switzerland for two seasons but it was his endurance as a Fells walker in the Lakes District that impressed Winthrop Young, although it seemed hardly the appropriate training ground for Everest. He was forty-six and had been severely traumatised by his experiences as a physician during the war.

Dr Thomas Longstaff was chosen as the expedition doctor, although he would admit after arriving in India that despite being technically qualified, he had never actually practised medicine. At forty-seven, Longstaff was too old to seriously tackle Everest although he had an impressive climbing record, not only in the Alps but in the Caucasus, Norway, Greenland, the United States and, importantly, in the Himalayas, where in 1907 he had been the first person to climb over 23,000 feet.

John Noel, the expedition photographer, was the son of a career army officer and grandson to the Earl of Gainsborough. He'd been christened Baptist Lucius but changed his name when he entered Sandhurst. He was a reluctant soldier (enrolling at the insistence of his father) who hoped that his posting to India would allow him to pursue his twin passions for exploration and photography, and in 1913 he had disguised himself and travelled with two local guides to find an eastern route to Everest, getting within fifty miles of his goal before being turned back by angry tribesmen. It was his lecture in 1919 concerning this adventurous trek that had reignited public interest in the conquest of Everest.

As expedition leader, General Bruce exercised his right to choose the support staff, selecting mainly soldiers with the experience and local knowledge to be able to handle logistics such as transport and translation services. His first choice was his cousin Captain Geoffrey Bruce, a 25-year-old Indian Army officer who was about to receive a Military Cross for gallantry during the Third Afghan War (although his performance review in 1920 had described a soldier 'not decidedly above or below average in any respect'). Geoffrey Bruce had never climbed a mountain but was considered to be a fine athlete, able to spear a pig between the shoulder blades from the back of a horse. He had youth and bravery on his side but time would tell if he could turn from horseman into mountaineer.

Captain John Morris was the antithesis of Geoffrey Bruce, a young bank clerk who'd been so bored with his job that he'd enlisted in 1915 and spent the next two years enduring the harrowing life of the trenches of France before joining the Indian Army. The killing hadn't stopped during the Afghan Wars and the smell and sight of shredded men would haunt him for the rest of his life. His salvation was an obsession with Tibet and its cultures, and the skills he'd acquired in pursuing that passion had impressed Charles Bruce when Morris had shown an interest in the expedition. At twenty-seven, he and Geoffrey Bruce would be the youngest in the party.

The last member of the support staff was Colin 'Ferdie' Crawford, a Cambridge graduate aged thirty-two who had fought with the Gurkhas during the war and then joined the Indian Civil Service. He had climbed for seven seasons in the Alps as well as in Kashmir and, like Morshead, had accompanied Harold Raeburn during his Himalayan expedition in 1920.

Although he had not met, let alone climbed with these men, George Finch would find the respect and support from a number of them that was sorely missing from those in charge.

* * *

On December 27, a week after the grandeur of the Queen's Hall reception for the 1921 reconnaissance team, George attended a much more private ceremony that would have a much more lasting impact on his life and legacy. For the third time in six years he took the vows of marriage in a registry office, rushing through a brief ceremony before two witnesses, but no friends or family. This time he knew he had chosen the right partner in Agnes Bubbles Johnston, which may be why, vexed by a combination of regret, shame and fear that he might never be happy, George could not bring himself to reveal the secrets of his past.

19.

THE POLITICS OF OXYGEN

In the summer of 1820 a London-based Russian physician named Joseph Hamel organised a party to climb Mont Blanc, in part to confirm the imposing mountain's height as the greatest in Europe but also to test his belief that a lack of oxygen contributed to muscle weakness at altitude.

'Mountain sickness' had first been documented in 1624 by a Jesuit priest and explorer named António de Andrade who reported that while crossing the Himalayas some members of his expedition had become ill because of what local tribespeople described as 'noxious vapours that rise'.

Little had been done scientifically in the two centuries since to solve the mystery, but Hamel, a savant who had previously published works on mining, education and the manufacture of potassium, wanted to conduct various experiments including measuring oxygen levels in the blood of his fellow climbers. He had also hoped to carry compressed oxygen to test its effects as his party neared the 15,780-foot summit, but couldn't find a suitable container that could be carried up the mountain.

It was an adventure that began full of promise but would turn to tragedy when three guides in the party, during the final ascent, were swept away by an avalanche. Hamel's experiments went with them, and though the guides' bodies would be recovered some years later, the reputation of Hamel, whose conceited attitude was blamed in part for the accident, never did.

It would be another fifty years before mountain sickness was again considered scientifically, but this time in a laboratory. In the mid 1870s the French zoologist Paul Bert used a steel tank pressure chamber to test and prove his theory that hypoxia was caused by low oxygen pressure. Bert mostly used animals and even insects in his experiments but also risked his own life, on one occasion reducing the chamber pressure to the equivalent of that at the summit of Mount Everest (although he didn't know it) and remaining conscious inside the tank by using piped oxygen.

Bert's findings were demonstrated in horrific fashion in 1875 when three daring aviators attempted to make a record balloon flight. Gaston Tissandier was a chemist and flying enthusiast keen on setting a new height benchmark. Joseph Croce-Spinelli and Théodore Sivel wanted to study the effects of breathing oxygen at great heights to prevent asphyxiation, so they carried bagged oxygen and planned to use it as the balloon neared the target of 26,000 feet.

The men were already feeling dizzy as the balloon rose past 23,000 feet and they entered the so-called 'death zone', but instead of reaching for the oxygen bags they cut free more ballast. The balloon shot skywards and the men fainted before they could get to the bags. Tissandier awoke as the balloon finally began to descend but Croce-Spinelli and Sivel were dead, their faces blackened and their mouths filled with blood.

Altitude experiments continued through the nineteenth century but it wasn't until 1907 that oxygen was used on a mountainside when the British climbers Arnold Mumm, Thomas Longstaff and

Charles Bruce (the latter two both members of the 1922 Everest expedition) climbed the main peak of Mount Trisul in the Indian region of Kumaun, at 23,359 feet.

As well as supplies, tents, sleeping bags and even a stove, Mumm carried an oxygen mask, as he later wrote: 'I took out, as my special contribution to our outfit, some oxygen generators, or pneumatogen cartridges. They are intended to be employed in mines where the air is foul, but I thought they might be useful at great heights. However, I never could get any of the others to take much interest in them, and no really good opportunity offered itself of testing their efficiency.'

Longstaff and Bruce were both dismissive of the idea of climbing with oxygen – an attitude that would later have great significance for George Finch – but Mumm persisted and would write about the night spent in his tiny tent while a storm raged outside high on the mountain: 'In the interests of science I tried whether a dose from the pneumatogen cartridge would assist me to enjoy a pipe. I think it certainly did; and I found I could smoke with satisfaction for several minutes continuously, which I had not been able to do before inhaling the oxygen.'

But that would be it, and Mumm's research went no further than the end of his pipe.

In the spring of 1916, a few weeks before the beginning of the Somme Offensive, a short, slight and bespectacled Scotsman gave a speech to members of the Royal Geographical Society in London. It was Dr Alexander Mitchell Kellas, who in 1921 would join the Everest reconnaissance party, and he had been invited by Arthur Hinks, already the society secretary, who had suggested a topic in his invitation: 'If you could give us a paper with some general title like "The possibilities of climbing above 25,000 feet" it would be a subject of first-rate interest, especially since no one perhaps in the world combines your enterprise as a mountaineer with your knowledge of physiology.'

There is no record of what Kellas said that day or of how many members, all men and mostly in uniform, were present, but the invitation seems to have piqued Kellas's own interest because a year later he proposed a scientific experiment in which he would erect a wooden hut on the summit of Mount Kangchenjhau (22,703 feet), where he would live for several months while conducting experiments on the physiology of acclimatisation.

The experiment never happened, cruelled by the continuing war, but Kellas was persistent and two years later was involved in a four-day study held in a low-pressure chamber at the Lister Institute in London. It resulted in a paper that was delivered during an Alpine Congress held in Monaco in 1920 and initially published in French. It began by posing the question: 'Is it possible for a man to reach the summit of Everest without adventitious aids?'

In the paper Kellas discussed the theoretical composition of air in the lungs of a climber as he reached the summit of Everest, the amount of oxygen in his blood and its rate of consumption by the body. Kellas even made predictions about the speed of climbers making their way up the mountain, encountering ever-thinning levels of oxygen, concluding: 'Mt Everest could be ascended by a man of excellent physical and mental constitution in first-rate training, without adventitious aids if the physical difficulties of the mountain are not too great, and with the use of oxygen even if the mountain can be classed as difficult from the climbing point of view.' (It would take almost six decades to confirm that Kellas's calculations were remarkably accurate when, in 1978, the Italian Reinhold Messner and the Austrian Peter Habeler became the first to ascend Everest without supplementary oxygen.)

In the years immediately after the Great War thoughts once again turned to peacetime frontiers, and an attempt on Everest and the use of artificial oxygen to get there became the source of great debate. Was it humanly possible to reach some altitudes and was it cheating to rely on artificial supplies of oxygen to defy nature's physical boundaries?

Kellas would try again, this time on the remote Mount Kamet (25,446 feet), tucked away on the Tibetan Plateau. In the autumn of 1920 he took seventy-four tanks of oxygen with him, each weighing twenty pounds (nine kilograms), and tested the effects of their use when he reached an altitude of 21,000 feet. The conclusion was emphatic and pessimistic: the cylinders were 'too heavy for use above 18,000 feet and below that altitude they are not required. They would be quite useless during an attempt on Mt Everest.'

Kellas conducted two other experiments at about 20,000 feet. The first was overly simple: he took a breath from a 'rebreather' – a rubber bag filled with the chemical compound oxylithe to help create oxygen – and then climbed thirty feet. He then climbed another thirty feet without taking a breath from the bag: 'The times were practically identical,' he concluded. 'The excess amount [of oxygen] in the lungs at starting was of negligible value in promoting ascent.'

But when he carried the bag beneath his arm and continually used it while climbing, the results were very different: 'The gain while using oxygen was quite decisive, the advantage being up to 25 per cent ... and clearly indicates that the light oxygen cylinders might be of considerable value as regards increase of rate of ascent at high altitudes.'

Kellas, of course, never got to test his theories on Everest, dying in the early stages of the 1921 reconnaissance mission and buried within sight of three giants he had climbed, his equipment abandoned as the others moved on toward the behemoth. His analysis lived on, however, eventually being published in the *Geographical Journal* back in London and read by George Finch as he fumed over being dropped from the expedition team.

* * *

It was in the superficially polite surroundings of Lowther Lodge, the Royal Geographical Society's headquarters in Kensington Gore, that the question of whether the 1922 Mount Everest expedition would use artificial oxygen was discussed on January 26, 1922. There were a dozen men around the oak table that dominated the council room, upstairs along the corridor, past the glass-walled exhibition rooms and well-stocked library, but only eight of them would vote on this most contentious aspect of the 1922 assault. It was clear that Percy Farrar would say yes to oxygen, just as Arthur Hinks would say no, but the remaining committeemen – Francis Younghusband, Edward Somers-Cocks, Colonel Jacks, Charles Meade, Norman Collie and John Eaton – were harder to pick.

The three others in the room were there to persuade the committee members to follow Farrar's lead. Howard Somervell, one of the climbers chosen for the expedition, had been convinced of the need to take bottled oxygen by the continuing research of Georges Dreyer that had again shown the benefits of oxygen. Along with George Finch, Somervell had recently submitted to testing in Dreyer's steel tank. This time the altitude was set at the level of the base camp on Rongbuk Glacier. George did the step-up test first, doing twenty repetitions with a thirty-pound (fourteen-kilogram) pack on his back to simulate carrying oxygen. Somervell followed but could only manage five step-ups before he collapsed and had to be given oxygen, recovering quickly.

George, backed by Percy Unna, outlined Dreyer's findings for the committee. It was the most accurate information at hand, albeit collected in the controlled and artificial environment of Dreyer's steel tank, and only an attempt on the mountain would prove the argument one way or the other. The minutes of the meeting, pasted roughly into an archived scrapbook, recorded the outcome in a matter-of-fact manner:

> After discussion the committee requested Captain Farrar, with the assistance of Messrs Somervell, Unna and Finch, to proceed with the scheme for the use of oxygen by the climbing party at a cost not exceeding £400 and to report progress to the committee. It was resolved to apply to the Air Ministry, the Department of Scientific and Industrial Research and the National Physical Laboratory for any assistance possible.

The minutes did not capture the passion of the debate inside the room that day, as Sir Francis would recall bitterly a decade later at another meeting of the committee as it planned a new assault on the mountain. He grimaced and snarled at the memory as the committee launched into yet another debate about the use of oxygen, revealing that the vote had been tied at the 1922 meeting. He, as president, had held the casting vote. The minutes in 1932 would record: 'The committee took into consideration the question of oxygen. Sir Francis Younghusband said that he gave the casting vote for oxygen in 1922 and had regretted it ever since. He was now definitely against oxygen ...'

The division among the expedition members in 1922 was palpable. Bruce and Strutt were against the idea from a moral perspective, Wakefield was distrustful and Longstaff, who with Charles Bruce had dismissed Mumm's 1907 experiment on

Mount Trisul, wanted his opposition noted formally, worried that any interruption to a supply of artificial oxygen would be fatal to climbers. George Mallory fumed at the decision, telling Sir Walter Raleigh, the chair of English Literature at Oxford, 'the physiologists might explode themselves in their diabolical chamber, but we would do well to explode their damnable heresy'.

But the decision had been made, if with some suspicion and regret. Ignoring the background rumblings George now turned his attention to the task of designing, manufacturing and testing the cylinders that would carry the oxygen that would be strapped to the backs of men attempting to scale the world's highest peak in the icy tempest that swirled around its upper reaches even during summer.

He retreated to Oxford where he and Georges Dreyer quickly ruled out trying to create oxygen through chemical reaction and instead opting for either producing liquid oxygen, which had to be generated on site, or taking compressed oxygen in steel cylinders from England. The first option was impractical and expensive but the second had already proved successful with pilots during the war. The challenge was to design cylinders that were light and did not leak.

The British company Siebe Gorman, which manufactured equipment used in the mining industry and in marine salvage, was chosen to build cylinders to George Finch's design. The cylinders were made of thin carbon-steel, each with the capacity to carry sixty-three gallons (240 litres) of compressed oxygen that would last a climber approximately two hours. Critically, each cylinder would weigh only five and a half pounds (2.5 kilograms) when full – barely one-quarter of the weight of the cylinders carried up Mount Kamet by Alexander Kellas. The carrying frame, hitched to the climber like a backpack, was made from the aluminum alloy duralumin, and weighed six and a half pounds (three kilograms), while the valves and hoses added another six and a half pounds. A full rack of four cylinders, which would provide a climber with oxygen for eight hours, would weigh only thirty-five pounds (sixteen kilograms).

To ensure a continuous flow of oxygen, George attached two hoses, which could be regulated by a pressure gauge and switched by opening and closing a simple valve, to the central cylinders. This would provide four hours of oxygen from two cylinders before the climber had to find a resting place where he could exchange the two near-empty cylinders with the remaining pair. The oxygen was almost pure, distilled from liquid air and cleaned by spiralling it through cooled metal coils to ensure that in the frigid environs of Everest there would be no residual moisture that could turn to ice and block the hoses.

Amazingly, the equipment was designed and manufactured within a month, the air compressed to 120 rather than 150 atmospheres to allow for the change of temperature between England and India and ten sets of four cylinders were packed carefully into wooden trunks and shipped on February 21. Another set was kept by George to train his fellow climbers during their own voyage a week later.

Some expedition members had already left for Marseilles where they would all gather to travel together to India, but most were still in London on February 22 when George presented his creation to the committee. That morning Hinks sent a letter to Bruce to discuss the departure of the expedition. He could not resist another dig at Finch: 'This afternoon we go to see a gas drill. They have contrived a most wonderful apparatus which will make you die of laughing. Pray see that a picture of Finch in his patent climbing outfit with the gas apparatus is taken by the official photographer.'

The climbing outfit ridiculed by Arthur Hinks was another piece of unrecognised genius on George Finch's part and another example of establishment ignorance and bile. On February 13 Hinks had taken delivery of a bulky parcel from the London firm SW Silver and Co, 'outfit contractors and manufacturers of camping equipment', with an accompanying letter: 'We are sending you herewith an eiderdown lined coat, trousers and gauntlet as per instruction from Capt Farrar. These garments have been made to the order of Captain Finch of the Mount Everest Expedition.'

George Finch, who had already stitched together his own duvet sleeping bag, had designed a knee-length padded jacket, mint-green in colour and made from the gossamer fabric used for hot air balloons, its carefully stitched layers filled with down and topped with a wide fur collar that could be wrapped against the neck when the Everest gales blew. There were matching trousers and gloves which created a largely windproof suit which contrasted sharply with the attire of the other members of the expedition, who were hoping to climb to more than 26,000 feet above sea level in various layers of pullovers, scarves and even pyjamas, topped with a Norfolk tweed suit. George Finch's creation would be a forerunner to the staple of modern alpine garb and urban streetwear – the puffer jacket – but it would be another two decades before anyone realised his brilliance.

20.

'WHEN GEORGE FINCH
STARTS TO GAS'

The men had been at sea, aboard the SS *Caledonia*, for three days before George Finch unpacked his precious oxygen tanks and called the climbing party to the main deck for a drill. The adventure was finally under way and he held what he believed would be the key to their success.

George had said goodbye to Bubbles in the afternoon of March 2. They had embraced hurriedly as a cold wind hustled across the main platform at Victoria Station and although nothing was said between them, both were keenly aware that he might not return. George was not afraid. He had faced death many times in his relatively short life but his third marriage, barely two months old, had significantly changed his outlook. There had been a time when he hadn't seriously contemplated the consequences of his death, the achievement of a daredevil ascent worth far more than the risk. But now he had a reason to return.

The world for now seemed at peace: bright sunshine, calm waters and dolphins at play, surfing on the bow wave of the white-hulled vessel as she steamed south across the Mediterranean toward Egypt. At Port Said they would turn down the Suez Canal before heading across the Arabian Sea to the teeming city of Bombay on the west coast of India. The voyage would take two weeks, more than enough time to ensure the men knew how to use and take care of equipment that would keep them safe at altitudes never before attempted by a human being.

George was keenly aware of the controversy surrounding the use of artificial oxygen, but the decision had been made and its implementation should be taken seriously. But it was clear from the first morning that Arthur Hinks had successfully sowed the seeds of distrust and, therefore, disharmony. The others attended George's training session but were visibly uninterested and dismissive. His cause had not been helped when a pressure valve had leaked slightly, even though George quickly repaired it. The following morning, March 7, was the same, as he noted in his diary, the first he had ever kept: 'Progress is somewhat slow because most of the others think it is all so simple that it does not need concentrated practice. However, today some made rather fools of themselves and got a bit muddled over the question of the valves. So shall probably do better next time.'

George's optimism was not well placed, though he continued to call daily drill sessions over the next week, sometimes scheduling them as early as 6am to beat the heat of the day. He had always planned his climbs meticulously in an effort to eliminate errors in this most dangerous of pastimes. He could not understand why the others were so laissez-faire in the face of such gigantic odds, preferring to sleep, to stroll the decks, read, gamble and even play cricket on a ship that was designed to carry 400 passengers in relative luxury but was largely deserted. Wakefield, one of the climbers, and Strutt, Bruce's deputy, were particularly venomous behind his back.

Only Somervell seemed fully supportive. In his subsequent book, *After Everest*, he recalled lengthy discussions about oxygen, and outlined his own views:

I, as a physiologist, could not help feeling – in conjunction with many physiologists much more experienced and distinguished than myself – that it was extremely doubtful whether human beings could live and move upwards at a height anything much above 23,000 feet, the highest point attained by any mountaineer up to that time. We all hoped the additional power given by the oxygen it [Finch's apparatus] supplied would more than counterbalance the awkwardness of so heavy a load, and would make up for the actual extra work expended in raising it along with our own body weight. Anyway, we decided to take it with us.

Even so, Somervell couldn't resist penning a light-hearted poem as he watched George doggedly battle the cynicism around him, the men preferring their games or drinking to addressing the serious challenges of the task ahead. Even though Somervell signed the ditty '*HS. A mon ami G.F*', George would not take it well.

The anchor weighed in the Port of Marseilles
When we started to verify travellers' tales.
The weather was fine and we all were at ease
And prepared for a fortnight's good rest on the seas.
But Hark! What was that? It's six bells without doubt
And soon all our holiday's gone up the spout;
For whether we're resting, or reading or ill
We're ruthlessly summoned to Oxygen Drill.
Are you lounging at ease or trying to sleep?
Are you watching the porpoises play in the deep?
Are you busy increasing your beverage bill?
Come away, for it's time for the Oxygen Drill.
Are you eating your breakfast or playing deck tennis?

Are you trying by guessing the Run to get pennies?
Never mind what you're doing your time for to kill
You've got to be present at Oxygen Drill.
Have you theories precise on the subject of gas?
Respiration, and so on, and action in mass?
The exactest of thought will appear rude and boorish
Compared to the latest in science from Zürich.
Do you think that you know about altitudes high
And what kind of glass keeps the sun from your eye?
On such questions your ignorance really is crass
But you'll soon be made wise when George Finch starts to gas.
So put down your books, come along learn the knack
Of hoisting the cylinders on to your back.
For if you'd be the victor of Everest's hill
You must finish each morning with Oxygen Drill.

As they eased down the Suez Canal, the dry, clean heat of the Mediterranean was replaced by baking desert temperatures, cooling only under the clear black night skies. The rains began at the Gulf of Aden, adding to the humidity as they neared the Equator: 'Hotter and damned moist,' George recorded briefly as he finally admitted defeat and ended the oxygen drills.

George Mallory had watched them with distaste – 'I sicken with the thought of the saliva dribbling down. I hope it won't be necessary to use it' – but also with a measure of sympathy for a man he had been told to dislike, as he wrote to his wife on March 15:

> I must say that in this company I'm amused by Finch and
> rather enjoy him. I'm much intrigued by the shape of his
> head, which seems to go out at the sides where it ought to go
> up. He is a fanatical character and doesn't laugh easily. He

greatly enjoys his oxygen class and talks about what he has got to do about it somewhat egotistically. However, the drill is being abandoned so perhaps we shan't hear quite so much about the subject – which nevertheless is very interesting – and Finch has been very competent about it. After endless discussion as to the volume of air one can breathe in a minute, the proportion of oxygen, I have very good hopes it will serve us well enough without psychological dangers from a camp at 25,000 feet.

Despite his previous cries of heresy, Mallory appeared to be softening his attitude and coming to accept oxygen as a legitimate tool that he might be prepared to use, although he was sceptical of Finch's belief that they all required a fortnight's training: 'Of course this is fantastic nonsense – two days would be ample training,' he told Ruth.

* * *

The *Caledonia* docked in Bombay on March 17 and after buying some supplies at a British army and navy store and several books from Thacker's publishing house (including *Hindu Manners, Customs and Ceremonies* and *Rifle and Romance in the Indian Jungle*) George and the others caught the first of several trains travelling north-east across the central plains to the city of Darjeeling, where Charles Bruce, his cousin Geoffrey and the other Indian Army officers, John Morris and Colin Crawford, waited, passing the time by choosing a team of cooks, interpreters and dozens of porters to carry the stores of food and equipment including the reconnaissance mission's tents that had simply been patched.

It was a three-day journey from Bombay to Darjeeling, in relative comfort but for the spiralling dust that invaded the carriages. It gave George his first taste of the poverty of the undeveloped world and of the complexities of Indian culture. Travelling through rich agricultural plains he observed that people seemed incapable of making the best use of the land and lived 'little better than animals', in sharp contrast to the people living in the hills: 'The hill men here are totally different; they are fine, well set-up, self-reliant men,' he wrote.

They reached Darjeeling on March 20 to find Charles Bruce eager to leave as soon as possible and begin the expedition. It would take a week to finalise arrangements but any delay beyond that would limit or even thwart an attempt on the summit, particularly with the monsoon due in early June and the mountain still 300 miles away.

But there was a problem: the oxygen equipment had been delayed, shipped around the coast of India and unloaded in Calcutta to reduce the overland train journey and avoid breakages. Someone – George Finch – would have to stay in Darjeeling until the tanks arrived while the rest of the party went on ahead to the hill town of Kalimpong, thirty miles north, from where they would begin the real trek across the Tibetan Plateau. George didn't question the decision; after all, the oxygen was his responsibility. Crawford, as a support officer, would wait with him.

As he waited in the lush hill station, the Himalayas forming a jagged white backdrop to the dense green of the region's famed tea plantations, George Finch recorded his assessments of the others in the party in his diary, even while conceding to himself that they were preliminary estimates only and he was prepared for the possibility that he might be wrong.

Some like Charles Bruce and Thomas Longstaff were 'non-starters', unable because of their age and ill health to climb higher than base camp. Others, like the photographer John Noel, Geoffrey Bruce, Crawford, Morris, Strutt and Heron, would go higher, but were support staff and unlikely to have ambitions to get to the summit. Geoffrey Bruce, for example, was a fit young man but had never climbed before.

George regarded the real climbers as Mallory, Morshead, Somervell, Norton and himself, although his assessment gave none of them – not even himself – a chance of reaching the top, at least not without oxygen.

The assessments were not intended for anyone's eyes except his own, and typically for George Finch, his conclusions were candid:

Captain Geoffrey Bruce: Good for 23,000 feet. Too young [lack of stamina], lung capacity not very pronounced [he is slightly narrow in chest from back to front]. Not a climber.

Captain Morris: Good for 23,000 feet. Wears glasses. Not a climber. Rather clumsy. Body long, legs short.

Captain Crawford: Good for 22,000 feet. Nervous disposition tending faintly to hysteria. Informs me he has much difficulty in sleeping above 19,000 feet. To judge by appearances is now suffering from mild insomnia.

Major Norton: Good for 23,000 feet. Trunk long, legs short in relation. Stamina good. He may do 24,000 feet but he is no mountaineer.

Colonel Strutt: Would be good for 24,000 feet or even more but for the fact that his opinion of himself is rather a gloomy one. He lacks full confidence in himself and that may very well stop him at 23,000 feet.

Dr Wakefield: Will not make 23,000 feet. Very nervous, distinctly hysterical and thus not likely to properly conserve his power. Age very much against him, more than it really should be.

Mr Mallory: Good for between 24,000 and 25,000 feet, perhaps a little more but not over 25,500 feet. I am inclined to look upon him as the strongest of all if he learns to go slow and not fluster himself.

Mr Somervell: Good for 24,000 feet. Rather heavy and likely therefore to become muscle bound. 23,000 feet in tank at Oxford finished him, and given time 21,000 would have done so judging from Dreyer's records of diastolic and systolic blood pressure.

Major Morshead: Don't know. Was fairly fit last year at 23,000 feet but is no born mountaineer.

Major Heron: Won't make 23,000 feet to judge from reports from last year's members.

Captain Finch: Would, I hope, hold my own with Mallory. But also I hope I won't be called on to make an attempt without oxygen.

* * *

George also wrote to Bubbles from Darjeeling. The letter, the first he'd written since leaving England almost three weeks before, began 'Beloved wife' and then launched into a list of instructions for dealing with the hundreds of photographs he planned to send back – 'films galore', he said. He had already begun taking photos as he strolled around Darjeeling, resplendent in his sturdy tweed knickerbocker suit, tie and pith helmet and carrying two pocket cameras.

By the end of the expedition he expected there would be more than 1500 images, all of which should be carefully developed by Bubbles with amidol, a crystalline powder, before the images were marked on the back by number to match the negatives and then filed in numbered envelopes with paper sheets between each photograph. What George required was 'thorough developing, fixing, washing, drying and handling after to avoid scratching, soiling or finger-marking any film'.

To anyone else, his demands might have seemed over the top, but Bubbles knew it was simply her husband's perfectionism speaking. She had fallen in love with a man she believed was a genius, and he needed her support. It was a role she wanted to perform.

George also sent Bubbles pages from his diary, insisting that Percy Farrar be the only other person allowed to read them 'until he has censored out what should not go further'. He wrote in wonderment at the scenery around Darjeeling and the exotic animals – buffalo, elephants, tigers, panthers, cheetahs, two types of bear and an Indian bison called a Gaur – that lurked in the jungles down by the Tista River.

He told her he had been busy, if not with his own equipment then helping to repair the equipment of others, and was excited at the chance to test the eiderdown jacket he'd designed, now packed in a trunk until he reached the Rongbuk Glacier. But the letter made no mention of the chance to conquer Everest; instead, its overwhelming sense was one of loneliness, George's distance from his new wife a more powerful feeling than the excitement of the adventure ahead:

> My darling, I am hoping anxiously that the first mail from
> you will arrive here before I go on trek ... You don't know
> how I long for you, how everything seems to be pulling me
> back to you — I feel so empty, so forlorn. I ought to tell you
> when reading my diary don't think I'm down in the mouth
> or really worried because I'm not. You are really always with
> me, and everything that comes along is just being accepted
> & taken on without question on my part. I love you, my
> dear darling heart with just that one great love of which I
> had never had the faintest idea of its existence but which I
> have known since you came into my life bringing happiness
> untold.

His sense of isolation was exacerbated by the underlying disunity of the expedition team. He was an outsider, unwanted by the team leaders, and he knew it. Worst of all, George did not trust the two men he would most likely be climbing with – George Mallory and Howard Somervell:

> It seems to me that [reconnaissance expedition leader
> Colonel Charles] Howard-Bury has left something of a
> legacy of gossip for me to live down. I like all the members
> of the party except Mallory & Somervell neither of whom
> are straight, especially not the latter of whom I can tell you
> something when I return. Young Bruce & Morshead I don't
> know, having only seen them for a few moments: but I think
> they are all right, even though Mallory is very thick with
> Morshead.

Not everyone was suspicious of him. John Morris immediately liked Finch and was disturbed by the behaviour of some of the others, particularly Colonel Strutt, which he witnessed one morning when the weekly parcel of English newspapers arrived. In one of them was a two-page feature written about George and his exploits in the Alps. It was the piece in the *Illustrated London News* that Hinks had chided George about five months before, slipped into the mailbag for no other reason than to create more friction and give the impression that George had broken the publicity embargo. Strutt seethed, as Morris would recall in a book he wrote later about the expedition:

> Strutt's objections were based upon Finch's unusual
> background. He had been educated in Switzerland and had
> acquired a considerable reputation for the enterprise and
> skill of his numerous guideless ascents. Besides, he was by
> profession a research chemist and therefore doubly suspect,
> since in Strutt's old-fashioned view the sciences were not a
> respectable occupation for anyone who regarded themselves
> as a gentleman. One of the photographs which particularly
> irritated him depicted Finch repairing his own boots. It
> confirmed Strutt's belief that a scientist was a sort of a
> mechanic. I can still see his rigid expression as he looked at
> the picture: 'I always knew the fellow was a shit,' he said,
> and the sneer remained on his face while the rest of us sat in
> frozen silence.

The incident made Morris keenly aware of George's demeanour during the few days they were all together in Darjeeling:

> He seemed ill at ease at first, probably knowing that his
> presence was not particularly welcome. But it was at once clear
> that his whole approach to the problem with which during the

next few months we should be confronted was different from
that of the rest. His attitude was thoroughly professional,
and although this was his first visit to the Himalayas, his
scientific training had led him to consider a number of matters
the importance of which was barely sensed by some of the
others. It was his misfortune to be of the right age to attempt
Everest in 1922. His ideas of how such expeditions should
be conducted were in advance of his time. He would have
been more at home in one of the highly planned expeditions
of later years, especially if he had been the leader. Even
so, his contribution was considerable. He was an advocate
of climbing with the aid of oxygen, which at the time was
considered by the old guard to be unsporting. Indeed, Strutt
was firmly of the opinion that if we reached the summit of
Everest only with the help of oxygen we could not claim to
have climbed the mountain. His dislike of Finch continued
throughout the expedition.

21.

THE ROAD TO KAMPA DZONG

Charles Bruce split the expedition into three travelling groups when they left Darjeeling. On March 27 he led the first group, which included Mallory, Longstaff, Morshead, Wakefield, Noel and his nephew Geoffrey, out of the city. The next day Strutt, Morris, Norton and Somervell boarded a train and headed to Kalimpong. That left George and Crawford to bring up the rear with the oxygen equipment, which had not yet arrived.

On the surface the idea seemed to have merit. Smaller teams meant quicker travel and increased the party's chances of getting to the Rongbuk Glacier and establishing a base camp with enough time to prepare for an assault on the mountain before the monsoons arrived, as expected, in early July.

But there was also a downside, as George attempted to explain to General Bruce, as tactfully as possible given his tenuous relationship with the expedition leader – 'I do not wish to appear to be an unruly nuisance.' The first two groups were well equipped with medical support but George and Crawford would have none and were likely to be several days' march, perhaps a week or more, behind the others.

It was the opposite issue with the oxygen equipment. George and Crawford would be carrying everything, with no chance to test the equipment or complete the training for the other climbers unless they caught them along the 250-mile trek to Rongbuk Glacier. George estimated it would take a fortnight to train the others properly, but that was now going to be almost impossible because it was unlikely, based on travelling calculations, that he and Crawford would arrive at Rongbuk until May 20, giving them barely a month to prepare for and make a climb before the expected rains in early July.

The diplomatic approach failed. General Bruce stuck with his plan and made it clear that it was up to George and Crawford to catch up, if and when they could. He and Strutt had also made a major decision about the climbing strategy. The first attempt to climb Everest would be made by a team led by George Mallory and it would be without oxygen. If he was ready, George could follow later.

'I should mention at this stage that the attempt (or at all events the first real attempt) is to be made without oxygen,' George wrote in a diary entry on March 22 as he sat in his room in the suitably named Everest Hotel:

> I gathered this impression yesterday in conversation with General
> Bruce and it was confirmed today by Longstaff in the course
> of a conversation between him, Norton and myself. I can also
> mention that Longstaff thinks it is a great mistake to have oxygen
> at all. Oxygen is not popular and I doubt very much if anyone,
> excepting myself, places any reliance upon it as a help in reaching a
> high altitude.

After the others left Darjeeling, George became more and more despondent. He packed and repacked four times, including his supply of 1000 cigarettes, shot and developed dozens of photographs in a makeshift tank as an experiment, made waterproof maps of the area by pasting them to canvas and coating them with layers of a thin rubber compound, and even whittled himself a slingshot to use as protection against the jackals he could hear wailing at night outside the hotel.

He bought the bladders from toy footballs in case he needed a back-up breathing system for the oxygen tanks and rearranged the nail tread on his boots to improve their grip and then tested them by climbing to the top of Tiger Hill, a seven-mile trek from the town, where on a clear day it was possible to get a glimpse of the tip of Everest as it peeked through the wall of rock and ice immediately confronting the expedition.

George even began drawing, sketching and painting, as he explained to Bubbles in a series of letters: 'I got up at 6am & went to Observation Hill armed with sketchbook and pastels. The result of my labours, especially after applying fixative, is very horrid, but in spite of my obviously absolute inability in this field I'm going to stick to it, chiefly because it affords a certain amount of amusement.'

He also referred to the financial problems at home, which highlighted the sacrifices he'd made to go on the six-month expedition. Most of the participants were independently wealthy men, like Charles Bruce, Strutt, Longstaff and Somervell. Others had been drafted in from the Indian Civil Service or the British Army and remained on full pay. George, by contrast, was on half pay and it was clear that Bubbles was already struggling, worried about meeting the £10 per month payment on a car, an open-top Humber that George had bought in his flush of excitement when they married:

> I rang up before leaving to say that I was not going to
> resume payments until October. Sell the Humber when

you like & for what you like, only keep back my tools! In
any case, beloved wife, you may do anything you think fit
and you need never be afraid that I shall criticise what you
do – provided you look after yourself & don't worry or fret.
I know how awful this separation is. Almost ever since last
writing to you I've been fighting off an almost insufferable
attack of loneliness. Beloved heart. Like you I find my way to
you and dreamland in the still dark hours, wondering at the
strangeness that leaves me so often much alone. I love you,
love you & wonder sometimes at my undeserved happiness
in having the love of you.

On March 31 George received word that the oxygen tanks had
finally arrived in Calcutta and would be railed almost 400 miles to
reach Kalimpong by April 3. It meant he and Crawford would be
eight days behind the others by the time they left. Perhaps all was
not lost, after all, as he wrote to Bubbles:

My beloved wife,
The oxygen has turned up sooner than I had dared
to hope so tomorrow sees the real commencement of our
trek. Dear darling Bubbles, I love you as you know & I am
so utterly proud of you. I am getting this letter off tonight
because after today postal arrangements will not be so good!
Somehow I have felt all the time that you are with me &
partaking in all the things I see and experience. I feel I go
forward now to achieving my best – whatever that may be.
We have a longish trek tomorrow [to Pedong] and as it's
getting late I must begin to say goodnight. I long & long
for the time when I can once more fall asleep in the happy
shelter of your arms. Darling wife, be happy as is possible –

I think of you and am so often with you. Do not worry, I will
be careful & God will keep me well for your dear sake.

* * *

George faced a dilemma as he and Crawford set out from
Kalimpong on the morning of April 4. They had to find a balance
between haste, so they could catch up to the main parties that
were both now approaching the Tibetan fortress town of Phari,
100 miles north and another 6500 feet above sea level, and care, to
avoid damaging the precious tanks with their life-giving oxygen.

He could hear the hollow clank of metal on metal as the
cylinders rubbed together, carried by porters on their shoulders
along the rough track. George ordered a halt and using a penknife –
the only tool Charles Bruce had bothered to leave him – prised
open one of the boxes. It confirmed the worst, that the cylinders
had already been damaged.

They had to be repacked, and it was a six-hour task to secure all
of them using a makeshift padding of ropes and rags. Otherwise
the tanks would not make it to the base of Everest, let alone the
summit, as George wrote: 'The inevitable explosion would not
only cost us the cylinders' precious contents and maybe endanger
lives but it would have discredited oxygen completely, and many
participants had a low opinion of and little love for oxygen as it
was.'

The condition and route of the trail compounded the problem;
it was a rough and rutted track alternately plunging through deep
valleys of lush green jungle and wild blue and silver rivers before
leading upwards so steeply they had to walk their ponies until they
topped a ridge, often to find a village of roughly hewn houses with
a tea house at its centre and surrounded by tiny plots of farmland.

George Finch had never seen country, weather or people like this although, typically, he had read about the region assiduously: 'Get Farrar to lend you [Douglas] Freshfield's book,' he advised Bubbles in a letter. 'It has lots to say about Darjeeling & is altogether a ripping book.'

He photographed everything, fascinated in particular by the faces of the local tribespeople, and spent hours under candlelight each night experimenting with makeshift methods of developing his film. His diary, until now filled with his frustration at the delays, recorded his wonderment as he and Crawford leapt into a mountain stream to wash off weeks of grime in the pristine waters:

> The surrounds of the stream are beautiful beyond all my powers
> of description. Both banks support dense jungle growth –
> magnificent trees, many of which have their life support sapped
> away by the luxuriant burden of orchids, ferns, creepers and other
> parasitical plants which they nourish. Dense shrub and fern
> undergrowth completely hide the ground and the lowest part of
> the tree trunk. Bamboo grows everywhere with many beautiful
> palms.

He also wrote about the mule drivers, porters and cooks who accompanied them:

> The twenty mules are rather small animals; they average little
> more than 14 hands but they are wonderfully fast goers, ever so
> sturdy and splendid weight carriers and are extremely well looked
> after by their two Tibetan drivers – cheerful, willing hard workers.
> The coolies are a mixed lot – one or two Nepalese and mostly
> Lepchas ... they come along all right and don't grouse. Our cook is
> a Sherpa. His name is Kang Cho. He is rather lame, the result of

a horse's kick. He is a very solemn figure with a lovely pigtail. He cooks well and is always usefully busy. His mate is a Lepcha, quite a boy and satisfactory in every way.

The days and villages passed by – Pedong, Rangli, Rangpo, Lingtam, Sedongchen and Lingtu – as the trail inevitably led upwards, through the land known as Sikkim toward Kangchenjunga, the world's third highest peak. The mountain's name, an interpretation of Tibetan pronunciation by members of the Kellas expedition in 1920, meant 'five treasures of the high snow' and the expedition members would have to work their way around the base of the five peaks of the mountain to get to their destination.

The scenery was changing, the forests thinning. The vivid dark red hues of the giant rhododendrons and the white, lilac, blue and yellow gentians were increasingly replaced by bare stony ground. And the temperature was falling as they climbed higher, the hazy skies and humidity of the hills and valleys now turned misty and overcast.

It began to snow on the afternoon of April 7 as they approached the hilltop village of Gnatong; slight flutters at first but thickening to cast a grim pall as they stood for an hour in the local cemetery, reading the inscriptions on the headstones of British soldiers who had lost their lives during the bloody campaigns of the late nineteenth century. George was taken by the fact that only one man had been killed in action, the others dying from disease or exposure. It highlighted the isolation and peril of the bleak, barren country they were about to traverse.

It was still snowing the next morning, forcing a delay as they arranged stockings and boots for the porters before the next climb across the Jelep La, the mountain pass linking India with Tibet. George was frustrated that his skis had been taken ahead against his express wishes – yet another example of his warnings about conditions being ignored. The climb itself wasn't difficult under calm skies, hence the name which meant 'lovely level pass', but by mid morning the snowfall had turned into a blizzard, the conditions now hazardous as the mercury plunged and the trail began to ice.

Dressed in his knee-length eiderdown coat for the first time, George took the lead. Accustomed to trekking through a snowstorm, he ploughed ahead and found a safe path down from the Jelep La, but his footprints were soon covered by the snowfall and he had to backtrack to find the porters and Crawford who had become lost as visibility was reduced to a few yards. It took them over six hours but eventually George led the descent into the village of Yatung at the entrance to the Chumbi Valley. They had reached Tibet.

* * *

The cold had also hit the two parties ahead, both of which had reached Phari by April 6 and had then huddled for two days, frozen and 'coughing in the ever thickening murk', as John Morris noted. Mallory in particular was unhappy, telling Ruth in a letter that he had been bored by 'the repetition of aesthetic experiences' of the trip and was longing to get to Everest. The men stayed the second night in Phari to celebrate Charles Bruce's fifty-sixth birthday with a bottle of 120-year-old rum that he'd brought for the occasion: 'If we had known what was in front of us, we should have put off the drinking of this peculiarly comforting fluid until the evening of the day after our first day's march from Phari,' he would later write, referring to the blizzard they would face.

They set off on April 8 on a three-day march to the fortress town of Kampa Dzong where, in 1903, Sir Francis Younghusband had attempted to negotiate a trade treaty with Chinese and Tibetan officials. He had taken five hundred troops and waited five months before giving up and going home. Now it was the gateway to the greatest adventure of all.

Charles Bruce again split the reunited expedition (save for the Finch–Crawford party) into two groups: he would lead the first, taking a higher and quicker route with fifty Chumbi mules carrying mostly luggage, while the second, under Colonel Strutt, would include a convoy of two hundred yaks loaded with stores and supplies, and would follow the lower, safer, but longer track.

General Bruce had likened the trek so far to a walk through the Highlands of Scotland, but that was to change dramatically. Soon after midday, the threatening weather broke and struck with a force they had not expected. No one was properly prepared; neither the Englishmen who were dressed in a motley selection of tweed suits and pullovers, nor the porters who still walked in sandals and light robes.

The bitter 'half-hurricane' winds pounded them for hours and made it almost impossible to marshal their animals. In the midst of the tempest three porters from the lower group were lost and presumed dead. The next morning they were found barely alive, having slept the night in the open, unable even to chip through the ice crust and start a fire.

When General Bruce's mule party reached Kampa Dzong on the afternoon of the 11th, his first priority was to check the grave of Alexander Kellas. He added extra stones to the mound over it to ensure its security against wild animals. He then set up a camp site at the base of a 300-foot cliff on which the old fortress had been constructed. Strutt's group was another two days behind with the yaks, and arrived during the morning of the 13th, just a few hours ahead of George Finch and Colin Crawford.

It had been a remarkable effort by Finch and Crawford to travel from Darjeeling in just ten days – a journey that had taken the others eighteen days – yet their effort to reunite the expedition was barely acknowledged by General Bruce other than to question the impact it would have on the porters and coolies, who, he worried, would arrive at the base camp exhausted and unable to 'do the work', while the oxygen equipment, he said, had been 'badly knocked about'. The general had intended leaving Kampa Dzong the next day but begrudgingly agreed to a rest day.

Unlike the sour Mallory and Bruce, George was ecstatic: 'Ye gods, I am fit!' he declared after describing how he rushed up and down a hillside to get a photograph of a Tibetan antelope that reminded him of a European chamois. The last few days had been challenging but exhilarating, cheered by the scenery of the Chumbi Valley as they crossed into Tibet which, blanketed by snow, reminded George of a Swiss Alpine gorge but otherwise left him at a loss for words: 'I wish I could describe more adequately our experiences and the beauty of the scenery we have been wandering through the last few days. But sometimes it seems quite beyond the powers of my pencil, and I must trust my photographs to make up some of the deficiency.'

The ugliness of Phari, where they had arrived on April 10, had stood in sharp contrast, although it had offered a place to sleep and to post a letter and confirmation that they were within touch of the others. Foregoing the chance to rest for a day, Finch and Crawford and their party of a dozen porters and mule drivers had chosen to face the ice-cold conditions and bitter, stinging wind to race along the higher track toward Kampa Dzong. On April 11 they had slept outdoors and on April 12 their accommodation had improved slightly when they'd been welcomed into a roofless monastery by a group of helpful if bedraggled nuns who spread George's eiderdown sleeping bag across an altar just beneath the partly eaten and decaying carcass of a goat.

At more than 16,000 feet above sea level it was akin to sleeping on top of Mont Blanc, but George was not complaining. On the contrary, his diary glowed with the pleasure of the scenery as it changed again, the blue skies revealing three giants – Chomolhari, Pauhunri and Chomiomo – across the flat, stony plain. George was by now encased in his eiderdown coat, trousers, gloves, flying boots and helmet, and was impervious to the cold and the altitude, as he noted: 'I need hardly say that the altitude has had no noticeable effect upon me. I feel and know by what I can do by way of muscular work that I am extremely fit, and in spite of regular shaving, my face is almost as dark as any Tibetan. Crawford and I get on splendidly together.'

In the five weeks since leaving London he had not once mentioned, in letters or his diary, the prize of Everest. It was as if reaching the summit mattered less than the experience and the desire to test scientifically his theories about oxygen. He worried constantly about the equipment he had helped devise and design and was frustrated at the apparent lack of interest by General Bruce. He wondered whether it would result in him missing an opportunity to use the oxygen high on the flanks of the mountain, above the so-called death zone. It was this scientific attitude and his determination to absorb as much as he could from the entire experience that set him apart from many of the other men. He did not believe he was superior to them, but realised he had a more complex purpose in joining the expedition.

George was a polymath, happy to apply his varied skills for the benefit of the team, unfazed by the strictures of class: he made himself useful around the camp in Kampa Dzong developing film for his colleagues, including Mallory, and repairing the cameras of

Morris and Longstaff; he applied his engineering skills to adjust the Primus stoves and didn't blink at helping to shoe the horses, readily involving himself in manual chores which would have been unthinkable for men such as Colonel Strutt.

But his first rest day since leaving Darjeeling began with him writing to Bubbles, his declarations of love even more desperate than usual:

> My own dear beloved wife,
>
> Crawford and I arrived here yesterday afternoon after three very long marches from Phari, during which the weather had been decidedly cold. We found all the rest of the party here. They were all glad to see us & were surprised at our speed.
>
> Mallory alone was obviously fed up. You know he does not like me. Today we are having a so-called rest day, but really there is so much to do that there is little rest about it. I took about six rolls of photos since leaving Phari. Two I developed here this morning – but they go very dusty drying so I'm keeping the rest until I get to some better spot. Beloved, I don't know how many times I have read your letter ... Please keep well darling. I am taking all possible care here – for whenever I am inclined to be careless you seem to be talking to me and telling me to pull up my socks. Dear darling beloved, you know how I love you, and I am coming back just as soon as possible to you. September is not far away & if it can be made sooner so shall it be. Beloved, we are just sending out a post & it is now just closing. I did not know one was going. Beloved, God bless you. I love you, love you, love you, kiss you my beloved. Your husband Geof

22.

GODDESS MOTHER
OF THE WORLD

The expedition was now travelling together and the lumbering great caravan of three hundred animals and their handlers moved off. The Europeans rode mules or ponies when they could, across the flat, desolate Tibetan Plateau, crossing a series of dunes and marshes where the Yaru and Arun rivers met and timing each march to arrive at a new village each afternoon. On April 16 they set up camp outside Tinki Dzong, a fortress built into a hillside with its imposing stone wall overlooking a shallow lake.

George decided to resume the oxygen drills that had been abandoned because of lack of interest before they had even reached Bombay. It was the first time the entire party had been together for any period of time and he hoped that being so much closer to their goal might change a few minds.

John Noel stood back from the rest to capture the scene with his camera: George with his head down, eagerly pointing out the features of his creation to those gathered around him, their limited interest clear as they stand with their hands shoved into the pockets of their tweed jodhpurs. A group of porters looks on, bemused. Behind them white tents stand in neat rows, surrounded by stacks of wooden crates and ragged yaks that have somehow found small patches of alpine grass to eat on an otherwise brown landscape.

As indicated by the photo, the response was not what George had been hoping, and the resumption of the drill sparked a heated debate that night during dinner, with Mallory and Longstaff the most vocal opponents.

George had been right about Mallory, at least to some extent: 'I'm bound to say I find Finch rather tiresome,' Mallory told Ruth. 'He is perpetually talking about science as practised in his laboratory or about photography. In fact it is becoming a little difficult not to acquire a Finch complex. I hope we shall manage to get on.'

Still, the anti-Finch sentiment was beginning to thaw. John Morris had already declared his liking for George and Crawford had become friendlier as the pair trekked across northern India and Tibet. Henry Morshead was another who was beginning to doubt what he had been told about George and indicated that others felt the same way, as he wrote in his diary on April 16 after the fractious dinner: 'Finch has been giving us a lecture on the use of the oxygen apparatus; we are to practise it every day from now onwards. Finch is a good fellow and I don't know how all those yarns about him originated last year. We all like him, and I personally consider him far more of a sahib than our local representative of the ICS [Indian Civil Service].'

George's struggle to be accepted was only heightened by his dress. The men had all been issued with thigh-high flying boots but nothing else was standard issue. John Morris had hurriedly bought a knickerbocker suit before leaving Darjeeling, made of 'shoddy Kashmir tweed'. He, like the others, wore woollen underclothing beneath his suit as well as several Shetland pullovers, which restricted their movements to a 'clumsy waddle'.

George could sense a change in the attitudes of the others toward his attire: 'Today has been bitterly cold with a gale of a wind to liven things up,' he wrote on April 18. 'Everybody now envies me my eiderdown coat and it is no longer laughed at. May it do its job well on Everest!'

Although he meant it innocently, envy was not an emotion he needed to foster. It is significant that Charles Bruce, in his memoir, wrote of his own 'very efficient mackintosh', but made no mention of Finch's clothing. His silence was loud, as he agreed that the clothing of most of the men was useless against the wind that 'simply blew through wool'. George Mallory, who had been complaining of the cold, took a different view, describing the men as 'snugly wrapped in their woollen waistcoats and Jaeger pants, their armour of wind-proof materials, their splendid overcoats, the fur-lined finneskoes or felt-sided boots or fleece-lined moccasins devised to keep warm their feet'. His comment was ludicrous: at best heroic and at worst disingenuous, serving only to highlight his jealousy of George Finch.

John Noel, however, looked at George in wonderment: 'Finch, who had a scientific brain, invented a wonderful green quilted eiderdown suit of aeroplane fabric. Not a single particle of wind could get through. Underneath he used to wear a suit of silk underclothes, then one of wool, then another, then a fourth of thicker wool, then a fifth of the thickest fabric he could find.'

Noel's growing admiration for George Finch also extended to his photography. Despite Mallory's carping (which was hypocritical, given that he had happily accepted George's offer to develop his film), Noel recognised George's skill and asked him to help with some of the photographic work. The panoramic shots were time-consuming: setting up the equipment and waiting for the right light, not to mention avoiding bad weather. And Noel was busy filming as well, in order to satisfy Arthur Hinks's desire to have a commercially viable movie of the expedition to help recoup some of the costs and perhaps even turn a profit.

Not only was George Finch capable of developing film but he was also a decent photographer, so Noel set him the task of capturing the 'topical' shots that Hinks also expected – photographs of people, both members of the expedition and the people of Tibet, as well as photos that would capture the essence of how the party travelled and lived as they moved ever closer to Everest.

George was excited by Noel's invitation, although he was wary of Hinks and the Everest Committee as he instructed Bubbles to get two mountaineering pals, Raymond Peto and Bentley Beetham, to make prints of the best shots, bind them in a paper book and arrange for Percy Farrar to offer them to the committee for publication:

> But do not let them have the film on any account, for I have suffered so much by way of stained, fingermarked, torn & even lost negatives through lending them to office people that I do not trust any more. If they demur about this, inform them that the negatives are made throughout with my own materials. And if they should get still nastier, don't let them have any at all, but keep them till I return. I hope, however, they are reasonable for I should very much like some of my photos to be published soon.

* * *

Back in London, Arthur Hinks had not let up in his campaign against George Finch and his oxygen, and was unapologetic in his attempt to influence Charles Bruce, even en route to Everest. On April 12 he wrote to Bruce complaining about an article Percy Farrar had prepared for the *Alpine Journal* in which he supported Professor Georges Dreyer's view about the use of oxygen. He planned to counter the article with one of his own in the Royal Geographical Society magazine:

> Dreyer seems to maintain that oxygen must be taken into use at 23,000 feet. The president [Francis Younghusband] and I believe that it is nonsense. Abruzzi went to 24,800 feet without it. Kellas and Morshead at 23,500 feet on Kamet felt quite fit to go a long way, and our opinion is that this year the expedition ought certainly with its far greater resources [be able] to beat Abruzzi's record without oxygen, though it might very well be that oxygen be taken up to the top. I write of this just to tell you what is in our minds, and to let you know that although we cordially agree with equipping the party with oxygen we think that a great deal can, and should be done, without it. I would gladly put a little money on Mallory to go to 25,000 feet without the assistance of four cylinders and a mask.

Two weeks later he tried again, revealing that things had got personal between himself and Farrar, who had accused him of making fun of the oxygen outfit. Hinks denied the accusation even though it was true: 'It is not intended to make fun of the oxygen outfit at all, as Farrar had first supposed, but some of us do feel that the oxygen people have relied too much on Dreyer … we shall be very disappointed if some of the party do not get to 25,000 feet or 26,000 feet without such artificial aid, and I hope they will bear that in mind.'

When the Royal Geographical Society article appeared it got immediate publicity in the wider media, with *The Times* reporting:

> The writer entertains doubts as to whether or not oxygen should be taken at all times above 23,000 feet and adds that

'it seems quite as important to discover how high a man can climb without oxygen as to get to a specified point, even the highest summit in the world, in conditions so artificial that they can never become legitimate mountaineering'.

It demonstrated yet again that Arthur Hinks, who had declared before the men left that 'anyone who climbs to 26,000 feet with oxygen is a rotter', was determined to find a way to sabotage George Finch. His acceptance of oxygen as a legitimate experiment was disingenuous and his machinations were potentially damaging to the expedition and the lives of the thirteen men who had been sent to seek glory on behalf of the Empire. His stance was even more damning considering that he was neither an expert nor had he ever experienced the effects of altitude on a climber's mind and body – and that he was trampling on the decision of a committee largely made up of men who had.

* * *

Mallory and Finch wanted to find reasons to like each other – after all they were kindred souls on a mountain – but their differences at ground level were becoming more and more entrenched as the expedition progressed. Not only were the two men divided on the question of artificial oxygen – one because of his own dogmatic character and the other because he was easily swayed by the arguments of others – but the manner and even the skills of each man were annoying to the other.

Mallory was a sublime natural athlete who moved instinctively and often without thought for the consequences. George moved quickly enough and with authority, but only after careful thought. Mallory was a creative spirit, who wrote like a dream and thought nothing of peeling off his clothes if the weather was too warm and trekking naked. He habitually left his belongings scattered around the camp site. George was a man of logic who preferred his camera to words. He was far from a prude, happy to bathe in a mountain stream. However, his preference was for order: he preferred hot water, hated the feeling of stubble on his chin and was perennially frustrated by the necessities of quick teeth, face, hands and arm washing after wading across rivers on long treks.

They were also rivals, both with a point to prove – to themselves and their philosophies. The rivalry bared its teeth on April 20 when the expedition arrived at Gyankar Nangpa, 'the usual collection of dirty squalid hovels', as George described the scene. In contrast, above the camp site rose an elegant mountain known as Sangkar Ri, which reminded him of the majesty of the Matterhorn.

The trek that morning had been barely six miles of easy terrain and the pent-up energy of the men bubbled over into a desire to climb the 20,000-foot peak as a training run for the challenges ahead. There was also the promise of an uninterrupted view of Mount Everest, which lay on the other side of the peak. They would have to camp overnight on the mountain and then strike out for the summit in the early morning to give them time to descend by 1pm the following day in order to move on with the rest of the expedition. Mallory, Somervell and Wakefield, as well as George, were all eager to go, so, with General Bruce's permission, the four men divided themselves into two teams – Mallory with Somervell and Finch with Wakefield.

Mallory would later write that the climb was his idea and that he and Somervell, having sought the permission of Bruce, were making their plans when 'two others' decided to join in, as if it was an intrusion. To make matters worse an argument then broke out between Mallory and Finch about the right way to tackle the mountain – 'a battle royal', as George would describe it – which was only settled by Bruce who, perhaps surprisingly, favoured the Finch proposal.

They set off at 4.15pm, the four men with six porters who would bring the equipment – tents and sleeping bags – back down the mountain the next morning while the climbers continued upwards: 'Mallory, of course, started to race so, just to show there was no ill-feeling, I acted as his runner-up and beat him by just over three-quarters of an hour in the three and a half hours it took to get to the site of our projected camp. It was dark by the time we set in to pitch our tents. The cold was intense,' wrote George.

George woke during the night feeling ill and admonished himself for not wearing his cholera belt, a piece of flannel designed to keep the abdomen warm and supposedly prevent the chills that were thought to lead to dysentery. The others couldn't sleep either because of the cold but preferred to stay huddled in their tents and ridiculed George's suggestion that they leave at 1am to ensure they had enough time to complete the ascent. The men finally emerged at 3.30am, ate and broke camp soon after 4am, but were slowed almost immediately when confronted by moraine, debris from an ancient glacier. It took them four hours to negotiate the unexpected obstacle and reach the steep slope that led to the base of a col they hoped would take them to the mountaintop.

By 9am the four men, still climbing in pairs, were only halfway up the passage and time was running out if they were going to be back at Gyankar Nangpa by the promised 1pm deadline. George was feeling ill again, vomiting several times. He decided to turn back with Wakefield while Mallory and Somervell went on. Mallory's report of the climb was laced with the perception that his rival had quit too easily: 'We had ascended not more than 1000 feet the next morning when one of the party decided he was too ill to go on; he exhibited the usual symptoms of mountain-illness.'

As it turned out, Mallory and Somervell were also forced to turn back only a few hundred yards from the peak, both suffering the effects of altitude sickness, although Mallory shrugged it off: 'I had come near to exhaustion, considering the difficulties of the climb, and had suffered from a severe headache, but certainly felt no worse than I expected at this stage in our training.' Finch and Wakefield had rejoined the main party and made their way to the next village, but Mallory and Somervell would only arrive late in the night after being helped across riverbeds – 'quicksands of evil repute' – by their porters.

The Sangkar Ri experience not only highlighted the increasing division between the two lead climbers but also the challenge they all faced to acclimatise to the altitude. The Tibetan Plateau has an average altitude of almost 15,000 feet, the equivalent to trekking across the top of the Matterhorn. The climbers were accustomed to the plateau's altitude and Sangkar Ri had been a chance to test themselves at the next level. Although he felt fitter than at any time in his life, it was clear that George Finch (and Mallory, too) needed more time to acclimatise and that performing an exercise at altitude in the controlled environment of a steel tank in Oxford was vastly different to the experience in the wild environs of the Himalayas.

There was another moment of importance the next morning soon after they struck camp and mobilised the caravan. The climbers were walking ahead, following the banks of the Yaru River, when they rounded a sharp bend. George caught sight of it first as a reflection in the calm waters, an enormous white pyramid that seemed to grow as they turned the corner. Everest.

The men stopped, transfixed. John Noel hurriedly set up his camera to capture the moment on film. Two of them – Mallory and Morshead – had seen the mountain before, but even they had not seen the Goddess Mother of the World from this perspective:

the full south face blanketed in snow, filling the horizon of the mountain pass they walked in, as if she had been lying in wait and now wanted to show her might. The bare red and brown mountains that had bordered their path for the past week seemed to melt away, puny now – 'a crumpled Egyptian desert', mused Charles Bruce.

George Finch had a strange, mixed response: 'A great and stirring sight,' he wrote. 'One which renewed the enthusiasm of all, perhaps a little dulled by our lengthy trek.'

Perhaps it was an anticlimax; after all, he had been imagining this moment for at least fourteen years, ever since Easter in 1908 when he and Max had sailed to Corsica to prepare themselves for the challenges of Everest in all her isolation.

George's response to Everest also revealed that while the mountain was overwhelming in mass, it was not quite the thing of beauty he'd imagined. He wrote to Bubbles a few days later: 'I have had several close-up views of Everest by now – it is not nearly such a fine-looking mountain as Mont Blanc.'

23.

THE FOOT OF EVEREST

Occasionally, George Finch reminisced about Australia. They were momentary flashbacks mainly; a sight or smell might take him home to the bush around Orange, where he had spent so much time as a boy, and in his later years he liked to tell tales of snakes and wallabies and swimming in Sydney Harbour.

On the road to Shekar Dzong, one of the last plains settlements before they began the climb to the base of Everest, he noticed clumps of a hardy shrub growing on the banks of the Arun River, its thorny, silver-green leaf and golden berries sparking a memory. He knew the plant well enough to name it – the sea buckthorn, or hippophae, which also grew in abundance high in the European Alps above the tree line where it could survive in dry air and with very little water. But this sight sparked a different and more distant memory of a morning on top of Mount Canobolas and a golden tree that symbolised his homeland: 'A wattle … a great sight in an otherwise treeless country,' he noted in his diary that night, as if reflecting on that twenty-year journey that was now so close to reality.

They were within a week of their first destination, the Rongbuk Glacier, where base camp would be established, and the weather was a confusing mix: warm and sometimes even hot under clear skies during the day then freezing cold after the sun set, with frequent whipping winds and frost. George had taken to wearing layers that could be added or discarded as the day progressed and conditions changed. By day he wore a sun-proof shirt and sweater, a cardigan waistcoat, long stockings, brogues and his plus-four suit as well as a soft felt hat. At sunset the hat, coat and brogues were replaced with his flying helmet and boots, his lambskin gloves and his now beloved eiderdown coat, 'frankly admired and desired by all!'.

Though his testy relationship with Mallory bothered George, there were further signs of his acceptance by others in the expedition. The morning after the climb up Sangkar Ri he had played the fool by riding a yak and a cow, as if to disarm his colleagues and distance himself from the serious lecturer he normally appeared to be. It was a deliberate effort to earn a 'sobriquet', as he admitted in his diary on April 22, and he was immediately dubbed 'Buffalo Bill', adding to the growing list of nicknames that had been assigned as the trek proceeded and the men relaxed into each other's company:

> We are all settling down well and I am glad to feel now that most
> of the legacy of hate that Howard-Bury left behind for me has
> not only vanished but would appear even to be recoiling upon
> its author. Nicknames have started. Mallory, on account of his
> appearance and peculiar mentality, is known as Peter Pan. Morris,
> who affects native head dress in the evening and has shorn his
> head of all except one lock, after the manner of the Hindu,
> answers to Babu Chatterjee, or the latter for short. Wakefield is
> usually referred to as the Archdeacon ... and General Bruce, of
> course, is the General. We could not have a better or more able
> leader.

George's glowing praise of Bruce was surprising, given their earlier clashes, but the fact that the general had backed him over Mallory in how to tackle Sangkar Ri had caused George to rethink his opinion of the team leader. Perhaps in hope more than anything else, he appeared oblivious to Bruce's obvious dislike of him and chose to blame Howard-Bury for spreading the poison that had actually been fed and fostered by Arthur Hinks, aided by Francis Younghusband, and had now been picked up by Colonel Strutt. George's new-found admiration for authority would not last long.

Shekar Dzong, with several thousand inhabitants, was the biggest settlement they'd seen since crossing the border into Tibet. White-walled stone houses wound their way up the side of a steep hill, reflecting the sunlight, true to the village's name (meaning shining glass), toward the fort set high above the plains. The expedition would stop here for three days, waiting for new transport.

George was happy enough with the delay because it gave him time to develop some film, a slow process given the brackish water he had to first distil and the continual dust devils that swept through the camp and threatened to ruin his work. He was also developing film for the others, including John Noel, with whose work he could not resist comparing his own, as he confessed in his diary: 'On the whole my photographs are very good and have improved ever so much since leaving Kampa Dzong. Noel's photos are, to my mind, not as good and they are far less numerous.'

He wrote to Bubbles for the first time in a fortnight, two letters in as many days, which he sent as they were leaving on April 27 and in which he enclosed some jewellery he'd bought at the local market, including two bracelets of brass and quartz, a bead and stone necklace, turquoise earrings and a small silver charm box. He was pleased with himself, 'awfully fit', and had finally had some time to relax and read from the 'little library' he'd brought, particularly the poetry of Elizabeth Barrett Browning and the sonnets of Robert Burns.

And as much as he looked forward to the challenge of Everest, it was home that was consuming his thoughts:

> How I long for the time when we turn our backs on Everest
> & we're homeward bound towards you. Gen Bruce has
> definitely settled that we all leave when the monsoons
> break – so set your mind at rest on that. Don't be anxious
> then, for you are always with me & I know that for your sake
> I must not only always be careful but that I must, come what
> may, come back to you in September.

* * *

Until now the expedition had been following the path forged by the Howard-Bury reconnaissance the previous year, but that was about to change. Worried by the approach of the inevitable monsoonal deluge, Charles Bruce decided to cut a shorter path to Rongbuk across a mountain pass known as Pang La, long used by travellers and merchants moving between China and Tibet but never before by Europeans. The trek would take four days and should have them at the mouth of the glacier by May 1.

They left Shekar Dzong on April 27 and headed south before beginning the ascent to the pass. The next morning, George Finch, Geoffrey Bruce and Thomas Longstaff went ahead of the main party, eager to clamber to the top of the pass where they sat for two hours, transfixed by the jagged white line that stretched across the horizon beyond the folds and shadows of the brown hills:

> Everest was in clouds, but the great ridge of the Cho Oyu
> and Gyachung Kang was perfectly clear and stood up to great
> advantage. Later on, Everest itself shook off its fleecy mantle,

at least in part, and to our astonishment we saw that its great northern flank east of the north ridge and the north peak was almost bare rock. One thing cheered us all up, and that was the thought that from Tashidzom onwards every step we took bore us up nearer to the summit of Everest; at an end were the ups and downs of the last month's trek.

* * *

The old man had an enormous face, seemingly twice the size of Charles Bruce's, and the general for once was showing humility. George watched, impressed by Bruce's diplomatic skills, as he fiddled with his camera to adjust the light settings, keen to take a photo of the 'impressive old humbug'. The two men were standing in the darkened monastery, the most sacred of temples in Rongbuk, the 'land of precipices and deep ravines'. Outside, the great slab of rock they had come to conquer loomed ominously, but here it was the fat-faced man who first needed to be conquered. The lama of Rongbuk, Dzatrul Rinpoche, was a living Buddha and the reincarnation of the mythical teacher Padmasambhava who'd brought Buddhism to Tibet.

General Bruce's recollection of the lama was perhaps kinder than the observations of George Finch, describing him as dignified and wise and keen to understand why his men wanted to climb the mountain. Bruce settled on the word 'pilgrimage' and concocted a series of 'gentle white lies' about vows his men had taken. Finch listened to the exchange: 'With perfect logic he explained that Everest's summit, being the highest point on earth, was also the spot closest to the heavens; and was it not natural that, at least once during our brief journey through life, we would try to get as close to heaven as we possibly could?'

George thought the explanation had 'satisfied the old gentleman', who gave them his blessing and later sent them meat, tea and flour, according to the local tradition of hospitality. The lama later wrote his own version of the meeting which highlighted the cultural chasm between the climbers and the spiritual leader who admired their efforts and 'magic skills with iron nails, iron chains and iron claws' but was perplexed by their motives: 'I felt great compassion for them to suffer so much for such meaningless work.'

The lama's permission may have been a formality, but their progress up the glacier was more problematic. George was sent with Somervell, Wakefield and Crawford to try to thread a route through a minefield of moraines so the cavalcade could reach a level plain that stretched out at the foot of the glacier, ideal for setting up camp. Much to George's frustration, his companions were useless – 'none of them has the slightest idea of route finding' – and he went off on his own to find a route, which he did, taking three trips to bring the entire caravan through the glacial debris. But that's where the trek ended for many of the local workers: 'Here the transport stopped and refused to budge another inch,' he wrote that night in his diary. 'No arguments or inducements by way of backsheesh were of the slightest use. Fear of devils and lack of grazing for the animals were insuperable obstacles. So back they went and here we are with all our kit and what now must become our home base.'

The base was almost exactly where the reconnaissance mission had pitched its tents the year before, although it had arrived a month later when the bare, rocky ground was cushioned by alpine grass and a wide running stream eased past, fed by thawing ice from above. Now there was no grass to be seen and the stream bed was virtually dry, save for some patches of snow. The men pitched their tents – eight in total – against the side of a steep rise in the hope it might act as a wind-break against the icy gusts that billowed from the glacier behind them.

Charles Bruce was sanguine: 'I do not think such an enormous cavalcade could possibly have mounted the Rongbuk Glacier before. There were over three hundred baggage animals, about twenty ponies, fifty or sixty men in our own employ and the best part of one hundred Tibetans. Finally, all were paid off and the expedition was left alone in its glory.'

They had arrived at the foot of Everest.

24.

THE RIGHT SPIRIT

May 10th

Mallory and Somervell start this afternoon upwards. They are to try to climb Everest without oxygen. In a few days time Norton and I start for the same thing with oxygen. Meanwhile, the great difficult problem is how to get our staff forward and keep all the advance camps replenished. Personally I am quite optimistic [that is, as far as the oxygen party is concerned] though I don't give Mallory and Somervell a foot above 25,000 feet. I am completely recovered and my tummy is quite normal again. Now for the mail!

George Finch had been wrestling with a bout of dysentery for the past four days, confined to camp where he had made himself busy studying weather patterns, tweaking the Primus stoves and testing the oxygen equipment while the others trekked upwards to find sites for the three camps they would need between the base, at 16,500 feet, and the bottom of the North Col, from where the attempts to the summit would be launched.

A week earlier he, Colonel Strutt and Edward Norton had walked, scrambled and climbed for almost four hours across a lunarscape of broken rock and ice hard enough to bend his best axe to find a suitable site for Camp I (at 17,720 feet) on the eastern edge of the giant glacier. The men had begun under sunny, clear skies but by the time they headed back down in the afternoon it had clouded over and a 'pestilential' wind had whipped up. It was a pattern that would be repeated over and over again during their six weeks on the mountain, the expected summer weather refusing to arrive as if the mountain devils were set against their intrusion.

Strutt, this time with Longstaff, Norton and Morshead, had then set off on a four-day hike to find two further sites, Camp II at 19,700 feet and Camp III at 21,000 feet. In the meantime Geoffrey Bruce and John Morris had led a conga line of fifty porters, carrying piles of dried yak dung for heating, to secure the first camp, constructing four stone shelters to save on tents. And so it went on as the expedition slowly but surely worked its way from base camp toward the North Col.

But behind the teamwork there was friction. The effect of the increased altitude had brought irritability into the camp and, once again, George Finch appeared to bear the brunt of it. Mallory by now could not stand him, so much so that he took Somervell off one day to climb a nearby peak rather than attend another of George's lectures. But it was at meal times, with appetites dulled by the altitude and the overly rich provisions, that the alienation really showed.

John Morris noted that only George Finch seemed to be able to digest the ludicrously luxurious diet more befitting a group of travelling English gentlemen than pioneering mountaineers. Meals regularly included items such as quail in aspic, sausages, ham, tinned herring and sardines, spaghetti, bacon and sweet biscuits, the men eating as if at a Sunday lunch in the English countryside:

At great heights most people become irritable and absurdly intolerant of each other's idiosyncrasies. It was not long before we began to find fault with such petty details as one another's method of using a knife and fork or a tendency to whistle. And a companion's obvious enjoyment of a solid meal at a time when one had lost all appetite invariably resulted in an exchange of words. Finch, who was a man of most equable temperament, was an almost permanent subject of sarcastic comment, since he alone was capable of eating anything at any time. Most of us learned to control our feelings, but there were several occasions when Strutt, who was naturally intolerant in even normal circumstances, was unable to keep his thoughts to himself. He always apologised for these outbursts but they nevertheless had a dampening effect.

Finch was doing himself no favours by pursuing experiments with an alternative oxygen system he had brought from England. The oxylithe bag, created by Leonard Hill, the professor of physiology at London Hospital, was supposed to be a back-up system to his own. Mixing water and oxylithe (or sodium peroxide) in a bag chemically produced oxygen, which could then be inhaled as needed. Instead, when George gave oxylithe to John Noel, it exploded in a blue flame and filled his tent with a mist of caustic soda. The effect was even worse when he tried using a bag himself, the resulting spray causing a fit of coughing and leaving a slimy taste in his mouth: 'I have therefore decided to condemn the Leonard Hill apparatus as not only being useless but, indeed, directly harmful at high altitudes.'

The damage had already been done, however, and even though the oxylithe bag had only ever been something George was experimenting with, he found himself more isolated than ever on the issue of oxygen. On May 7 Charles Bruce wrote to Francis

Younghusband, complaining about the cold temperatures which were delaying an attempt at the summit. Of the oxygen equipment, Bruce said: 'I am terrified by it. It seems to me to be so very easily put out of order and also so liable to be damaged by hitting against rocks or catching its Indian rubber tubing on rocks; also the changing of bottles on steep slopes when the apparatus has to be taken off and readjusted by very weary and hungry men seems a danger. However, Finch seems very confident.'

* * *

The arrival of the mail on May 10, so eagerly anticipated by George Finch, brought him equal amounts of joyful longing and angry despair. There were two letters from Bubbles with chitchat of her plans to redecorate their home. The car had finally been sold, which eased her immediate financial pressure, but she had some slight concerns about Christmas and the possible poor behaviour of a female relative. She enclosed a few photographs of herself as well as George's monocular, a hybrid telescope and magnifying glass that George used to help his bad eye, injured during the war.

George's reply – written almost immediately and noted, with light-hearted precision, as being sent from 'Base Camp, 17,000 feet 11 inches N of Everest' – was filled with words of love and assurances of his good health. His clothes were stout, the suit holding firm and his shirt hand-washed in Lux every couple of days, and he was gadding about after a few days with a 'chill'. He longed for fresh fruit and salad and filled his days developing films and preparing equipment while memorising Browning sonnets. There was no mention of the climb ahead, only of his desire to be back with her in London: 'Darling mine, they've just warned me that the mail closes in a quarter-hour so I must hurry off to get all the parcels ready in time. In the meantime darling heart, don't be the slightest bit anxious – don't worry, for I shall always be careful & ever mindful of you who are waiting for me. I love you, love you, and adore you ...'

But the mail also carried copies of Arthur Hinks's Royal Geographical Society magazine article, addressed to Charles Bruce with an accompanying letter, justifying the article: 'We felt that it was desirable to point out to people in general that there was as much interest in climbing as high as possible without oxygen as getting to the top with it.'

Bruce and Strutt read the article and handed it to Finch, without comment, the message clear that they agreed with the conclusions or at least felt compelled to follow the views of the Royal Geographical Society kingpins Hinks and Younghusband, even though both were members of the Alpine Club and supposedly loyal to Percy Farrar.

George read with growing fury, later writing:

Thus far our mission had been to undertake a determined assault on the summit with every and all available means. Overnight, the opinions of oxygen opponents have taken over and influenced the expedition participants to such a degree that suddenly an entirely new assignment seemed to have emerged: To find out what altitude a person could advance on this earth during a leisurely stroll ... The author of the article, campaigning against the use of supplementary oxygen, and wishing to give it a grand burial, had illuminated the problem in a new light and shaken our group's belief in its mission. Our only consolation lay in the fact that the author was no mountaineer himself. And so it came about that I remained the only one firmly believing in the power and indispensability of oxygen.

Meanwhile, George Mallory and Howard Somervell had made their way steadily up the glacier from camp to camp and by the early afternoon of May 13, nursing blinding altitude headaches and bracing themselves against a gale, they hammered poles firmly into the ice at the foot of the North Col and erected a tent to establish Camp IV at 23,000 feet – 'a symbol of our future intentions'.

The pathway to the summit of Everest had been opened, ropes now pegged to the steeper slopes from the glacier so porters could haul supplies to the next staging post. The two men retreated, exhausted, to huddle in their tent at Camp III for the next three days where they played cards and read to each other from Mallory's small collection of books, including *Hamlet* and *King Lear* and an anthology of poetry and prose edited by the Poet Laureate, Robert Bridges, called *The Spirit of Man*. It seemed appropriate as they waited, alternately sleeping and talking in the slow-motion atmosphere of high-altitude existence, for the others to arrive.

Back at base camp General Bruce and Colonel Strutt had again changed their strategy, and the news would be devastating for George Finch who had been struggling to overcome a relapse of his 'tummy trouble'. Teddy Norton would no longer partner him in the oxygen-assisted attempt on the summit, instead leaving base camp on May 14 with Morshead and Strutt to join Mallory and Somervell. Strutt would then make the final decision about the composition and size of the climbing team or teams.

Bruce would later insist that it was Strutt's suggestion, made because of a concern about the clearly worsening weather as well as ongoing doubts about Finch and his oxygen equipment. George had made a cursory check of the cylinders back in Darjeeling but it was only after arriving at Rongbuk that he discovered repairs were necessary before they could be used:

George's father, Charles Edward Finch, who sparked his son's interest in science. *Courtesy Mrs A. Scott Russell*

Laura Finch, George's bohemian mother. He ridiculed her beliefs but entrusted Peter Finch to her care. *Courtesy Mrs A. Scott Russell*

Max (front) and George learn about roping from the guide Christian Jossi in the Alps circa 1907. *Courtesy Mrs A. Scott Russell*

The two Finch boys in 1909, sunbaking on the roof of the Guggi hut, halfway to the summit of the Jungfrau. *Courtesy Mrs A. Scott Russell*

Two sides of George Finch: in a mountain hut in 1911, he looked the young rebellious figure who eschewed formality, as can be seen from his relaxed dress sense; and at ETH in 1912, where the young scientist was a student of Albert Einstein. *Courtesy Mrs A. Scott Russell*

George captured this image of Max leaping a crevasse down Mont Blanc in the summer of 1911. *Courtesy Mrs A. Scott Russell*

ABOVE LEFT: Even though it was taken in black and white, George Finch's official Great War portrait shows his piercing eyes steel-blue in colour. He was stationed in England for more than a year, but once at the Front in Macedonia he showed leadership and ingenuity, repairing the army's arsenal of mortars and bringing down an enemy pilot using a dummy balloon filled with explosives, for which he was later awarded an MBE. *Courtesy Mrs A. Scott Russell.*

ABOVE RIGHT: In June 1915, George married Betty Fisher who would become the mother of Peter. Betty modelled her looks on silent-screen stars.

Geoffrey Winthrop Young, one of the few vocal supporters of George Finch, introduced him to George Mallory. *Alpine Club Photo Library, London*

Percy Farrar, editor of *The Alpine Journal.*
Alpine Club Photo Library, London

George Mallory, the romantic, heroic but ultimately tragic climber whose respect for George Finch came too late.
Royal Geographical Society (with IBG)

Arthur Hinks, bullying secretary of the Royal Geographical Society who despised George and his science.
Royal Geographical Society (with IBG)

Sir Francis Younghusband, the elitist president of the Royal Geographical Society, reluctantly backed George's use of oxygen on Everest in 1922.
Royal Geographical Society (with IBG)

George and new wife, 'Bubbles', say goodbye as he sets off for Everest, in 1922. *Courtesy Mrs A. Scott Russell*

The 1922 expedition team at the foot of the mountain: the two Georges, Mallory and Finch, sit next to each other at the front left. *Royal Geographical Society (with IBG)*

George demonstrates his oxygen system to cynical team members while the porters look on.
Royal Geographical Society (with IBG)

1922 expedition members sit down to eat. Most found their appetites dulled, but not George.
Royal Geographical Society (with IBG)

North Col camp perched on the snow, showing the face of Everest that the climbers would take.
Royal Geographical Society (with IBG)

George (right) returning with Geoffrey Bruce from their climb up Everest, where they got to 27,300 feet, the highest point reached to that time. George is wearing his eiderdown jacket. Everyone else wore combinations of jumpers and even pyjamas topped with tweed suits.
Royal Geographical Society (with IBG)

George and Bubbles in the Alps in 1924. They would climb the Matterhorn together.
Courtesy Mrs A. Scott Russell

The three Finch girls in the 1930s, Felice (Collette), Paola (Moseli) and Anne (Bunty). *Courtesy Mrs A. Scott Russell*

George and Bubbles on their way to India in 1953. *Courtesy Mrs A. Scott Russell*

Peter Finch with his first wife, the ballerina Tamara Tchinarova, in their London apartment circa 1953. George never accepted Peter as his biological son but took custody anyway when he divorced Peter's mother, Betty Fisher.

NLA MS 9733, Series 5, Item 39

At first sight it would seem that it was not wise to send so many of the best climbers at once on the mountain before the oxygen apparatus was ready, but he felt (and I consider he was quite right) that as the weather was so bad and the monsoon was evidently arriving before its time, and as at the moment the oxygen equipment was in such a doubtful condition, it was far better to make an attempt than possibly to fail in making any attempt at all.

The explanation defied logic to George, given that the original plan was to use two-man teams and that Mallory and Somervell were already prepared to climb when the weather cleared, but there was little he could do but watch the others go: 'Until then I had firmly believed that it was indeed possible to conquer Everest but my hopes sank deeper and deeper as I watched the last climbers leave base camp.'

* * *

Strutt arrived at Camp III on May 16 anxious to get a report about the impending monsoon. Mallory and Somervell had trekked to the eastern side of the glacier to a pass called Rapiu La from where they could look down through the Kama Valley and get some sense of the weather approaching from the south. The two men insisted that conditions, while less than perfect, were reasonable, but Strutt was not convinced and accompanied them on another trip to the pass. The situation had changed, at least as far as Strutt was concerned, the clouds boiling beneath them in a grim, grey mass. Even Mallory had to concede the weather was worsening: 'The bitterest even of Tibetan winds poured violently over the pass at our backs. We wondered as we turned to meet it how long a respite was to be allowed us.'

Strutt was decisive in his anxiety, insisting that they stood a better chance of success if the men climbed as one team of four. Mallory agreed, arguing that if one man faltered and required help then at least two could keep going. The decision was made and there was no discussion about the impact on Finch's attempt. Weather permitting they would begin the next day by taking provisions to Camp IV on the backs of ten porters. They would have a rest day back at Camp III and then leave after breakfast on May 19, with the aim of climbing to 26,000 feet where they would camp overnight before striking out for the summit the next morning.

George Finch, now fully recovered physically and determined psychologically, made his move on May 16, leaving the base camp with Geoffrey Bruce, Arthur Wakefield, a Nepalese officer with the 6th Gurkha Rifles named Naik Tejbir Bura, who, along with the other Gurkhas, had been with them since Darjeeling, and a handful of porters to take the last of the oxygen equipment to Camp I. George had made up his mind. Despite being abandoned by the other climbers he would not come this far and miss the chance to conquer Everest. It was just a matter of who to take with him.

Years of guiding inexperienced young men like John Case, Will Sturgess and Guy Forster up the biggest mountains in Europe made him confident that he could take on the world's highest peak with men who had never before climbed a mountain, provided they were not only physically strong and fit but 'had the right spirit'. He decided he wanted to take the two soldiers, Captain Geoffrey Bruce and Lance Corporal Tejbir Bura, with him up Everest. He couldn't see why General Bruce would object; why would they be on the expedition unless they were prepared to climb?

Of Geoffrey Bruce George later wrote:

Tall and strong physique, the athletic man possessed unusual amounts of energy. Especially this last attribute was of great importance and value for the adventure that lay ahead of us. Additionally he was such a jovial fellow in any and all situations that, even though he had no experience in mountain climbing, he was a near-perfect comrade.

He regarded the quiet Nepalese as the most promising of the non-commissioned Gurkha officers:

Tejbir was a wonderful representative of the human race – 6 feet tall, broad shouldered and wide of chest – a splendid fellow from head to toe. I had discovered another endearing quality about him: the smallest encouragement would cause his face to break into a wide grin, even in uncomfortable and miserable situations. Like Bruce, Tejbir had never climbed a mountain before. But I am convinced that a man who knows how to laugh will always prevail, be it on a mountain or in life, much more than an individual who is an expert on the ins and outs of climbing but does not know how to laugh.

It was a strange assessment, given that George was regarded by many of the others as an example of the latter: a man who knew, or thought he knew, everything but was too serious about it to relax.

Ever the pragmatist, George had dissected the challenge ahead, and his initial awe of the mountain had been tempered by his study of its structure. Yes, Everest was huge, almost overpowering even from a distance, but there were two heights – absolute and relative. They didn't need to climb its absolute height above sea level, but its relative height of a little under 10,000 feet from the base camp, roughly the same height that Mont Blanc soared above its glaciers.

While others wrote poetry about Everest, George Finch had become disdainful, at least aesthetically:

> From the point of view of beauty there can be no comparison
> between the two mountains. Mont Blanc, seen from the
> north, is a wonderful, glistening mass of snowy domes,
> piled one against the other in ever-increasing altitude
> to a beautifully proportioned and well-balanced whole.
> No beauty or symmetry of form can be read out of the
> ponderous, ungainly, ill-proportioned lump ... of almost
> comical squatness and which carries, as if by accident, a little
> carelessly truncated cone to serve as a summit.

Having reached Camp I, George called a halt, opting for a 'rest' day to check and test the oxygen cylinders. Spying an ice slope on the edge of a frozen pond of glacial water, George decided to give his rookie charges a lesson in the use of climbing irons and ice-axes. Bruce and Tejbir eagerly attacked the slope with an enthusiasm that only bolstered George's sense that they were up to the task, but he was also reminded of the dangers ahead when Tejbir, overreaching, slipped and slithered down the slope, breaking through the ice and disappearing into the waters beneath.

It was a frightening moment, saved only by Tejbir's quick response as he kept hold of his axe and used it to clamp himself to the ice until he could be hauled clear and taken back to camp where he was stripped and thawed out under a pile of blankets. The problem then was to find a way to dry his clothes that had fused into a suit of armour in the sub-zero temperatures. It was too cold for the ice to melt but George realised that the air was so dry and rarified that the ice would evaporate just as water would on a hot summer's day at sea level:

Thus to dry Tejbir's frozen garments one only had to apply a little logic and scientific training. Take, for instance, his trousers. These were first of all hammered out flat and then placed in a vertical position against a little wall of stones. The moment they collapsed and fell to the ground, it was obvious that their stiffening of ice had disappeared and they were, therefore, dry. Who, after this brilliant example, would gainsay the uses of science?

George had initially planned to spend two nights in each camp on the way to the North Col but his little party felt so fresh when they reached Camp II without incident that he decided to push on the next morning to Camp III. The weather was still holding and an extra day acclimatising could be useful. They left at 8am on May 19 and by midday, under a summer sun that warmed their backs, had made their way past a series of yawning crevasses and through the puzzle of giant seracs that glistened in a rainbow of blue and green crystals to find the neat row of tents pitched on bare rock alongside the glacier wall.

The only expedition member there was Colonel Strutt, who emerged from his tent to explain that the others had left a few hours earlier 'to inspect the North summit'. George looked to where Strutt pointed, squinting against the light flaring off the white slopes above them, and could make out several static black dots – the tents of Camp IV. Scanning left he could just make out four more dots, this time moving, albeit slowly. It was Mallory, Norton, Morshead and Somervell: 'Apparently someone had decided to go for a little stroll up there,' he commented acidly.

Although George appeared to accept Strutt's assurances that the decision to send four and not three climbers together was for the good of the expedition, he was angry that the colonel was offering him Wakefield as a replacement climbing candidate. Not only was the doctor struggling physically in the extreme conditions but he had been one of the most vocal opponents of the use of oxygen. That night, tucked into his eiderdown sleeping bag, George scrawled a brief entry in his diary: 'Wakefield has come up with us. I don't know what he expects to do. He can barely crawl along, is always fussing and making a nuisance of himself. Generally speaking he is a busy old woman and good for nothing.'

George was determined to climb with Bruce and Tejbir – and leave the naysayers and backstabbers behind.

25.

A BLADDER AND A T-TUBE

George Finch's mood turned to dismay the next morning when all ten sets of oxygen units were unpacked and closely inspected for the first time. He had already opened some cases and knew there were problems to be addressed, but now he realised that all the cylinders were faulty. The combination of the pounding sea voyage, rough overland trip and see-sawing temperatures had weakened the metal joints, while the cold dry air of the mountains had caused the washers to dry out to the point they were no longer airtight. The flow meters and gauges did not work properly. Thankfully, the cylinders themselves had not leaked.

George might well have cast his mind back to Salonika in 1916 when he had been confronted with the problem of an armoury made useless by leaking fuses and had managed to co-ordinate the repair of thousands of shells in a matter of weeks. By comparison, re-soldering and re-sealing ten oxygen units, while frustrating, was achievable. Even on the side of a mountain. The ground outside the tents resembled a mechanic's shop as George set to work repairing the oxygen units with his makeshift toolkit and dodging a storm that suddenly swept through the valley, sending him scurrying into his tent to survive temperatures so cold – at times plunging to minus 56 degrees Celsius – that it was impossible to touch tools with his bare hands. Within twenty-four hours, however, he had four functioning sets, more than enough for himself, Geoffrey Bruce and Tejbir.

But there was a more serious issue – the breathing masks. He had packed two designs, the first one dubbed the economiser because it was configured to allow exhaled air to mix with the tank oxygen and therefore would use less of the precious mixture. By comparison, the second mask fitted across the bottom half of the face and fed a continuous stream of pure oxygen to the climber, whose exhaled air collected in a separate reservoir. Both masks had worked in the controlled surroundings of an Oxford laboratory but in the extreme environs of the Himalayas, the resistance caused by the complicated valve system of both designs meant the effort to breathe was simply too much for a climber already straining physically.

Without a working mask, the oxygen system was useless. Finch's dream was on the verge of collapse, had it not been for his technical genius. A month before, as he waited in Darjeeling, George had struck on an idea for a simple, back-up mask in case the others either did not last the sea trip or became unusable at high altitude. The concept was simple (at least in George's mind) and relied on the use of the toy football bladders he had bought at a local bazaar together with a small length of rubber tubing and a glass T-tube. The rubber tube was fitted between the oxygen valve and one end of the T-tube, the opposite end of which was placed in the climber's mouth. The football bladder would enclose the third end of the T-tube.

When the climber inhaled, the oxygen flowed directly from the tank through the T-tube into his mouth. On exhaling, he clamped the tube shut with his teeth, forcing the air into the football bladder which inflated. He then unclenched his teeth as he inhaled, allowing the mixture of oxygen and exhaled air back into his lungs, and so on. And by halting the flow, the oxygen from the tanks was not wasted.

No doubt Colonel Strutt would add George's mechanical tinkering to the growing list of his unattractive attributes, but the man himself was happy: 'The correct closing and opening of the rubber tube by alternately biting and releasing the pressure of the teeth upon it became, after a few minutes' practice, a perfectly automatic, subconscious response. The success of this simple mask pleased me greatly; without it, no really effective use could have been made of our oxygen supplies.'

Just after midday on May 20 George Finch and Geoffrey Bruce set out to test the repaired equipment by climbing to Rapiu La. It was the first time George had climbed using oxygen and he delighted in outstripping Strutt and Wakefield who trudged ever further behind Finch and Bruce as they made their way up the slope: 'The effect of the O$_2$ was remarkable. Though the apparatus weighed some thirty pounds we two went ahead like a house on fire.'

The view from Rapiu La warned them there was foul weather ahead – 'the valleys in the south filled with dark and heavy cloud banks, piled high upon each other like giant feather beds' – and they scurried back to camp just as a wild snowstorm struck. The blizzard continued for most of the next day, confining them to their tents. They wondered when it would lift and how badly it might be affecting the four men on the mountain. As sundown approached, they ventured out to scan the North Col for any signs of their comrades. At first they could see nothing against the white canvas, but eventually they spotted four black dots on the broad slopes of the lower ridge. They were descending, if slowly, clearly exhausted but alive. How far had they made it up the mountain?

The next morning George took Bruce and Tejbir with a group of porters to restock Camp IV in preparation for their own attempt. Strutt and Wakefield joined them to assist Mallory's group back to the camp. It was difficult to know what condition the men might be in, but they had appeared weary and hesitant in their movements the previous evening.

As happened the previous day, the positive effect of the oxygen was immediately obvious as the three men, George, Bruce and Tejbir, outpaced the porters who were carrying less weight, not to mention Wakefield and Strutt. In his excitement, George flippantly described the climb as akin to 'a brief Alpine ascent' as he cut steps easily into the ice to climb from the glacier onto the shoulder of the col. It was here that they met Mallory and the others: 'Most of them appeared to be at the end of their strength and were barely capable of speaking coherently. Only Norton, his skin a blackish brown from the cutting winds, his face showing the incredible strain he had been under, could give us a brief report of their adventure.'

They had not reached the summit, but had climbed higher than anyone before them.

George watched the weary men continue their descent, ensuring they were safely onto the glacier before he and his group continued upwards. It took three hours to reach Camp IV, well ahead of the porters who could not believe the speed of the men carrying tanks on their backs: 'We explained to the coolies that our phenomenal speed was due to our freely imbibing "bottled English air",' George later wrote. To prove the point, he released a spray of pure oxygen at the cigarette he was smoking, the end glowing a fiery red in response.

By casually smoking a cigarette at 23,000 feet he had inadvertently solved another question mark hanging over the equipment. What would happen if they suddenly stopped using oxygen? Would they be affected, perhaps even die if the equipment stopped working? The answer was an emphatic no: 'We were able on the Col to suddenly switch on or off our oxygen supply without experiencing the slightest inconvenience.'

The men stayed for less than an hour, ensuring the tents were solidly pitched and the supplies salted away before heading back to Camp III. The descent took just fifty minutes, including pausing for photographs, and their arrival was greeted with disbelief by the others who were sitting around a makeshift table, clasping mugs of hot tea against tortured fingers and warily eyeing a plateful of tinned ham that appeared as appetising as a serving of dog food. George captured an image of the blackened, weary faces as he sat down to listen to their story.

* * *

George Mallory had penned a letter to his wife the day before the four men had begun their climb to destiny. He was not optimistic: 'We shan't get to the top. If we reach the shoulder at 27,400 feet it will be better than anyone here expects.' The letter would not reach Ruth until well after she knew that he had been right.

Mallory was referring to the shoulder of the North Col, a ridge at which the climbers would turn right and face a ramp-like slope that appeared to offer a comparatively easy climb to the summit. But it depended on so many factors, the effects of altitude and the weather being the most obvious. They had now made three trips from Camp III to the foot of the col and, each time, Mallory had felt the leaden weight of oxygen-deprived fatigue. The climb seemed to get slightly easier but the improvement was marginal, and if they felt lethargic at 23,000 feet, then how would they be able to climb the 6000 feet of snow, ice and rock above them to reach the summit?

Still, he had been hopeful the first evening, pitching five dark green tents at Camp IV for the climbers and the nine porters who would accompany them for the first part of the climb and then lying in his sleeping sack, the tent flaps open to suck in the thin offering of oxygen, content that the skies were clear enough to see the outline of the mountain.

'I remember how my mind kept wandering over the various details of our preparations without anxiety, rather like God after the Creation seeing that it was good,' he would later reflect. 'It was good. And the best of it was what we expected to be doing these next two days.'

But the morning brought the first set of problems: the porters feeling the nauseating effects of the increased altitude and the breakfast cans of spaghetti frozen solid after being left outside the tents overnight. Only four of the nine porters would be fit enough to follow the climbers up the mountain, severely limiting the equipment they could carry and ruling out any chance of establishing any more camp sites between Camp IV and the summit.

They eventually broke camp at 7.30am, more than two hours late, which put more pressure on their hopes of climbing to the planned bivouac at 26,000 feet, just beneath the north shoulder, before sundown. Progress was steady at first, the lower slopes of the col firm and safe and the remaining porters able to carry between them two tents and double sleeping sacks, cooking gear and provisions for one and a half days.

But things began to go wrong again mid morning when they stopped for a rest and Mallory accidentally knocked Norton's knapsack containing the extra clothing he intended to wear as it got colder. It tumbled out of reach, back down the mountainside. It was already apparent that the men were woefully underdressed for the climb, their tweed suits, woollen pullovers, silk shirts and scarves little help against the bitter wind that blew across them from the right and seemed to grow with every passing minute – 'an old wind in the old anger' – although Mallory shrugged it off, insisting that his layers were enough to ward off the worst that could be thrown at him.

Their progress slowed as the wind grew and they were forced to lean forward into the gale to stay on their feet. The sun was now hidden behind clouds and frostbite was already a very real threat as fingertips, toes and ears began to throb. Mallory changed direction, slanting across the slope to find shelter from the wind. The ground was harder here and the blue ice difficult to cut, but he had no choice; they had left their crampons behind to save on weight and now had to cut their way up a 300-foot rise.

By midday, Mallory, Norton and Somervell had reached a height of 25,000 feet (measured by an aneroid barometer) and they stopped behind a wall of rocks to shelter and wait for Morshead who was struggling behind with the porters, badly affected by frostbite and altitude sickness. It had taken four hours to climb 2000 feet and the three men estimated that it would take another three hours to climb the remaining 1000 feet to their bivouac target.

They could go no further as the weather continued to close in, if only because the porters needed time to get back down the mountain to Camp IV before dark. It would take another two hours to find vaguely level places to pitch the two tents and they would spend a sleepless night, exhausted and in pain. They were not demoralised, Mallory recalled, 'but we had come through an ordeal'. Mallory nursed three frostbitten fingers in a tent with Norton who could only lie on his left side because his right ear was swollen to three times its normal size. In the other tent, Morshead was nauseous, frostbitten, and could not stop shaking.

He would pull out after a few steps the next morning, opting to remain in the tent while the others pushed for the summit, still 4000 feet away.

Progress was slow as they moved almost methodically, 'evenly with balanced movements, saving effort, to keep our form, as oarsmen say at the end of the race, remembering to step neatly and transfer the weight from one leg to the other by swinging the body rhythmically upwards'. They climbed in thirty-minute spells, then stopped for five minutes to catch their breath. It was an effort of will to keep going, particularly when Mallory had to stop to remove his four layers of socks so Norton could rub his toes warm.

There was fresh snow to contend with, half a metre deep in places, and it became clear as the hours ticked by that they were not moving fast enough to reach the peak in daylight: 'We were prepared to leave it to braver men to climb Mount Everest by night,' Mallory concluded.

Besides, in the rarefied atmosphere everything was happening slowly, mentally and physically. The men 'tacitly accepted defeat' but agreed to keep moving upwards until 2.30pm when they would head back down with enough time to reach Morshead and then descend safely to Camp IV. None of them wanted a second night on the mountainside.

Mallory called a halt at 2.15pm after climbing a short, steep section. The ridge they hoped would lead to the summit was just above their heads, but it seemed out of reach to men whose tongues hung out of their mouths trying to catch a breath. They shared the small amount of food they carried in their pockets – chocolate, mint cake, acid drops, raisins and prunes and a nip of brandy – and lay back against the jumble of rocks, luxuriating for a few moments and gazing around and down at peaks that had previously looked gargantuan but were now 'contemptible fellows beneath our feet'.

George Mallory, Howard Somervell and Teddy Norton had reached a height of 26,984 feet, almost 2500 feet higher than anyone had ever climbed. At that moment, though, none of them had a sense of triumph: 'It is impossible to say how much further we might have gone,' Mallory wrote after returning. 'In light of subsequent events it would seem that the margin of strength to deal with an emergency was already small enough. I have little doubt that we could have struggled up perhaps two hours more to the north-east shoulder, now little more than 400 feet above us. Whether we should then have been fit to conduct our descent in safety is another matter.' How right he was.

It took barely ninety minutes for the three men to descend to the tents where they had left Morshead, a quarter of the time it had taken to climb. Mallory felt it was quick and they had been moving freely, but realised later that his perceptions had been warped by altitude. Morshead insisted he was well enough to make it back to Camp IV where they would spend the night before returning to the relative comfort of Camp III where the other team members waited.

The men seemed safe, relieved almost, as they made their way down, Mallory in the lead, followed by Norton and Morshead with Somervell as the anchorman. Mallory was trying to follow the footsteps of the day before but fresh snowfall made it difficult. Their progress was slowed as it became necessary to clear the snow to ensure they were not stepping onto rocks that might cause a slippage. This was a danger period when fatigue made concentration difficult. And then it happened.

Morshead, the third man in line, slipped on a rock just as Somervell behind him was mid step. Both men fell and began hurtling down the slope that only stopped at the Rongbuk Glacier more than 3000 feet below. There was hardly time to call out as they slid past Norton who plunged his axe into the snow but could not hold their combined weight and was swept off his feet.

Mallory had heard 'unusual sounds' behind him and without looking wedged his axe into the snow and ice, managing to hitch his rope around the handle like a belay then brace himself against the slope before the others flew past: 'In 99 cases out of a hundred either the belay will give or the rope will break,' he later wrote. 'In the still moment of suspense before the matter must be put to the test nothing further could be done to prevent a disaster one way or another.' The axe gripped, the rope tightened but held. The men were safe but shaken.

Their relief was short-lived, however, as the descent slowed even more, because Morshead seemed almost unable to move. What had looked to be a relatively easy descent had now become a desperate race in slow motion to reach their tents at Camp IV before darkness. The way down had become perilous, their tracks from the previous day now obliterated under the new snow and their fears of a hidden crevasse forcing them to stretch the distance between them to ensure that only one would fall and could be saved by the others.

It was almost sundown when George Finch and the others at Camp III spied them on the lower slopes. They appeared exhausted and still some distance from the Camp IV tents, clearly unable to reach safety until after dark. It would be 11.30pm before they found the tents by candlelight, the last 600 feet taking an hour. Unable to swallow anything solid, they all desperately wanted water but the porters had taken the stove and there was no way to melt the snow. Norton tried to manufacture an ice-cream of sorts from a tin of strawberry jam, frozen ideal milk and snow, but the concoction just made them retch.

The descent resumed at six o'clock the next morning, another four hours of hesitant and weary progress through the thigh-high snow that had gathered as the slopes flattened toward the bottom of the col. The discipline that had kept them together and alive finally broke down at the top of the last slope, such was their desperation for fluid. In the rush, Mallory, who had overcome a shaking fit the night before, slipped and slid 100 feet before his axe once again saved him. His relief turned to annoyance when he looked up to find that George Finch, carrying his oxygen equipment, had photographed his 'ignominious glissade'.

Colonel Strutt, Geoffrey Bruce and Arthur Wakefield were with George and handed over two thermoses to the desperate men before Strutt and Wakefield guided them back to Camp III where they gulped down tea and told their story of triumph and survival. The next morning they would return to base camp to recover while George Finch, Geoffrey Bruce and Naik Tejbir Bura began their own attempt.

* * *

It would take more than a fortnight for news of Mallory's triumph to reach London, announced exclusively in *The Times* as per their commercial agreement with the Royal Geographical Society. 'Gallant explorers … in these tremendous altitudes more especially because they made no use of oxygen, that must be looked at as extremely good going,' the newspaper declared, outlining the barest of details from a note scrawled by General Bruce and transported by foot from the base camp back across the Tibetan Plateau to Darjeeling where it was wired.

Arthur Hinks was delighted: 'Nothing pleased us more than the exciting news which arrived on June 8 and was published the following day than the two words "without oxygen" reached 26,800,' he wrote to the expedition leader. Later that day he penned a note to Ruth Mallory:

> We send you hearty congratulations on the success of your husband reported in *The Times* this morning, and we are so very glad that he is able to break the record so completely without the use of oxygen. It does not seem impossible that at the second attempt they might get to the summit without it. I have always been willing to bet Captain Farrar that your husband would get higher without oxygen than Finch would with it. This is not because I fully believe it, but in order to rouse the oxygen experts.

Hinks's delight would be short-lived.

26.

THE CEILING OF THE WORLD

In contrast to Mallory's pessimistic letter to his wife, George Finch was cautiously optimistic about his chances on the mountain. His almost boyish enthusiasm was expressed in a letter sent with a runner to Charles Bruce detailing the success of his experiments with the oxygen cylinders and seeking formal support: 'In view of these excellent results, after consulting with Col Strutt we are pushing oxygen for all its worth, pending your approval. The plan is to dump oxygen at the 25,000 ft camp from which an attempt on the summit can be made with some prospect of success. Provided the weather brightens up.'

And that was the key. The weather. There had only been two days of warm, benign conditions since they had arrived almost a month ago, most days beginning calmly but deteriorating by early afternoon as slicing winds and brutal temperatures struck. George had stood gazing up at the mountain for hours, studying its folds and lumps and stratified ice. It did not provide the climbing conundrums of many Alpine peaks; in fact, it was more a steep uphill walk, from what he could see. The challenge lay almost entirely in its thin air and wild, unpredictable conditions.

It was late morning on May 24 when he, Geoffrey Bruce and Tejbir left Camp III with twenty porters carrying stores and equipment, including the precious oxygen bottles. John Noel was also with them. He had taken film of the returning heroes Mallory, Somervell, Norton and Morshead and now wanted to place himself at Camp IV and photograph the progress of Finch's men as they made their way up the mountain. George was pleased to have Noel along, not only for the photography but because he had agreed to use an oxygen set – 'a new convert to the true faith'.

They reached Camp IV without incident and settled in for the night. The skies had clouded over early in the afternoon, the temperature plunging as the sun disappeared and a brisk cold wind set in. The men ate hurriedly and dived for their sleeping bags and tents, the inner-tent warmth countered by the fact they had been pitched directly onto the snow. George underplayed the discomfort as 'fairly agreeable'.

John Noel felt lethargic the next morning, uninterested in his cameras as he watched, rather than photographed, the porters as they ate and packed in readiness for the first climb of the day to George Finch's planned oxygen dump site. As the others emerged from their tents he noticed their ponderous movements, as if everything was in slow motion. Eventually someone made breakfast 'at a ridiculously slow speed': 'I felt so done up that I went to my oxygen apparatus, opened the tap wide and took a quarter of an hour's heavy breathing of oxygen. This had the most marvellous effect. I became another being. I woke up and took notice, regained full strength and felt quite myself again. Finch also took oxygen.'

George didn't mention the oxygen fillip as he sent the porters ahead, confident that the climbers would catch up easily even though the oxygen tanks weighed more than the loads the porters carried. Instead, he regarded a second breakfast as more important, aware that the rations they would have higher up were meagre and that they needed all the sustenance they could stomach.

The skies were clear but the wind had already risen by the time they left at 9.30. They were ninety minutes behind the Tibetans, one of whom they found slumped, already exhausted, at the bottom of a small crevasse. He couldn't go on and had chosen to wait in the sun for the others to return later in the day. He was safe enough and the trio resumed their rhythmic plod, following the tracks of the porters as they stayed on the leeward side of the ridgeline to reduce the impact of the wind.

It was nearing noon when they caught the porters at 24,600 feet, just 300 feet short of where Mallory, Somervell, Norton and Morshead had been forced to camp for the night. Although conditions were similar, it had taken George, Bruce and Tejbir less than half the time of Mallory's group to climb roughly the same distance from Camp IV. The oxygen had already made a significant difference, as was shown by the reaction of the porters when they drew alongside: 'They greeted our arrival with their usual cheery, broad grins,' George wrote. 'But no longer did they regard oxygen as a foolish man's whim.'

A short rest, time enough for a few photographs, and George, Bruce and Tejbir were off again, outpacing the porters as they sought flat ground somewhere above 26,000 feet to pitch their tents for the night, so they would wake the following day within striking distance of the peak.

The joy and promise of the morning ended an hour later. They had climbed another 1300 feet when the wind, already sniping at them, suddenly rose to a howl, whipping the slopes above them into a frenzy of spindrift. Then it began to snow. A storm was brewing and would be on top of them soon.

George faced the same dilemma as Mallory had three days before, forced to cut short his advance and secure a camp site so the porters had a chance to get back to safety: 'Persistence in proceeding further would have run them unjustifiably into danger. This I would under no circumstances do, for I felt responsible for those cheerful, smiling, willing men who looked up to their leader and placed in him the complete trust of little children.'

Instead of making ground George began casting around for a secure camp site, the wind now so strong that it would have been impossible to pitch the tent anywhere but behind the ridge. He climbed another 250 feet, alone, in search of level ground, but found nothing suitable. In the gloom that had now descended the only option was to secure the tent at an angle on the leeside of the ridge backbone, on a ledge with a 5000-foot drop to the glacier directly below.

* * *

With the porters gone, supplies and oxygen tanks piled alongside the tent and the sounds of Tibetan songs drifting up from below, George checked the guy ropes one last time and crawled into the tent with Bruce and Tejbir. They removed only their oxygen backpacks and boots in the tight space, huddling together to try and keep some warmth. Within a few minutes they were covered in a layer of fine spindrift as the wind, now near hurricane strength, forced snow through the tiniest fissures.

There was no respite from the violence as night set in. The men created enough space to light the Primus stove and melted snow to make tea. Conversation was muted as they sipped the lukewarm liquid and smoked cigarettes, the nicotine hit welcome. There was little to say as their individual thoughts turned from hopes of a triumphant ascent to the very real possibility that they might not survive the night.

There would be no sleep. The blizzard grew, forcing the men to remain vigilant as the wind reached beneath them like a living, clawing beast to lift one side of the tent and then the other. It took their combined weight to stop the ground sheet from being lifted completely, tearing them from their flimsy hold on the ridge and hurling them into the chasm at their feet.

It was hard to know for certain but the storm seemed to peak around 1am, the tent flaps slapping with a sound like machine-gun fire. Although huddled tightly together, the men could hardly hear one another as they shouted their warnings. Some of the guy ropes had worked their way loose, but there was no time for fear as George donned his eiderdown jacket and, without oxygen, crawled outside into the teeth of the gale to secure the ropes by fastening them around boulders on the ridge: 'The effort was all I could manage and I returned to the tent chilled to the bone and utterly exhausted.'

As dawn approached, grey and grim, the snowfall began to slow, and there were gaps between wind gusts, as if the storm had done its worst and worn itself out. The tired men inside the sagging canvas triangle peeked out. Was it over?

The answer came swiftly and brutally; the monster was just drawing breath and within an hour had returned, more fearsome than before. The guy ropes were again loosened, but each man could only spend two minutes outside at a time in the effort to re-secure them. A great hole was torn in the roof of the tent, and the flaps were stripped of their fastenings. Yet inside, the trio remained 'cheerful', perhaps content to let Everest decide their fate.

George sat as if in the calm eye of a cyclone. While his companions thought of survival his questing mind turned to science. He had realised that breathing at this altitude was a voluntary rather than involuntary action, and that he had to continually *think* to take a breath, otherwise he would end up in a coughing fit as his lungs gasped for air. And yet with a glowing cigarette in his mouth, the problem seemed to go away. Why?

The answer was logical, he decided. The lack of oxygen effectively starved the body's supply of carbon dioxide and that, in turn, exhausted the nerve centre and its ability to co-ordinate involuntary actions. There must be a component in cigarettes that stimulated those same nerves into action, as the effect of a single cigarette lasted three hours. As incongruous as it appeared, his observation would be valued by other scientists as one of the many stepping stones toward understanding human capacity in extreme situations.

Respite came just as suddenly. Shortly after 1pm, almost twenty-four hours after they had made camp to shelter, the wind dropped back to a stiff breeze, cold and yet blissful compared to the previous fury. Now was the time to make their escape and head back down the col, alive and ready to try again if the weather improved. George carefully considered the two men beside him: the Nepalese Gurkha officer who had placed unshakable faith in his leader and the stoic soldier who would not yield in the face of the improbable.

The decision was easy. They would stay clinging to the mountain for another night:

> Very cautiously and tentatively I broached my wish with
> Bruce, fearful lest the trying experience of the last twenty-
> four hours had undermined his keenness for further
> adventure. I might have spared myself the anxiety. He jumped
> at the idea, and when our new plans were communicated to
> Tejbir, the only effect upon him was to broaden his already
> expansive grin. It was a merry little party that gathered round
> to a scanty meal cooked with the last of our fuel. The meal
> was meagre for the simple reason that we had catered for
> only one day's short rations and we were now very much on
> starvation diet.

* * *

There were noises outside the tent. Geoffrey Bruce had woken with a start and prodded George Finch who was half asleep himself, even though it was still only 6pm. It made no sense and they both nestled back down, keen to catch up on lost sleep before the push to the summit the next morning. But there it was again; faint, but clearly the sound of human voices.

Pushing back the tent flap, George found six sherpas standing outside, led by a man named Tergio, with whom he had struck up a friendship. Tergio and his friends had left Camp IV that afternoon after the storm passed, carrying thermos flasks filled with tea and beef tea prepared by John Noel. It was a rescue mission; Noel and the sherpas were worried about the trio's safety and the sherpas had come to escort the climbers back down the mountain.

The actions of these men touched George: 'That is just one more example of the many ways the porters proved daily their self-sacrificing, courageous and truly selfless devotion. Tergio possessed a rare combination of qualities that made the little man especially dear to me.'

It took the climbers an hour to reassure the sherpas that they were strong and safe enough to stay on the ledge and to attempt the final climb in the morning. Eventually, the six men headed off into the darkness with orders to return at noon the next day. It would take them five hours to reach Camp IV, getting lost along the way and barely escaping with their lives.

Getting back to sleep was not easy, and not only because of their concern for the sherpas. As he lay down, George felt the impact of physical exertion in such extreme conditions, not to mention worry, lack of sleep and very little food. A coldness crept up his body; he felt it take hold of his heart and create a sensation he had never known. Dread. He looked over at Bruce and Tejbir; it was clear that both of them felt similarly.

A thought popped into his head. Oxygen. They hadn't used it since making camp because they were stationary, but surely it would have a reviving effect. He retrieved a backpack and offered Tejbir the mouthpiece and watched the impact as the exhausted man's face brightened almost in an instant. Bruce responded likewise before George sucked down on the rubber tube and felt a prickling sensation and warmth as the oxygen coursed through his body.

'There is no doubt whatsoever that oxygen saved our lives that night,' he wrote later. 'Without it, in our well-nigh exhausted and famished condition, we would have succumbed to the cold.'

Still, rest was difficult. They set up the oxygen so each could sip when the need arose, but it meant dozing rather than sleeping and they were stirring before dawn, not so much eager as sensing that time was short. Their problems began immediately. George had brought his boots inside the tent to ensure they were malleable but the others had left theirs outside where they had frozen, and it took an hour over candlelight to mould them back into shape.

At least they did not linger over breakfast – there was none to be had – and the men set off just as dawn touched the sagging tent pole. It was clear, but a fresh wind cut across them as they moved upwards toward the shoulder of the ridge 1600 feet away where Mallory's group had been forced to abandon its attempt. George and Bruce each carried about forty pounds (eighteen kilograms) in equipment, including the oxygen, cameras and tools. Tejbir carried two extra oxygen cylinders, although George only intended that he would climb as high as the shoulder where he would dump the tanks and head back to the tent to wait. George and Bruce would carry on.

Tejbir lasted barely 300 feet before slumping face forward into the snow, his endurance finally shattered. George was at first angry, but then realised the brave soldier deserved a kinder response. He could not go on, but after being revived was fit enough to get back to the tent, which they could still see from the slope. George watched him descend, ready to help if necessary, as he and Bruce rearranged their loads to carry an extra cylinder each. Satisfied that Tejbir was safe, they continued up the slope to the shoulder.

Conditions were changing quickly, the wind rising as they made their way up the relatively easy slope of broken rock toward the shoulder. The problem was not the terrain but the realisation that if they continued onto the ridge itself they would be exposed to the wind at its worst. It was simply too powerful to stand against, let alone climb along to the peak. The only option was to change direction and seek some form of shelter.

They had reached 26,574 feet, still below the shoulder where Mallory, Norton and Somervell had finished, when George saw an opportunity and signalled to Bruce that they would traverse the face of the mountain, away from the wind, and then look for a chance to climb straight up from beneath the summit itself. It was a longer and more difficult climb, but would be in calmer conditions.

At first it was relatively easy, as their path across the stratified rock angled downwards. They were losing height, but getting closer to the wall just below the summit. George was constantly aware of the inexperience of his young charge and kept him close behind. Bruce seemed to be coping, although the terrain was getting more difficult, sloping upwards now, the rocks covered in a fine powder that formed a thin, dangerous crust.

They stopped occasionally to rest, take a height reading from the aneroid barometer or unhook an empty cylinder, which they sent bouncing into the abyss, enjoying the satisfying clang of metal on rock. At least on this route the wind was less of a factor, prompting George to unrope them. It was a risky strategy and meant that a slip by either man would be fatal, but George judged Bruce to be sure-footed and it would save time.

George was buoyed by their slow but sure progress and could not help but think of his brother, Max, and their early climbs. They had planned for this moment as long ago as 1908. And here it was, happening for George but not for Max. George suddenly felt a great longing for what might have been. Geoffrey Bruce was a fine man, but he would much rather have been climbing with his brother.

They had moved halfway across the north face of Everest when George stopped again. They were now at an altitude of 27,100 feet and the peak was directly above them. They had to take a chance and head upwards, toward a spot along the ridge close to the summit.

George had gained about 300 feet and reached a ledge crowned by a stone slab when he heard a cry. Geoffrey Bruce was sixteen feet behind him and was clearly in trouble: 'I'm not getting any air,' he called out, grasping at the rocks to get a safe purchase. George acted swiftly, climbing back down from the ledge and reaching Bruce's side just as he began to topple. He grabbed his companion by the shoulder, hauling him back from the edge of oblivion. Where had he found the strength?

Bruce was unconscious. George shook him awake and, calling on all his reserves, shoved him against the wall and helped him up to the safety of the ledge, clambering up after him. Both men sat heaving.

'I'm not getting any air,' Bruce gasped again, weakly.

George offered him his mouthpiece and began inspecting Bruce's oxygen backpack to find the problem. Nothing seemed wrong; the tanks were unharmed and the flow meter was still pumping out oxygen at 80 fluid ounces (2.4 litres) per minute. Still, something was amiss. He took out his axe, preparing to slice off the flow meter and connect the valve directly to Bruce's breathing tube when something made him stop. He was weakening quickly and needed a shot of oxygen. He took the tube back from Bruce, who was looking better, and took a few big breaths until he felt refreshed.

George needed to find a way for them both to breathe from the same functioning cylinder, so he inserted a spare T-tube and rubber hose that he was carrying in case of such an incident. He then resumed his search for the fault in Bruce's equipment, now unwilling to cut the tube. It was the right decision. A few minutes later he found the problem: a glass connector tube used in the construction of the improvised masks had broken. Bruce must have bumped into some rocks. Again, George was carrying a spare and was able to replace the tube. Bruce's oxygen supply was returned, but at what cost?

As they rested, George looked closely at his companion. Until then he had been aware of his movements – how he walked and climbed – but now he looked beyond the mechanics to the man himself. Geoffrey Bruce was spent. The realisation hit George hard: 'It never occurred to me for a moment that we might not be able to reach our goal. We had made rapid and steady progress. The summit stood before us. Just a little further and we would be standing on the peak – atop the highest mountain in the world.'

The two men were standing on a narrow ledge beneath the ceiling of the world, as high as the cruising altitude of a commercial aircraft where the temperature hovered around minus 50 degrees. Above him George could see 'the individual stones on a little patch of scree lying underneath the highest point'. In his mind, he could almost reach out and touch it. Beneath his feet to the west was the mighty summit of Cho Oyu which reared 26,900 feet. Mount Pumori, at 23,494 feet, was 'an indistinguishable bump of ice'.

They could not give up, not yet anyway. He still had a camera in his pocket, the film inserted that morning, ready to capture the moment of their triumph. But now, with their lives in peril, was not the time for photographs. Bruce was on his feet and they began upwards again but it was clear within a few yards that he could go no further. He sat down as George looked up, the temptation that he might go on alone flashing across his mind. Then it was gone. He could not leave his companion whose eyes had filled with tears. 'Turn back', George called.

27.

'MY UTTER BEST. IF ONLY ...'

Shortly before 5.30pm on May 27, George Finch and Geoffrey Bruce walked arm-in-arm into Camp III at the foot of the North Col. George smiled for John Noel's camera, his chin unshaven for a change, his boots untied to release the pressure on his freezing feet and his precious fur-collared coat grimy but otherwise intact.

Bruce stared vacantly ahead as if unaware of his surroundings, his hat still wrapped around the bottom of his face and his hands shoved deep into the pockets of his tweed suit – he was alive, but clearly distressed. He would later write to George: 'I can never thank you enough for electing to take me with you on the climb, or for the perfectly astonishing way you pulled me through it all. It was wonderful.'

The pair had descended almost 6500 feet in just five hours, pausing occasionally to rest stiff and weary legs and stopping briefly at Camp IV to ensure Tejbir, who had been guided down by Noel and the sherpas, was safe and to slurp down tea and share a tin of Heinz spaghetti – their first food in almost two days. Now back in the relative comfort of the lower camp it was only hunger and a letter from Bubbles that kept George awake for the next few hours. He pored over her words of love and domestic chat while wolfing down four fried quail truffled in pâté de foie gras, and nine plump sausages, after which he insisted he was still hungry. He went to bed with the letter in his hand and a thermos of coffee and tin of toffees at his elbow and slept for fourteen hours.

The next day Arthur Wakefield physically assessed the men, including Tejbir, who had also descended safely. They had all come through the ordeal better than the Mallory party although neither had escaped unscathed. George had four small patches of frostbite on the soles of his feet where the cold had penetrated through his boots and three pairs of socks. Bruce was worse and could not walk. He would have to be dragged on a sled much of the way down the glacier until the terrain became too difficult and the sherpas were forced to take turns carrying him on their backs through the treacherous moraines while George shuffled painfully behind.

In contrast to their speedy descent down Everest, it took two days to reach the base camp where Mallory, Somervell, Norton and Morshead were still recovering. Their health had regressed in the first few days after returning, such was the impact of the ordeal on their bodies. Somervell was doing the best of them, while Mallory was nursing several badly frostbitten fingers. Norton, whose frostbitten ear would recover, could hardly walk, while Morshead, who would lose three fingers to frostbite, was so bad that Thomas Longstaff believed he should be evacuated as soon as possible.

Longstaff was worried not only about the men's external injuries but the impact on their internal organs. Mallory and Norton were both showing signs of heart trouble, as was George, whose heart was beating erratically, and would later prove to have become dangerously enlarged. George would take a fortnight to recover; some of the others took several months. And so, the first attempt to climb Mount Everest appeared to be over.

Charles Bruce, under pressure from Arthur Hinks to provide frequent updates to satisfy media commitments, had already sent a telegram to *The Times* via Darjeeling with the bare details of the Finch–Bruce climb. It would reach London on June 15 and be published the next morning in an article which noted the 'heroic failure' of George Finch and Geoffrey Bruce, who had balanced, exhausted and battered by crosswinds, on a ledge 27,320 feet above sea level, higher than any humans before them.

The term 'failure', in whatever context it was written, was an abomination for a climb that Douglas Freshfield, a doyen of mountaineers and former president of both the Alpine Club and the Royal Geographical Society, would later describe as 'one of the most surprising and bravest feats of mountaineering'.

George Finch and Geoffrey Bruce had climbed at almost three times the rate of Mallory, Norton and Somervell, even though they had carried forty-four pounds (twenty kilograms) on their backs. They had also climbed in much worse weather conditions, spent an extra night on the mountainside and gone without food. To compound matters, George Finch had been climbing with two novices because the others had gone ahead, not only at the suggestion of Colonel Strutt but with the encouragement of George Mallory and the approval of Charles Bruce.

General Bruce was still questioning the success of the oxygen experiment when he wrote to Arthur Hinks on June 1, although he praised George Finch: 'The whole oxygen apparatus was not altogether satisfactory and apparently if he had not bought in Darjeeling certain football bladders and he had not been an extraordinarily handy and accomplished person the oxygen apparatus would have come to complete grief. As it is, it has done yeoman service.'

Surely Finch's efforts deserved better and wider recognition. His ability to adapt in the field verged on genius, and his achievement in getting so close to the summit under such fierce conditions was remarkable. Pulling out of the attempt in order to save his companion, rather than seek individual glory, was laudable and the mark of a true gentleman.

General Bruce added a surprise rider at the end of his letter: 'I'll just state that I shall be very relieved indeed when this last attempt is finished because to tell you frankly I am afraid of Everest under the present conditions with the monsoon only within days of us.'

Last attempt? Surely Longstaff's concerns about the health of the men were enough to end the mission before a tragedy occurred: 'Must put my foot down,' Longstaff would write in his diary. 'There is too little margin of safety. Strutt agrees.'

* * *

George Mallory had been contemplating a second attempt even before he had begun his first, but the thought that George Finch would outdo him had driven his desire to a new level. On May 26, while recovering at base camp, his frustration spilled out in a letter to Ruth:

> We are waiting for news of Finch and Bruce who is with him.
> I think they will certainly break our record – they have had
> very good weather – but I don't expect them to have reached
> the top at the first attempt. All depends on whether they
> succeed in dumping cylinders ahead of them. I shan't feel
> in the least jealous of any success they may have. The whole
> venture of getting up with oxygen is so different from ours
> that the two hardly enter into competition.

His letter was disingenuous on several counts; he knew, for example, as he was writing from his tent, that Finch and Bruce were weathering a storm far worse than he had encountered. His declaration about a lack of envy was equally false, as he had shown on numerous occasions since leaving England. He didn't like Finch and loathed his science lectures, and the notion that he would be bested, particularly knowing that the likes of Hinks and Younghusband depended on him, did not rest easily on his shoulders. In fact, the single word in the letter that best expressed his feelings was the last one – competition. George Mallory wanted to be the first to stand atop the roof of the world, particularly if it could be at the expense of the annoying Australian. And if it involved his using oxygen, then so be it.

As much as he despised the idea, George Finch had provided undeniable proof that oxygen was a significant aid in such extreme conditions and, given that they were all struggling physically, it made sense to make use of the spare tanks. He had already proved his point about human capacity by having reached almost 27,000 feet. A second attempt was a bonus.

Mallory conceded that Longstaff was probably right in his assessment that none of the men were fit to climb again, but he wanted a second opinion, convincing Arthur Wakefield, who had now returned to base camp, to re-examine the three most likely climbers – himself, Somervell and Finch – and give them the go-ahead to mount a third attempt. George Finch overheard Mallory's scheming – 'a pretty little plot concocted in the tent next to mine', as he would note in his diary. 'Wakefield examines Mallory & me & finds us both fit for another shot (yet M's fingers are all frostbitten!).'

Charles Bruce fell for it, if somewhat reluctantly, on the condition that the main purpose of the attempt on the mountain would be to evacuate the camps and bring back the tents and any leftover supplies. If they reached Camp IV and the conditions were fine then they could make an attempt, as he wrote to Hinks: 'At this moment we are actually sending off a third attempt but by way of prophecy I do not expect it to do better than the previous two. The flower of the men's conditions must have gone, also the weather is distinctly getting rougher and when it is rough on Everest it is really rough.'

Mallory wrote again to his wife after General Bruce gave the go-ahead. He knew the climb would be a risk but dismissed doubts, quipping 'the game is worth a finger'. His bigger fear was that George Finch would get on his nerves, and he launched into a scathing assessment of his rival's climb:

> I wonder what you think of Finch's show with Geoffrey Bruce. They made a stout effort on the last day – but in some ways managed very badly. It was initially a mistake carrying up a fresh camp to 25,500 instead of moving the one we had already established; and they put it on the wrong side of the ridge, exposed to the wind. And then by some mismanagement – shortage of supplies both at the North Col and 25,500 feet I believe – coolies were sent up from the North Col at 4pm! They did well to get back at 11pm. But the idea of coolies wandering about up there in the dark with none of us to look after them fills me with horror. The story of the Gurkha officer is pretty bad too – the plan was to take him from 25,500 camp carrying six cylinders of oxygen for 1000 to 1500 feet by which time it was supposed he would be exhausted; he was then to be sent down by himself drinking oxygen from one cylinder! Finch seems to have an altogether different standard of caring for the coolies from mine. I'm determined he will run no risks with their lives during this next adventure.

The criticism smacked of the jealousy Mallory professed not to harbour, ignoring the fact that his own assault had stripped Finch of experienced climbers, porters and supplies. The sherpas, led by the stoic Tergio, had been sent up after the storm by John Noel, not Finch, and could not have stayed at the ridge camp because they had no tents. And George had watched to ensure that the Gurkha, Tejbir, was safely back at the tent before he and Bruce went on.

Against his better judgment and almost certainly convinced that the decision to use oxygen signalled a form of acceptance of him, George agreed to join Mallory and Somervell in a final attempt on Everest on Saturday June 3. He had only been back at the base camp for four days and knew, deep down, that it was not humanly possible to make another attempt so quickly. This probably explains why he made no mention of the plan when he wrote to Bubbles the night before they were due to leave:

> My own darling beloved,
>
> I fear I must have missed a post, or even two – I have been up for almost a fortnight, as my diary will tell you. An account of my doings will have appeared in *The Times* long before you get this. In addition to what that account contains I have little to remark beyond saying that in getting to 27,300 feet I had done my utter best and that that best would have been more if only I had had better backing – Bruce, splendid fellow though he is, being an absolute beginner was hardly the backing I ought to have had – and yet he was the only available man as all the others were *hors de combat* or in any case useless through their inability to put up with even 27,000 feet.
>
> Now I have had four days solid rest & am quite my normal self again. But the weather is very indifferent –

it looks as if the monsoon were upon us, so that further climbing should be out of the question. In any case Somervell & I are the only sound members of the party left. All the others are really out of it with more or less serious frostbite.

As far as I can make out we are all going to move to Kharta on the 11th June & will leave there for Darjeeling before the middle of July, so I should be home with you towards the end of August – It's so good to think of that! In the meantime, darling wife, I have had three beautiful letters from you. Can you guess how much they mean to me out here! One reached me at Camp III at 21,000 feet, the other two I got on our return halfway between Camps II and I, where I was feeling like nothing on earth, so tired and footsore that I could hardly walk. As soon as I got them I sat down & spent two hours reading them on the E Rongbuk Glacier & then went on my way again feeling just ever so much fresher.

Today it looks very much as if the monsoons are arriving fast – the whole sky is overcast & now & then a few flakes of snow fall. Darling, darling mine I love you – Now at last I feel that the turning point in my travels has arrived & that now every moment is bringing me back nearer to you. I am very backward now with photos but am sending you on those that are ready – I took none above our 25,500-foot camp, being too busy & too cold! & now I deplore my lack of energy, if one can call it such!

You will see that I am still troubled with occasional bulging of films – I'd like to wring Kodak's neck & shall certainly take it up with them when I get back. I am writing this in the quiet spell after lunch – it's very cold but I've got my precious eiderdown suit & flying boots on so that I'm probably the warmest member in the camp. Dear darling beloved wife of mine when you get this letter you will know that I shall be on my way back to you – perhaps even in Darjeeling and then in three weeks I shall be with you. Oh how I long for that time to come! I love you, love you & may God bless you, my own darling. I love you.

Your husband Geof

* * *

The sky was grey and heavy the next morning when the men trudged out of camp and back toward the mountain, now hidden behind a dense mass of cloud. The optimism and purpose of the first two attempts had been replaced by a weary wariness, and it was obvious within an hour of leaving base camp that George had made a mistake. Longstaff had been right. The frostbite patches on the soles of his feet had not healed and he was forced to hobble behind the others as they made their way back to Camp I. Wakefield and Crawford, who were making the trip as support officers, had gone on ahead and by the time the three climbers arrived at 3.30pm George was exhausted.

To make matters worse it had begun to snow heavily. The five men sheltered uncomfortably in one of the stone huts, its deficiencies apparent as the snowfall invaded the tight space. By morning George had made the obvious decision and abandoned the attempt, opting instead to head back to base camp and join the party led by Longstaff that would convey the injured Morshead and Colonel Strutt (who was also struggling health-wise) back to Darjeeling as quickly as possible.

Before he left Camp I, George took Somervell once more through the oxygen drill that the men had so cavalierly dismissed on the way to Everest. Eventually satisfied that they could manage the equipment, he headed back to base camp, pausing to say goodbye to the sherpa Tergio who had climbed the slopes of Everest in a blizzard to rescue his sahib.

Mallory and his party would shelter for another day at Camp I, hemmed in by heavy snowfall that only abated on the morning of June 5. The men emerged from their hut to find the snow lying heavy and wet on the ground, warmed by the winds that promised the monsoon season was upon them. As they contemplated whether to go on or yield to the conditions, George Finch was on the back of a donkey, making his way back to Darjeeling – and Bubbles.

* * *

George Mallory's reasoning was simple. If there was a chance, however small, of getting higher on Everest then they should keep going, even if there was an element of danger: 'To retire now with the smallest chance remaining to us would be an unworthy end to the expedition.'

At first the going was easy, but the snow lay thick and was still falling as they approached Camp III. Grey skies had set in, Everest hidden in the clouds which only cast further gloom when they arrived to find the tents sagging under the weight of the fresh snowfall and their supplies buried. With boots already sodden with melted snow, the men spent the next few hours clearing the camp site and establishing some semblance of order.

That night they discussed abandoning the attempt. The snow outside lay 16 inches deep and the trek up to the North Col to reach Camp IV would be difficult, let alone the climb to the summit. They decided to sleep on it – as best they could, having cleared the tents of snow and ice – and wait to see if the weather had improved by morning, aware that the imminent monsoon meant conditions were still variable.

The morning broke warm with clear blue skies and the decision was made. They would keep going, albeit with amended plans. George Finch believed oxygen should be used from the North Col camp onwards, but Mallory reckoned they could get at least as high as 25,000 feet before taking short sips of oxygen and then using it steadily from 26,000 feet, near the North Col ridge shoulder where he wanted to establish an overnight bivouac.

First, though, they would have to cross the rest of the Rongbuk Glacier and ascend the steep slope onto the col itself. The conditions were poor; ploughing through the deep snow would be exhausting and the party would have to travel slowly to avoid crevasses hidden by fresh falls. The danger of avalanches from snow lying loosely on the steeper slopes would be ever-present. Mallory was particularly worried about the final slope linking the glacier to the col.

Mallory and Somervell, joined now by Crawford and fourteen porters, set off at 8am on June 7 and quickly realised they were going to struggle even more than they had anticipated in their trek across the glacier, plunging knee-deep into snow with each step. It took more than two hours just to reach the base of the slope Mallory feared would be the most dangerous. The climbers went ahead, testing the surface by cutting a trench across the base of the slope, encouraging any loose snow to give way. It held solid and the party moved on.

As Mallory later wrote: 'The thought of an avalanche was dismissed from our minds.'

They paused just before 2pm, satisfied that the slope had flattened out somewhat, but aware that they still had 600 feet to climb to get to the camp site. Somervell was leading, followed by Wakefield and then Mallory, advancing straight up the slope rather than criss-crossing back and forth in the manner often employed in avalanche-prone areas. The climbers moved in virtual silence, the only sound their laboured breath in the thinning air, even though the conditions remained still and bright.

Mallory's account of the next few seconds is chilling:

> We were startled by an ominous sound, sharp, arresting,
> violent and yet somehow soft like an explosion of untamped
> gunpowder. I had never before on a mountainside heard such a
> sound; but all of us, I imagine, knew instinctively what it meant.
> In a moment I observed the surface of the snow broken where
> it had been even for a few yards to the right of me. I took two
> steps convulsively in this direction with some quick thought of
> getting nearer the edge of the danger that threatened us. And
> then I began to move slowly downwards, inevitably carried on
> the whole moving surface by a force that I was utterly powerless
> to resist. Somehow I managed to turn out from the slope so
> as to avoid being pushed headlong and backwards down it.
> For a second or two I seemed hardly to be in danger as I went
> quietly sliding down with the snow. Then the rope at my waist
> tightened and held me back. A wave of snow came over me and
> I was buried. I supposed that the matter was settled.

Mallory was tumbled down the slope like a surfer in a boiling wave, his senses confused until he felt the pace slacken and the snow close up about him. The avalanche had slowed and stopped. His arms were free and he began struggling, worming his way toward what he perceived to be the surface. He broke free and stood up, the rope taut around his waist until the porter who had been immediately behind him stood up. Somervell and Crawford emerged nearby, but where were the others?

They looked down and could see a group of sherpas standing 150 feet below. They had been the closest to the climbers and were pointing back down the mountain, where another nine had been swept by the wave of ice and snow. They had been roped together in two groups, and as Mallory and the others quickly descended it became clear they had been washed down an ice cliff and into a crevasse now covered in snow. It was an icy tomb unless they could be dragged out quickly. The process was heartbreaking. Seven of the nine were dead, among them the brave Tergio. The 1922 mission was over.

PART IV

28.

THE UNLIKELIEST OF HEROES

The closer he got to London, the briefer the entries in George Finch's diary would become. What began as a document full of the wonders of new lands, strange people and exotic customs, and evolved into a story of stoicism in the face of prejudice and achievement against the odds, turned into a weary notation of the towns and villages passed during the long trek back to India. Even the first of many celebratory dinners on June 26 in Darjeeling barely rated a mention: 'Lunch at Gov House and packing.' The diary entries petered out altogether after July 1 when the men boarded the RMS *Macedonia* at Bombay for the voyage home.

Finch travelled with Longstaff and Strutt, who had been among the more vocal opponents of oxygen. Yet by the time they docked at Dover on the evening of July 16, they had become friends of sorts. Longstaff was now an admirer and a supporter who believed it was only bad luck that had kept Finch from reaching the summit of Everest.

Strutt, who had been so willing to dismiss George as an uncouth cad, quietly acknowledged his achievements in the last days at base camp when he filled out an Alpine Club membership application for George, naming General Bruce as the proposer, himself as seconder and four other climbers, including Mallory, as supporters. Under the heading 'Qualifications for Membership', Strutt noted: 'Everest expedition, record height 27,300ft, many various in the Alps, Corsica etc.' Despite their differences, the two men would maintain cordial relations over the years.

But the welcome home was far from warm. Two days before they docked, news reached London of the avalanche and death of the sherpas. Charles Bruce, ashamed and worried, had held back the information for several weeks and was now trying to play down the accident and the culpability of the climbers, particularly Mallory. In public he defended the decision to climb and dismissed the accident as the revenge of Everest – 'a terrible enemy' – but privately he blamed it largely on an error of judgment by Mallory that had tarnished the expedition's other achievements. In a letter to Francis Younghusband he concluded: 'It is altogether a rather humiliating and I am sorry to say a quite unnecessary ending to the expedition.'

Arthur Hinks, in particular, was furious. The time gap between events at Everest and the information arriving in London had been frustrating enough without the general's delay in revealing the awful truth that now had to be massaged through the media. Hinks had already fired off an angry letter to Bruce, demanding an explanation about the composition of the first two climbs, both of which he regarded as reconnaissance rather than real attempts and ignoring the fact that his own interference had influenced the decisions of Colonel Strutt, backed by Bruce.

The early return of Longstaff, Finch and Strutt only heightened Hinks's ire and he sent them all telegrams demanding their appearance the following morning before the Everest Committee. At a time when they desperately wanted a quiet reunion with families they had not seen for more than four months, the three men instead found themselves fronting a boardroom inquisition in Kensington Gore.

It was an angry affair, at least at first, as Hinks accused a group of men whom most would regard as brave heroes of being irresponsible, questioning why they had left the expedition earlier than expected and demanding an explanation for Finch climbing with Geoffrey Bruce instead of Howard Somervell or Teddy Norton. Strutt insisted it was due to a combination of factors, including Finch's illness, worries about the weather and doubts about the oxygen equipment.

Longstaff angrily defended his medical evaluation of the climbers, which had proved accurate, and labelled the decision to approve a third attempt as reckless, as proved by the resulting tragedy, which the trio had been unaware of until they arrived at Dover. The official minutes of the meeting would reveal little of this debate and certainly none of the emotion, although Longstaff later gave an account in a letter to Sandy Wollaston, his medical counterpart in the 1921 mission, in which he castigated George Mallory as stout-hearted, 'but quite unfit to be in charge of anything, including himself'.

He was not the only man to critique the expedition's charismatic figurehead: the next day, Hinks sent a memo marked 'Private and Confidential' to Norman Collie, Charles Howard-Bury and Edward Somers-Cocks in which he outlined the sequence of events, and the impact of George Finch's bout of dysentery on the plans:

> This explains why Somervell and Norton went for the first climb. When Finch recovered, he chose Geoffrey Bruce as being the most reliable man with oxygen to accompany him. Bruce made a considerable effort but was slow because untrained in Alpine work, and Finch thinks that if he had Somervell or Norton with him he would have got a good

deal higher, which seems very likely. In fact Finch's sickness for a while is probably the most important mishap from the point of view of complete success. Finch has given very much useful and thoughtful information and seems to me to have come out of it very well. A contributory cause of his failure to get beyond 27,300 feet was the want of food. They thought of many things but overlooked the fact that consuming oxygen would make them exceedingly hungry.

Hinks, perhaps deliberately because of his own Machiavellian contribution to the debacle, had disguised the real reason for George picking Geoffrey Bruce – that he was the only fit man left. He then went on to make judgments about Mallory:

> The people who have come back think Mallory's judgment in purely Alpine matters was bad and much inferior to Norton of whom everyone speaks very highly, and they are inclined to attribute the accident to this. They evidently had sharp disagreements about the proper way to ascend the North Col, Finch going a different way from Mallory.

Collie replied a few days later, agreeing that George Finch had earned their admiration:

> Finch was the most able person besides being a first rate climber; he was I am sure of the greatest value to the expedition, a man who could turn his hand to anything, and a man who was at once capable of sizing up probably correctly the possibilities of any situation that turned up. Before he went out I saw how he at once understood about possible difficulties and how to meet them, and never made

any foolish remarks about things. I am sincerely glad that he got on satisfactorily with other members of the expedition.

Charles Bruce had also offered his verdict by letter. As usual, his comments on George Finch damned him with faint praise:

> Probably the best snow and ice man on the expedition but has a curious constitution. On his day can probably last as well as any man but apparently very soon shoots his bolt. I should say not a very robust man for a long strain and has a delicate inside. Is extraordinarily handy in all kinds of ways outside his scientific accomplishments. A convincing raconteur of quite impossible experiences. Cleans his teeth on February 1st and has a bath on the same day if the water is very hot, otherwise puts it off until the next year. Six months course as a Lama novice in a monastery would enable me to occupy a Whymper tent with him.

It was an ugly, graceless assessment of a man who had climbed higher than anyone else, rescued the general's own cousin from certain death, pitched in to help others with photographs and repairs of equipment and survived the attempt on Everest in better physical condition than all but one man. And yet even Charles Bruce could not hide from the conclusion that George Finch, a boy from the Australian bush, had emerged the unlikely hero of the first attempt to climb the world's biggest and most fearsome mountain.

* * *

If George Finch had expected that he would be allowed to simply disappear into the background to wallow in the anonymous comfort of wedded bliss, then he was sadly mistaken. The astounding aspect of his Himalayan adventure, over and above his climbing achievement and scientific genius, was how little it appeared to matter to him compared to his new home life, perhaps as it came after the failure of two previous marriages. For him, the conquest of Everest was important, a realisation of the exhilaration he had felt that spring morning as a thirteen-year-old atop Mount Canobolas. But it was his new life with a petite Scotswoman with curly hair and a can-do spirit which was the goal he could envisage from the summit that day.

There would be barely enough time for George and Bubbles to settle into their tiny Kensington flat as man and wife or for George to reacquaint himself with the staff and students at Imperial College before he was dragged away to attend endless rounds of meetings, grand public dinners and newspaper interviews and to give the first of dozens of paid lectures. Arthur Hinks and his cohorts might not have admitted it, but George, like Mallory, was a hero and the public wanted to hear first-hand his story of monster mountain winds, the bone-chilling deathly cold and the attempt, inch by inch, to stand on top of the world.

The fact that neither man had made it to the top seemed to make little difference, and the tragedy of the deaths of the sherpas seemed only to add to their tale, as did the ongoing dispute about the use of oxygen tanks.

When Mallory arrived in London to present his side of the story in *The Times* on September 4, he argued that a mountaineer was 'bound to take risks' but in doing so 'must be sure himself that the risks he takes are within reason'. The three climbers – himself, Somervell and Crawford – were all entitled to believe the slope was safe after testing it, he maintained. Privately, he struggled with the accident, as he wrote to Ruth: 'Do you know the sickening feeling that one can't go back and have it undone and that nothing will make it good?' Ultimately, however, he accepted no responsibility and the issue quickly disappeared.

Mallory was also keen to play down the difficulties of climbing at altitude – and thus the need for oxygen – insisting that the reason he did not climb the final 3000 feet to the summit was not because of altitude but because of the effort already expended in getting to 26,000 feet: 'The factors which will tell against the climber on this last section are his efforts on the previous days, from which it may be supposed he will not have recovered completely and, possibly, ill effects from sleeping at these very high camps.'

It seemed that the unquestionable success of oxygen only intensified the opposition to it, *The Times* even adding parentheses around the word 'record' when describing Finch and Bruce's climb, as if it were not legitimate. Not one to stay quiet, George used the pages of Arthur Hinks's *Royal Geographical Journal* to hit back at the 'anti-oxygenists' in an article laced with sarcasm:

There are those who do not believe in oxygen. Perhaps it is because simple obvious facts render them uneasy in their unbelief that they rush into print with a wholesale condemnation on the grounds that its use in high mountaineering is what they rather loosely term 'artificial' and therefore unsporting. Now, few of us, I think, who stop to ponder for a brief second, will deny that our very existence in this enlightened twentieth century with all its amenities of modern civilisation is, in the same slipshod sense of the word, 'artificial'.

Most of us have learned to respect progress and to appreciate the meaning and advantages of adaptability. For instance, it is a fairly firmly established fact that warmth is necessary to life. The mountaineer, acting on this knowledge, conserves as far as possible his animal heat by wearing specially warm clothing. No one demurs, it is a commonsense thing to do. He pours his hot tea from a thermos bottle – and never blushes. Nonchalantly, without criticism, he doctors up his insides with special heat and energy-giving foods and stimulants.

From the sun's ultraviolet rays and the wind's bitter cold he boldly dares to protect his eyes with Crookes' anti-glare glasses; further, he wears boots that to the average layman look ridiculous. The use of caffeine to supply just a little more buck to an almost worn-out human frame is not cavilled at despite its being a synthetic drug the manufacture of which involves the employment of complicated plant and methods.

If science could prepare oxygen in a tabloid form or supply it to us in thermos flasks that we might imbibe it like our hot tea, the stigma of 'artificiality' would, perhaps, be effectually removed. But when it has to be carried in special containers, its whole essence is held to be altered, and by using it the mountaineer is taking a sneaking, unfair advantage of the mountain!

In answer to this grave charge, I would remind the accuser that, by the inhalation of a little life-giving gas, the climber does not smooth away the rough rocks of the mountain or still the storm; nor is he an Aladdin who, by a rub on a magic ring, is wafted by invisible agents to his goal. Oxygen renders available more of his store of energy and so hastens his steps, but it does not, alas, fit the wings of Mercury on his feet.

By contrast to the British coverage, the American newspapers trumpeted the achievement, explaining to their readers that the men had got 'within four or five city blocks' of the summit: 'No more desperate or magnificent effort against the mountains was ever made,' said the *New York Times*. 'A fearful struggle but with great heroism succeeded in climbing higher than man had gone afoot before,' said the *Washington Post*.

The Australian media was also captivated by the adventure, although none of the Sydney or Melbourne papers realised that George Finch was a home-grown hero. It was only the regional papers that made the connection, like the *Northern Champion* in Taree which trumpeted him as 'a native of the western district' and the *Gundagai Independent* which declared 'Australia will be there!', suggesting the unlikely scenario that George had shouted the name of his homeland from the icy heights.

* * *

In the days when cinema was in its infancy, and decades before the technology that would create television, the lecture tour was a form of entertainment that brought to life the stories of daredevil adventurers. Thousands queued in villages, towns and cities across the United Kingdom to see and hear their heroes, who more often than not used the revenue raised to help fund the cost of their adventures to come or pay for those just completed.

Gerald Christy was the best known of the London managers who arranged these tours, his agency at one time managing two hundred celebrities, including the likes of Robert Falcon Scott, Douglas Mawson, Ernest Shackleton and even Winston Churchill.

It was to Christy that the Everest Committee turned to convert the public fascination with the Everest climbers into a commercial gain that would help pay the bills of an expedition that had cost £12,500. The lecture tour and film following the 1921 reconnaissance had turned a decent profit, which had paid for that mission and gone some way toward covering the cost of the 1922 adventure, although there was still a shortfall of around £9000.

Arthur Hinks was keen to involve as many of the climbers as possible, but not all were available, willing or capable. Henry Morshead was still recovering in India, where Howard Somervell and John Morris had also remained 'John Noel was in Tibet and Teddy Norton in Constantinople. Geoffrey Bruce had rejoined his regiment, Arthur Wakefield had headed straight for his country home in Cumberland, Thomas Longstaff wasn't interested and Edward Strutt, according to Hinks, 'would not do it well because he is a bad lecturer'.

That left the two Georges, and to a lesser extent Charles Bruce, to be the public faces and financial hopes of the expedition. Both men had suffered financially more than the others: George reduced to half pay and Mallory, having resigned from Charterhouse, earning nothing while he was away, pinning his hopes on making a living from his celebrity status. Both were happy to accept the committee's offer of 30 per cent of the net profits plus travelling expenses inside the United Kingdom, as per the agreement they had signed before leaving.

The rush of interest was only heightened by an announcement in early September that there would be another expedition, either in 1923 or more likely 1924, and that Charles Bruce would again be the leader. Given their climbing success and their status as the stars of the lecture tour, it was assumed that Mallory and Finch would again be the chief climbers.

Over the next three months George Finch travelled widely, often catching a train after lessons finished at the Imperial College, to appear in town halls and schools up and down the country. The accounts books of the Royal Geographical Society show that he visited towns and cities in Wiltshire, Gloucestershire, Kent, Worcestershire, Nottinghamshire and Leicestershire, reaping significant income for the Everest Committee.

Mallory was also busy, speaking at events in Wiltshire, Cheshire, the Midlands and Berkshire before he embarked on a three-month tour of America which proved somewhat less successful financially but would result in one of the most famous lines in mountaineering history. When a *New York Times* reporter asked him why he wanted to climb Everest, Mallory replied, 'Because it's there.' He then expanded on his much-quoted response: 'Everest is the biggest mountain in the world and no man has reached its summit. Its existence is a challenge. The answer is instinctive, a part I suppose of man's desire to conquer the universe.'

As his rival headed across the Atlantic, George Finch sailed to the Continent with Gerald Christy, where he was fêted, delivering five lectures in as many nights in Delft, Rotterdam, Amsterdam, Arnhem and The Hague before travelling to Switzerland to speak at three events, each in Geneva and Basel and two in Zürich. Then it was on to Gothenburg and Stockholm in Sweden before events in Paris and Marseilles, all of which earned the committee more than £1000. Returning to England, he began travelling again on weeknights and on weekends, visiting Cumbria, Surrey, Lancashire, the West Midlands, Yorkshire and Warwickshire, and venturing up to Glasgow.

By March, George Finch had given eighty-three lectures and delivered the bulk of the profits that would help pay for the expedition, yet earned just enough himself to compensate for his loss of income and to cover the £200 he had paid for photographic stock out of his own pocket before the trip.

And yet his efforts seemed only to irritate Arthur Hinks, who, despite pocketing a £250 bonus for managing the expedition from behind his desk, turned down George's request for a minimum fee of £25 per lecture while overseas and then ordered Christy not to accept any more engagements because 'he has had a good run'.

There was further angst behind the scenes when Charles Howard-Bury, despised leader of the 1921 reconnaissance mission, twice referred in public to Mallory as being 'the most distinguished climber' of the expedition, completely ignoring George's contribution. To compound matters, the official account of the expedition contained three chapters written by George and also used his photographs – for which he received nothing despite having spent his own money on equipment and photographic stock and in the face of Hinks's assurances that he retained ownership of his work.

Nevertheless, George was capable of his own high-handedness. When Mallory asked if he could use George's photographs during his own lectures, George wrote him a lofty and sarcastic letter, saying he had carefully considered the request but rejected it in the interests of the committee, arguing that his and Mallory's lecture styles were different and it would 'plagiarise them in the eyes of the public' if anyone besides himself showed them. It was a spurious argument, but the only ammunition George had to fight back the barrage of criticism waged against him.

Mallory complained to Hinks, asking him for a copy of Finch's report of his climb, because he was unsure of the detail and feared 'I have made rather a mess of it'. Hinks replied the same day: 'I certainly have not got Finch's verbatim reports. I would not touch them. He is now sad because Howard-Bury referred to you as the greatest climber on the expedition and did it twice. He asked me how I justified such action on the colonel's part.'

Hinks could not do so because the evidence was to the contrary, but it seemed the truth only worsened George Finch's situation. In March he took a break from lectures for a few weeks with other matters on his mind.

Bubbles was pregnant.

29.

THE BASTARDY OF ARTHUR HINKS

In the late autumn of 1935 a young man named Scott Russell arrived at the rooms of the Alpine Club in Savile Row to introduce himself as a prospective member. His mid-morning timing was deliberate as the club was largely empty before noon when the older members would begin filing in for lunch and an afternoon of reminiscing. The club was usually filled by late afternoon, particularly on Tuesdays when there was an evening lecture.

It was unnerving for the fresh-faced 22-year-old to be ushered into the first-floor lounge and reading room, the wood-panelled walls lined with bookshelves filled with accounts of the splendid adventures of members over the eighty years since the club's founding in 1857. There were a few stalwarts around and Russell found himself chatting with the Honorable Sydney Spencer, a 73-year-old former club secretary and librarian and now vice-president.

Spencer was pleasant enough and curious about the young man's background. And Russell obliged; after all, he needed to convince the club committee of his climbing pedigree if he were to be accepted as a member. Russell was London-born, he assured Spencer, but raised at the bottom of the world in New Zealand where the family had moved when he was a young boy, in search of a better climate because of his father's ill health. He had returned to London to study botany at the Imperial College. His love of climbing had developed in the wild hills behind Nelson on the South Island and been inspired by the adventures of two Alpine Club icons, Geoffrey Winthrop Young and George Finch.

The mood in the room suddenly chilled. Spencer paused, the veneer of friendliness gone in a moment. Winthrop Young was a perfectly reasonable choice and well regarded by his fellow members, but Finch was another matter altogether. No one liked him and he was barely tolerated as a member. The man simply didn't belong: 'I hope your proposers told you that in addition to being the oldest mountaineering body in the world, the Alpine Club is a unique one – a club for gentlemen who also climb,' Spencer explained. His voice was icy, disdainful. Although there was no mistaking his point, Spencer wanted to ensure the young man understood him perfectly. He glanced out of the first-floor window into the street below where a street sweeper was clearing the pavement: 'I mean that we would never elect that fellow even if he were the finest climber in the world.'

Russell would not forget the encounter, partly because of its ferocity but more so because he would not only meet Finch and fall under his thrall but, many years later, would become his son-in-law. Spencer's comments, therefore, became rather personal.

It is little wonder that Spencer hated George Finch, given that he represented all that George had railed against in his 1913 article in *The Field* – a 'professional man of comfortable means and adequate leisure', as he would be described after his death in 1950. The two men had interests and experiences in common, particularly their love of the Alps, but their generations and social attitudes held them apart. Both had known the legendary Swiss guide Christian Jossi, although their relationships with him were in complete contrast. George Finch regarded Jossi as a mentor, and remained forever grateful to the Swiss for teaching him and Max the art of ice climbing before they took off to explore the Alps. Sydney Spencer simply paid Jossi for the twenty-two summers and fourteen winters he led him safely across mountaintops, including the year they found a new route to the peak of the Aiguille de Blatière near Chamonix in France. The climb passed along a passageway later named the Spencer Couloir, a lasting reminder of the days when, as writer JH Doughty once remarked, 'the titular honour of a new climb was given not to the man who led it but the man who paid to do it'.

Both men were also avid and pioneering photographers, but it was their differences which mattered most in the early months of 1923, a dozen years before the meeting with Russell, as planning began in earnest for the next attempt to scale the world's highest peak.

Spencer had become the secretary of the Alpine Club at its annual general meeting in December 1922, succeeding Captain John Eaton who was a friend of Percy Farrar and, therefore, a supporter of George Finch. But times, and political numbers, had changed, and when Charles Bruce succeeded Norman Collie as the Alpine Club president at the same meeting it meant that George's already fragile support on the Everest Committee was lost, as shown by a missive from Bruce to Spencer on March 1 with his preliminary list of climbers: 'Somervell, Mallory, Norton, Finch (I am sorry to say but it is those scientific requirements) and Geoffrey Bruce,' he wrote, adding there was a need for two first-class snow men: 'Finch is one, Norton, I think is another.'

Given his stinging assessment of George's personal hygiene habits in his report some months earlier, Bruce was obviously reluctant to include him – but his own words of praise had trapped him. It was clear that Finch was not easily dismissed from the reckoning. Not only was he the best credentialled climber for the snow and ice near the summit of Everest, but he was also the only man capable of taking care of the fragile oxygen equipment. And, as Charles Bruce himself had pointed out, he was the best man in a tight spot, able to turn his hand to fixing clothing and equipment and adaptable in adverse situations.

From an objective point of view, George should have been the first man chosen. This was galling for men like Sydney Spencer and Charles Bruce, who despised what he stood for, as Spencer would make plain with his street sweeper analogy more than a decade later. George Finch had no breeding; he was a rebellious colonial from the bush of New South Wales, educated on the Continent rather than at Oxford or Cambridge, and he not only repudiated the role of gentleman climber but was critical of those who embraced it as a birthright. Percy Farrar's sheer force of personality had won Finch a place on the 1922 team, but if they could help it, Spencer and Bruce, along with Arthur Hinks, would not let it happen again.

George Finch was keenly aware of the resentment around him. Publicly he said nothing, but privately he would always refer to his nemesis as 'Little Hinks', not only because he towered over the bureaucrat but because he regarded him and his behaviour as beneath contempt. George was not interested in class, simply in ability, and what others interpreted as arrogance was a self-belief that could not be shaken – no matter the consequences.

* * *

In hindsight, Thomas Longstaff would probably regret writing to Sydney Spencer in late February 1923, asking for a special item to be placed on the agenda of the Alpine Club's meeting on March 6 to appoint a committee to select the climbers for the 1924 expedition. The reason, he wrote, was that the Royal Geographical Society had an enormous list of tasks to prepare for the trip, including improving equipment, logistics and food as well as selecting team members in support roles. It made sense that the Alpine Club select the climbers.

A few days before the meeting he wrote again to Spencer, repeating his request but this time revealing he had a hidden agenda. The public reason, as he wrote, remained the same: the club was simply helping the Royal Geographical Society in what was a complicated task. He then added:

> PRIVATE My real reason for making a move is that there
> is some dissatisfaction in the club in that they feel that
> they were not sufficiently directly represented – and kept
> informed as to plans of – the small Everest Committee.
> Especially this is the case as to the selection of the climbers.
> I therefore told the complainers I would move some such
> motion openly at the ordinary meeting.

Although he was not mentioned by name, the subtext was clearly the controversial selection of George Finch, an upstart who was not a member of either club when selected for the 1921 and 1922 missions. There were others who wanted to go to Everest, and believed themselves capable, and although none would challenge the iconic figure of Mallory, Finch had to be deposed.

Just after 5pm on March 6, as George prepared for a lecture in front of a decent crowd seated politely inside the town hall of Burton-on-Trent, Staffordshire, the Alpine Club elders met in London and agreed that a sub-committee of ordinary members and committeemen should make the decision about which climbers would represent the club on the next expedition, because 'it would give the members of the club a better opportunity of taking a personal interest in the expedition'. Among the twelve appointed to make the decision was George Mallory, who was still in the United States on his lecture tour and would only arrive home in early April as the committee met to make its recommendations. These were passed to the Everest Committee in time for its monthly meeting on May 2.

Percy Farrar was not in attendance when General Bruce read out the selected names. Three of the four men were from the list Bruce had submitted on March 1 – Somervell, Mallory and Norton, who had climbed together without oxygen. There were two other names: the geologist Noel Odell and the ornithologist Bentley Beetham. Odell, who had climbed mainly in England, was a member of the Alpine Club committee and about to leave with an Oxford University team on an Arctic expedition. Beetham was a good friend and climbing partner of Somervell.

George Finch's name had disappeared. There was no comment or minuted discussion about why he had been omitted, noting only 'names of other candidates would be submitted for consideration early in the autumn'.

Farrar promptly resigned from the committee, although he would later make one last attempt to have Finch included in the climbing party as a late consideration. In a letter to Spencer he wrote:

> We must not assume that there are plenty of men available or forget that he rendered splendid service and brought his party safely out of a most perilous adventure. With a less competent and resourceful leader than Finch we might have

had to record the loss of other than porters. I put his name forward with a full knowledge of his thorough competence in Alpine matters so that nothing should occur to prejudice the name of the club. That is always my main concern.

Spencer did not reply.

The formal minutes of the Everest Committee's meetings give no hint of any dissent or that anyone even raised George Finch's name. He had simply disappeared from all discussion.

Perhaps, the answer lay in a letter written more than three decades later by Alice Bullock, widow of Guy Bullock, the man drafted into the 1921 reconnaissance at Mallory's insistence to replace George Finch. Together, Mallory and Bullock had managed to climb to the North Col, but their relationship was not as close after the expedition as it had been beforehand.

In September 1960, Mrs Bullock wrote to the Alpine Club in response to a request to publish her husband's diary of the 1921 mission – the only diary kept by a member of the party. Bullock had refused to let Mallory use it as a reference during his lectures after they returned, insisting that he had not read it himself, but Mrs Bullock hinted at a different reason:

> My husband considered Mallory ready to take unwarranted risks with still untrained loaded coolies in traversing dangerous bits of ice. At least on one occasion, he [Bullock] refused to take his rope of coolies over the route marked by Mallory. Mallory was not over-pleased. He did not suffer a critical difference of opinion readily. In the second expedition Captain Finch as a physiological chemist considered that Mallory did not know what he was talking about in his opinions on the use of oxygen at high

altitudes. The result of this was, according to Mallory's own statement to us, when the third expedition was being prepared, Mallory refused to join it if Finch were to be a member.

George Finch's expulsion was complete.

* * *

Within his steely and intellectual character there seemed to be a touch of gentle innocence about George Finch, borne out by his belief during the 1922 expedition that Charles Bruce was an ally and by his writing that despite the party having conflicting views on oxygen, 'complete harmony existed among us – too valuable a thing to be disturbed by the friction into which, under the circumstances, a sense of rivalry might well have degenerated'.

He also seemed unaware of his rejection by the Everest Committee; either that or he was holding out a forlorn hope that his name would be added to the expedition list later in the year, because he accepted an invitation to attend the committee's meeting on June 14 to explain his plans for the use of oxygen. The committee had already given him the task of improving the design of the cylinders and he had also agreed to work on his designs for 'cold-resisting clothes' and more appropriate food.

In spite of doubts he may have felt about whether he would be selected, and without his champion, Percy Farrar, in the room, George presented a lengthy and passionate twelve-point report detailing his strategy for conquering Everest by establishing two main camps, one at the base of the North Col and the other at 26,000 feet, using a transport officer and a team of porters carrying tents and oxygen bottles.

Waiting below would be six designated climbers working in pairs, as he and Geoffrey Bruce had the previous year. The first pair would begin using oxygen at 21,000 feet and climb past the second camp to 26,500 feet where they would dump six or seven cylinders atop a small shoulder where they could be seen, then return to the 26,000-foot camp.

The second pair – the designated summit team – could then pick up four of the cylinders on their way to the peak. Assuming they made it to the top, the men could dump the empty cylinders when they descended to 26,500 feet, pick up fresh ones and make their way down to the main camp in triumph. If the attempt failed, then it was hoped the men would leave the spare cylinders at the shoulder, enabling the third pairing to make an attempt.

The plan was simple – a relay of sorts – and relied on teamwork as much as individual effort. It was a commonsense approach that would provide fresh oxygen at critical moments without the need for the climbers to haul the cylinders up the mountain.

When Finch was finished, George Mallory gave his views which differed quite markedly. Mallory was concerned about the weight of the cylinders, even though he had never climbed with tanks on his back, and believed the answer lay in acclimatising for four or five nights at 23,000 feet where there was no difficulty sleeping and oxygen was not necessary. The key then was to ensure that a second advance base was established higher up the mountain, at 27,000 feet near the shoulder of the North Col ridge. He insisted that porters should be able to carry equipment that high even though none had been able to do so in 1922. He also wanted three men in each climbing party.

The meeting ended without resolution. It would be the last time that George Finch was asked by the committee for his opinion.

30.

A DREAM IS DASHED

On April 12, 1923 Bubbles gave birth to a baby daughter, almost forty weeks to the day since her husband had arrived back in London from the Everest expedition. Despite their delight, neither could agree on a name for their newborn, so Joyce Nanette Ingle Finch was named by compromise – given names both parents could live with but neither particularly cared for – but it mattered not at all because she soon became 'Bunty'. She was the first child for whom George Finch would accept full parental responsibility.

He was still making payments to his second wife, Gladys May, who had celebrated the fourth birthday of their son, Bryan, just two days before Bunty's birth. And little Peter, the boy whose paternity would remain in doubt for the rest of his life, had recently turned seven and was exploring the Vaucresson wonderland in the care of George's mother, Laura, who would be told of her new grandchild and in later years would make sudden – and brief – appearances in England.

Peter's mother, Betty Fisher, had recently married Jock Campbell and moved to India with her second son, three-year-old Michael, who, like Peter, would always believe that George was his father and cite his name on the birth certificate as proof. One of the few photographs of the young boy would show a genteel afternoon tea in Jhansi, in central northern India, where Campbell's Poona Horse regiment was stationed. The wide-eyed, angelic boy is smiling in wonderment at the camera, standing at the side of the handsome Jock, clearly the senior officer of the group of officers resplendent in white dress uniform and lounging in wicker chairs. Betty is seated next to them, the only female adult, smiling coyly and dressed in flowing white chiffon. In another, taken around the same time, Michael wears a pith helmet and stands shyly between Betty and the grim-faced Jock who would divorce his mother several years later, always insisting that although he had bedded and loved Betty Fisher, he was not the father of either of her two sons.

Back in London, Bubbles knew only portions of her husband's unsettling past as she nursed their first-born. A friend of George had told her about his first disastrous marriage, probably at George's request, but the existence of Gladys and Bryan would always remain hidden, not out of any shame on George's part but from a misguided desire to protect his wife. While she took responsibility for communications, George kept his hand firmly on the family's financial tiller.

George was her champion, a man of action, intellect and romance in equal measure, as he had shown with his desperate, heart-torn letters from Everest. So Bubbles didn't hesitate when George, tired physically by the pace of the lecture circuit and worn out psychologically by the continuing sniping of officialdom, encouraged her to bring their baby and accompany him on a summer climbing trip to Switzerland.

He would spend six weeks rediscovering a corner of his Alpine playground, tackling some of his favourite mountains in a non-stop program of almost two dozen peaks, even encouraging Bubbles to leave Bunty with a sitter while he led her carefully up and over a small peak, the Riffelhorn, in the hope that she would get a sense of the exhilaration of his passion.

It was merely the beginning. A few days later she found herself on a climb via the Swiss Ridge to the summit of the Matterhorn, 'something not of earth but suspended in the air, splendidly detached from the lowly haunts of men. I could not have imagined myself scaling its precipitous slopes.' And yet Bubbles was seized by the challenge, as she would write soon afterwards: 'I was not going to climb the Matterhorn unless I could do so with zest and enjoyment. If one respects a mountain, one ought to approach it with a joyful mind.'

It was a moment that defined their relationship in many ways. Betty Fisher would never have ventured out of the hotel let alone to the summit of one of the biggest mountains in Europe, and the unfortunate Gladys May was not someone whom George believed would share his vision. Bubbles, by contrast, was a resolute and adventurous woman who was clearly a partner in life for George Finch rather than simply his domestic manager.

A letter to a young grandson written many years later would show her strength of character and her deep affinity with her husband. The letter was written to Francis, Bunty's son, for his first birthday and offered some grandmotherly advice, imploring him to not stand by silently if he thought something was wrong but to 'shout your head off'. She told him that: 'The vast majority of folk lack imagination, the most important single thing in one's mental makeup … It is my earnest hope that you will be blessed with this gift.'

Of her Matterhorn climb, Bubbles would delight at the peak's dark and quiet beauty – 'as quiet as whist' – while embracing the thrill of danger as a landslide of rocks crashed past the hut in which she and George slept, exploding onto a glacier below. She marvelled at her husband's skills and the sense of security he engendered:

I soon began to lose all consciousness of effort, my body felt light as the cool night air; my feet and hands, as if instinctively, sought and found hold. We mounted higher and higher – right out of ourselves, so to speak. There was none of the straining and panting that I thought must mark my climbing attempts. Here and there, as we seemed to wind our way in and out amongst the rocky towers of the ridge, I was aware of the tingling depth of precipice or chasm, and once I made a false step and dipped my right foot over into nothingness.

It seemed audacious in the extreme taking his wife, a beginner, up such a mountain, let alone so soon after giving birth, but such was George's confidence, and hers in him. And George wasn't finished with breaking the establishment's rules. At the Monte Rosa Hotel in Zermatt he insisted on taking Bubbles into the male-only confines of a room set aside for members of the London Alpine Club, the same men who had all but discarded him. Ignoring the surprised looks, he sat her down for dinner in the midst of the men, Charles Bruce among them. None protested. It would be another fifty years before the next woman was admitted and the sexist bar removed.

* * *

A MOUNTAINEERING FEAT
Zermatt Aug 4: Captain Finch (of the Mount Everest Expedition of 1922), Captain Forster and Mr Peto yesterday made the first ascent of Dent d'Hérens (13,175 ft) by the north face.

A more devious man might have planned to make one of the few 'first ascents' remaining in the Alps as a slap in the face to his detractors back in London, but George Finch's bold clamber up the north face of the tricky Pennine peak, which made the front page of *The Times*, was yet another example of his simple joy in a challenge.

In fact, the climb had been in the making since the summer of 1911, when an afternoon lazing in the summer sunshine, scanning the surrounding mountain-scape from a Zermatt hotel, had drawn George 'irresistibly ... as if for relief, from the solemn, dark magnificence of the Matterhorn to the white purity and graceful curve of the hanging glaciers of the north face of Dent d'Hérens'.

He'd then realised, after reading what he called 'mountain literature', that the face was unconquered. 'Here truly was a grain fat enough to satisfy the greediest appetite, and I made up my mind to secure it.'

In 1913, he'd surveyed by sight a route from the Schönbühl Hut below the main slope, satisfying himself that there was indeed a way around the giant ice cliffs from a hanging glacier that dominated the face. Then the war had intervened and so it wasn't until 1919 that he returned and began once more to map an attack. In 1921, he had returned again after being removed from the Everest reconnaissance expedition, but had run out of time to make an attempt.

So here he was for a fourth time, licking his wounds from another unfair mauling by his Alpine elders by challenging social norms and tackling another dangerous climb with a beginner. This time it was a former student and friend named Raymond Peto, nine years younger than George and keen to follow his famous mentor into, or rather up, the unknown. They would be joined by Guy Forster (Smith-Barry), who, fittingly it seemed, had been a sounding board for George's Everest disappointments in the summer of 1921.

Their first attempt on July 29 from the Schönbühl Hut was abandoned in haste after a few hours, the climbers fleeing the slope as the morning sunshine loosened seracs above them and sent ice, rocks and snow tumbling over their heads. They arrived back at the hut to a chorus of 'we told you so' from other climbers, preparing for easier ascents, who declared the north face climb 'unmöglich' – impossible.

Undeterred, the trio tried again on August 2, Forster holding a candle clenched between his teeth to light the way while George cut steps into the ice as quickly as possible across the slope before the sun rose, to reach a point where they could climb directly to the summit. It would take more than fifteen hours, and at one stage Peto, the beginner, braced himself against the mountain to hold George steady so he could swing his axe without hand-holds. They celebrated by shouting their triumph into the recesses below, their voices echoing off the stone walls.

* * *

Arthur Hinks was fuming. It had come to his attention that George Finch, against his instructions, was planning to conduct lectures in Switzerland during the autumn. He had made it clear in March that he was against the idea of Finch doing any more lectures and that the Everest Committee would not sanction them, particularly as John Noel's Everest film was now being shown across Europe. To make matters worse, Finch was apparently planning to break the confidentiality agreement he had signed as a condition of his selection and was intending to sign as an individual with Gerald Christy's agency and keep the proceeds to himself.

There had been an angry exchange of letters between Hinks and Christy in late May when Hinks demanded to see a written copy of the script Finch was using to introduce his lectures. He'd questioned the wording, insisting that it be made clear that the lectures were under the auspices of the Everest Committee. He had then edited the wording of Finch's promotional brochures to eliminate anything that might be regarded as 'boastful'.

Christy wrote back, perplexed and exasperated that Hinks seemed unable to grasp the notion of promotion: 'I am sorry you have cut out, more particularly from the Finch circular, anything which might be described as a "write-up", either of Finch or the subject. This sort of thing is very necessary – although it may be distasteful – when one makes anything in the nature of an appeal to the public. One has to blow one's trumpet a bit.'

Christy also disputed Hinks's claim that lectures by Finch would harm the film: 'I should have thought it would have been shown in all the big cities so that Finch giving some lectures in September next could hardly have any serious effects on his film. If anything, it might revive an interest in the expedition generally and make it possible for him to show the film again in some towns.'

But Christy's assurances did nothing to placate Hinks, who, behind the scenes, was under financial pressure. The film had been well received in London but its broader release had been delayed, which was a mistake. Extra costs had come in late for the expedition, too, including a dubious bill for almost £400 for the hire of mules and the discovery that an accountant hired by Hinks had embezzled £700. Even taking into account the success of the lectures that had paid for the 1922 expedition and left a reasonable surplus, the committee was struggling to find a way to pay for the 1924 expedition which Charles Bruce had insisted would cost £1000 per man.

But instead of embracing George Finch's popularity in Europe, perhaps even allowing him to front the film as suggested by Christy, Hinks saw it as further proof that he was not suitable for the next Everest expedition. He sent one last stinging letter, demanding that 'it be fixed', and left for a month's holiday.

George had stayed out of the debate to this point, preferring to allow Christy to bear the brunt of Hinks's attacks in the hope that the bureaucrat might see reason. But as he prepared to leave for Switzerland with his wife and baby daughter, George decided he'd had enough and fired off a blistering letter to his nemesis in which he revealed he had spoken to his lawyers about his obligations. He knew the move was provocative, but what else could he do?

> I am advised by counsel that the agreement which I entered
> into with the committee on joining the expedition is not
> legally binding in respect of the restraint of my activities
> contained therein, on the grounds that it is neither
> reasonable as between the parties nor consistent with the
> interests of the public. I myself always understood that
> the restraint was not intended to stand for more than one
> lecture season following the return of the expedition and
> in these circumstances I consider myself now free, morally
> as well as legally, to lecture on my own account, free from
> control of the committee. I therefore should be glad if you
> will inform the committee that I propose to do so on or
> after July 16th next (which is one year after my return from
> the expedition) unless before that date the committee take
> steps to obtain an injunction. If the committee decides to
> take this latter course, in view of the advice I have received,
> I shall defend the proceedings and my solicitors, Messrs
> Warren, Merton, Miller & Foster of 45 Bloomsbury
> Square, have instructions to accept service on my behalf.

In the absence of Hinks, the letter landed on Sydney Spencer's desk with a thud. The Everest Committee had never faced a crisis like this. No one had ever had the audacity to question its authority.

A hurried meeting was organised and a prominent lawyer named Withers, a member of the Alpine Club, was engaged to give his view of the strength of the agreement signed by the expedition members. His opinion was swift, as Spencer reported a few days later to Hinks and Charles Bruce:

> Withers said that our position was anything but a strong one as the agreement which Finch signed contained no stated limit of time and area and consequently [is] too indefinite and of very little value, and he thought it was very doubtful whether we should obtain an injunction. On this point I must say that Bruce expressed a very strong wish that the matter should not be taken into court and one or two of the others seemed to share his feelings.

In the meantime, Percy Farrar had implored George to withdraw his initial missive and pen a slightly more diplomatic one: 'There has been, as I anticipated, constant friction with Hinks, who is a man of great ability and strong personality, though not of equal tact in handling men of independent spirit,' he wrote to Spencer, adding that the new letter should be given 'every consideration'.

The replacement letter was much longer than the first, withdrawing the threat of legal action but pointing out that the issue had come to a head because Hinks had refused to allow George to lecture, even though he was happy to do so under the terms of his agreement with the committee: 'This proposal was declined, of course to my loss.'

George explained that Hinks had told him he was bound by the agreement 'until the mountain is climbed', which was excessive, particularly as he had already completed more than eighty lectures on behalf of the committee, written three chapters for the book and allowed the publication of his photographs. He had also earned an income from lecturing long before he went to Everest, as confirmed by Christy, so the agreement was unfair.

Hinks's reply was swift and pugnacious: the committee would not yield. The contract had not been written as a legal document but as a gentleman's agreement which he was expected to honour. It was imperative that the committee maintain control over publicity because the Everest expeditions were self-funding. Yet he was still refusing to allow George to lecture in Switzerland even though there were a dozen events already booked and the committee desperately needed money.

The hammer came in the third paragraph of page two:

> Any breaking away from the agreement by a single member
> of the expedition would do some damage to the future
> of the enterprise as a whole, but infinitely more damage
> to the station of the individual by his comrades and the
> committee. The committee believe that you have not
> taken into account these wider aspects of the question
> and that you will now be willing to agree that for the
> next two years at least you should not lecture in public on
> your experiences on the Mount Everest expedition except
> under the auspices of the committee on the same terms of
> division of profits.

The threat was clear: either toe the line or forget about going back to Everest.

George waited until he was back in London before he replied. He was happy to continue lecturing in England and for the committee to take its share of profits from the European lectures – exactly as he had proposed back in March when Hinks had tried to block him. But he would not be held to an agreement for another two years:

> If I may understand that the 3rd para of page 2 of your letter sets me free of any further obligation to the committee I am content. I understand indirectly that for reasons doubtless sufficient to the committee I am not to be asked to join the next expedition, notwithstanding the relative success gained by my own party and my subsequent very willing services in connection with the improvements in the new oxygen apparatus.

It was remarkable that for once he managed to contain his understandable anger and dismay, because, for George Finch, the Everest dream was over.

31.

THE TRAGEDY OF
GEORGE MALLORY

George Mallory was having second thoughts about George Finch. His dislike of the man who, logically, should have been his climbing partner had been tempered by the ongoing personal assault by Hinks and others on the Everest Committee. It was boring, he told Hinks in one letter – '*La question Finch m'ennuie*' – although he stopped short of protesting because, unlike George Finch, Mallory knew his place and the value of loyalty.

There would be accounts in later years that Mallory *did* protest about the treatment of Finch and refused to climb unless he was also chosen, forcing the intervention of a member (never identified) of the royal family. But there is no evidence of this other than hearsay. Certainly, Mallory now sensed that Finch was not the selfish scoundrel he had been made out to be, but instead was misunderstood and unfairly treated by men who didn't know what it was like to struggle financially.

As if to illustrate this point, Mallory revealed to Hinks that while in India he had lent Finch £2, and had been repaid with a cheque which promptly bounced, an unforgiveable sin in a society that valued honour above all else. But Mallory *did* forgive: 'He has since made good by postal orders ... but this explains part of his conduct,' he told Hinks, suggesting it had been an honest error made by a misjudgment of the financial borderline which they both constantly negotiated, rather than a dishonest ruse. It was naive of Mallory, of course, to believe that Hinks would be as understanding; instead, he used the tidbit to further malign Finch, particularly when Charles Bruce revealed that he, too, had made a small loan to George, who, in the general's mind, had taken too long to repay the money.

Mallory's doubts were more about himself than the other climbers. He was racked with guilt about the months he had already spent away from his wife and three young children on what had begun as an adventure but had become a war against an unyielding opponent. He had also come to the realisation that he was not infallible and might not survive another attempt on Everest, confessing to friends that he had doubts but felt obliged to go on the 1924 expedition as if it were his public duty to defeat the mountain on behalf of England and Empire. Ruth also had premonitions of his death, and Mallory's sister, Mary, begged him not to go. On February 13, just a fortnight before the expedition party's ship, SS *California*, sailed from Liverpool, he finally signed up to the ill-fated venture.

On the eve of departure, Mallory asked his wife to invite George and Bubbles Finch to their home, Herschel House at Cambridge, the weekend after he returned. He told her that if he succeeded in conquering the mountain, he wanted to ensure that George's contribution was properly acknowledged.

The weekend meeting would never take place. However, Ruth Mallory would not forget her husband's wishes. In 1937, she met George Finch in a chance encounter at the Gorphwysfa Hotel at Pen-y-Pass in Wales, where Geoffrey Winthrop Young was hosting his annual Easter weekend. George and Ruth sat together in quiet conversation for most of the evening, clearly emotional given the tragic end to the Everest campaign that had unfolded thirteen years before.

When they finally parted ways, Ruth Mallory spoke with Scott Russell, who had been watching from the other side of the room, and told him that she had revealed to George her husband's plans, the misgivings Mallory had expressed about George's treatment and his regret that he had not spoken out in protest. He had also expressed a desire to climb again with George when he returned from Everest, perhaps in the Alps as they had done in 1919. She had wanted to write to George after her husband's death, but a letter had seemed inappropriate for such an important message.

Russell was flabbergasted, not just about what Ruth Mallory told him, but because she had wanted to explain herself to a 24-year-old student who had only known George Finch for two years. (They had met shortly after Russell's ugly encounter with Sydney Spencer at the Alpine Club and had organised events together for the Imperial College mountaineering club.)

'Why are you telling me all this?' Russell asked her.

Ruth Mallory reflected for a moment, as if choosing her words carefully: 'Because you're like him [Finch]; you know what it's like to be an outsider and you would best appreciate the problems he has faced.'

Russell knew what she meant. Although born in England he would be forever defined by his New Zealand childhood. Their Antipodean backgrounds had created a bond between the two men, which was made even closer after World War II when Russell would meet and marry George's oldest daughter, Bunty. He was the son that, to George's mind, he had never had. Russell did not speak to George about the evening with Ruth Mallory but later noted that his father-in-law's greatest regret about Everest was that 'in their youthful impetuosity, he and Mallory had let others create trouble between them'.

Some years after his father-in-law's death, Russell would republish George's memoir, *The Making of a Mountaineer*, and pen a foreword that attempted to correct some of the misinformation that still swirled around George. In doing so, he would have his own tussles with bureaucracy; documents inexplicably went missing from the Alpine Club archives when Russell tried to access them and were later discovered in the personal papers of a club official.

Despite his personal loyalty, Scott Russell strove to be an objective observer of George Finch:

> At first sight he seemed rather formidable. Over six feet
> two inches tall, broad-shouldered and very erect, he made
> the rest of us look rather puny, but it was his strong finely
> drawn features which impressed me the most, especially
> his expressive cold-blue eyes, which inspected me rather
> dauntingly at our first meeting. Later I came to realise that
> they were an excellent barometer of his mood that sometimes
> changed rapidly. Interest, amusement, suspicion or disapproval
> were unmistakably conveyed with an appropriate change in
> voice; silence and a blank, rather stern expression indicated
> that he was deep in thought. It was no surprise that he
> inspired great friendships and equally great enmities, for his
> personality and his appearance made it scarcely possible for
> him to be ignored in any company.

* * *

George Finch not only had to be replaced as a climber but as the man responsible for the oxygen equipment. Despite his disappointment at being excluded from the expedition, which was never expressed publicly even in the memoir he was now writing about his experiences, George indicated a willingness as late as December 1923 to keep working on the oxygen equipment that the team would use without him on the trip. The Everest Committee chose to ignore his offer and assigned the responsibility to Percy Unna, who had long been a believer in the benefits of oxygen. But Percy was an engineer, not a scientist. The equipment would be redesigned without any involvement by George Finch and then built in neglectful haste as the departure day loomed. It was not surprising that the cylinders arrived in India broken, half empty and leaking.

Oxygen management during the expedition would fall on the broad shoulders of a 23-year-old Oxford university student named Andrew 'Sandy' Irvine. There was no doubt that Irvine was a brilliant and capable young man, something of a genius mechanically, who at the age of fifteen had designed a mechanism – an 'interrupter gear' – that allowed machine guns to fire between the blades of a moving propeller, much to the surprise of military officials to whom he sent details. He was a member of the winning crew in the annual Oxford and Cambridge Boat Race and had excelled during a 1923 university trip to the frozen Norwegian island of Spitsbergen.

But Irvine was no mountain climber; in fact, the highest peak he had climbed was just 6500 feet. He had come to the attention of the Everest officials because an expedition member, Noel Odell, had led the Spitsbergen trip and been impressed by the young man. Odell had first met Irvine four years earlier, in 1919, when the then seventeen-year-old rode a motorbike to the top of a Welsh mountain, the Foel Grach, while Odell and his wife were climbing it on foot. Odell was impressed by Irvine's bravado and felt he could be the future of Everest expeditions – a youthful 'superman' to whom he was happy to delegate responsibility for the oxygen equipment.

He put Irvine's name forward to the committee and the young man was accepted within a month, just in time for the expedition party to be formally announced. Not everyone agreed with the choice, one committeeman, Godfrey Solly, noting Irvine was 'a very nice, strong looking fellow, but only twenty-one. I think twenty-one is rather too young and so does Somervell.' But Hinks was delighted because it killed off Finch and satisfied George's own arguments for youth and science in a single blow. Any potential dissent about Irvine's inexperience could be crushed by referring, in a cruel twist, to George's achievement; after all, it was Finch who had taken Geoffrey Bruce, a novice, almost to the top of Everest and brought him back safely.

Irvine embraced his job as oxygen officer by taking home a sample oxygen unit, stripping it down and making a series of recommendations to the manufacturer, Siebe Gorman, for improvements. It was impressive work, but behind the scenes Irvine made it known that he despised the use of oxygen as much as Hinks and co: 'I really hate the thought of oxygen,' he would write to a friend. 'I'd give anything to make a non-oxygen attempt. I think I'd sooner get to the foot of the final pyramid without oxygen than to the top of it … still, as I'm the oxygen mechanic I've got to go with the beastly stuff.'

* * *

As preparations continued there was a ceremony that almost passed unnoticed and yet embodied the incredible achievements of the 1922 campaign as seen by the world outside the fusty British establishment. The first Winter Olympic Games was held in Chamonix in late January 1924, and twenty-one members of the expedition, including the seven dead sherpas, were awarded gold medals for 'the greatest feat of alpinism'.

Colonel Strutt was the only expedition member to attend. He accepted the medals on behalf of the others in a ceremony hosted by the International Olympic Committee president and architect of the modern Olympics, Pierre de Coubertin. Arthur Hinks may have regarded George Finch and his oxygen as unsportsmanlike but the father of the world's greatest sports event did not hold the same opinion. Science and heroism went hand in hand:

> We salute the most beautiful kind of heroism, that which
> confronts scientifically calculated danger step by step without
> hesitation or sensationalism. At the foot of the highest
> mountain in Europe, we present you and your wonderful
> companions with this small testimony of the admiration
> with which all nations have followed your journey towards
> the untouched peaks of the highest mountain in the world.
> We accompany this gesture by prayers for the completion
> of a work that will honour not only your country but all
> humanity.

George's medal, eventually delivered by mail, did not suffer the same fate as his Eidgenössische Technische Hochschule honour which had been melted down for its gold to fund his Alpine escapades. It is still kept in its green velvet presentation box by his family, nestled among a dozen more of varying importance bestowed on him for his achievements in science and mountaineering. On inspection it is clear that de Coubertin regarded the ceremony as significant in Olympic history. It was not the medal handed to the winners of the various sports at the Winter Games, but marked *VIII eme Olympiade Paris 1924* – the gold medal handed to the winners of the Summer Games held in Paris a few months later. Among the various athletic images on the front of the medal are a ski pole and skis. Appropriately, the back of the medal features a triumphant athlete helping another athlete to his feet. It might as well have been George Finch saving the life of Geoffrey Bruce.

* * *

George Mallory arrived at Rongbuk Glacier with the other expedition members on April 28. The journey had been full of regret and worry about his marriage, compounded by the curse of dysentery that had felled his companions one by one: Bentley Beetham, Noel Odell, Edward Shebbeare and even the youthful Sandy Irvine. He'd had his own health scare, a brush with what he feared was appendicitis, and Charles Bruce had been struck by malaria and replaced as leader by Edward Norton.

But it had all turned around on the road between Kampa Dzong and Tinki in late April while Mallory pondered how best to attack the mountain and how to split up the climbers. In a moment of epiphany, George Mallory suddenly became a convert to oxygen. It was a brainwave, as he explained to Ruth before thrashing out a plan with Norton that would involve twin attempts on the summit, one with oxygen and the other without. In a complete reversal of his earlier position, Mallory wanted to lead the oxygen party – and take Sandy Irvine with him – perhaps in a piece of one-upmanship on Finch's climb with beginner Geoffrey Bruce.

It may have surprised the others but Irvine had impressed Mallory as a man who could be depended upon 'for everything perhaps except conversation'. Besides, he was the only one capable of managing the problematic oxygen apparatus with which he had continued to tinker.

But a month later his mood had changed and the fear of failure or worse had resurfaced. By May 21 Mallory stood atop the North Col, eyeing the ramp-like slope to the north-west ridge beneath which he had been forced to retreat two years earlier. Four camps had been established from base camp to 23,000 feet, with plans to establish three more advance camps, the highest at the altitude reached by George Finch and Geoffrey Bruce, from where Mallory would launch the final assault.

But they were running out of time and morale had been sapped by the extreme cold that plunged temperatures to minus 56 degrees Celsius, and by the debilitating effects of altitude sickness. Mallory had dismissed predictions of an early monsoon as the rantings of 'meteorological people', but he was wrong. On May 24, after risking their lives to rescue four stranded porters, the men were driven all the way back to base camp by a blinding snowstorm.

The men were thin and weak; Mallory and Somervell both had bronchitis and Irvine diarrhea, Odell was not sleeping and Beetham had not recovered from dysentery. Only Geoffrey Bruce was fully fit, according to Mallory, who penned what would become a telling appraisal for *The Times* on May 27 as the party made plans for an assault as soon as the weather cleared.

The article, published on June 16, read like a soldier's letter home from the Front: 'The issue will shortly be decided. The third time we walk up East Rongbuk Glacier will be the last, for better or worse. We have counted our wounded and know, roughly, how much to strike off the strength of our little army as we plan the next act of battle.'

Mallory was now partnered with Geoffrey Bruce and Somervell with Norton. A third, reserve, group of Odell and Irvine would wait at Camp III while the two lead teams made separate attempts on consecutive days, supported by the remaining sherpas who would carry tents and supplies to establish two advance camps. Oxygen had been abandoned because of the loss of men to carry the cylinders up the mountain.

Mallory and Bruce set out from Camp IV just after 6am on June 1 and were immediately confronted by a wind that bent them double as they forced their way up the 45-degree slope. At 25,000 feet four of the sherpas sat down, unable to go on. Mallory and Bruce kept the others moving but could go no further than another 300 feet where they pegged a site for Camp V and erected two tents. Six of the porters were then sent back down while the remaining three crawled into one tent and Mallory and Bruce the other. The next day, June 2, was clear and bright, but the sherpas would not budge. All hopes of establishing Camp VI at 26,800 feet had gone and the attempt was abandoned.

Norton and Somervell set out under the same clear skies on the morning of June 2 but soon found themselves battling a gale almost as fierce as the day before. They passed Mallory and Bruce who were on their way down, exchanging few words as they crossed to save energy and because of the futility of trying to be heard above the roar of the wind.

They spent the night at Camp V and were able to continue upwards the next morning as the wind died and the skies cleared, reaching 26,800 feet where they pitched a single tent to mark Camp VI. Only Finch and Bruce had been this high and Norton and Somervell were in excellent spirits that night as they watched their sherpas descend to safety and pondered their chances of reaching the summit the next morning.

June 4 dawned clear and still but with a cold that neither had previously experienced. They broke camp with optimism, deciding to traverse across the face and stay below the ridgeline where they would be less exposed if a wind developed. Despite the favourable conditions, the combination of thin air and heavy snow made progress painfully slow.

At 28,000 feet Somervell was defeated, barely able to breathe. He sat down on a ledge and urged Norton to keep going alone. Norton nodded and plodded on, battling not only the conditions but deteriorating vision because he had removed his goggles and was becoming snow-blind. He managed to reach 28,126 feet before he turned back, realising that he had no chance of climbing the extra 900 feet and descending safely in the fading light. He had eclipsed Finch and Bruce's height by 800 feet and without oxygen, a record that would last almost three decades, but he would barely make it back alive.

While he waited anxiously for news below, George Mallory was hatching a plan for one last attempt, even though he was exhausted, having been ill for much of the past month and having already spent almost a week at high altitude. It bothered him that oxygen had not been used in any of the attempts, however frail the apparatus, and he felt he had been wrong about George Finch, led astray by men like Arthur Hinks who were not mountaineers. It might be possible to climb Everest without the benefits of bottled oxygen but not on this visit, he concluded: the weather and conditions were against them as was their poor health. However, there was a window, albeit a small one, to conquer the beast with gas. Mallory had by now climbed with the tanks and experienced the sweet rush of air that made him feel 'surprisingly fresh'. He wanted to grab the chance and vanquish the merciless peak. Sandy Irvine might have had very little experience, but he was young, rested and strong. Besides, if Finch could take a novice climber like Geoffrey Bruce, then he surely could take Irvine.

Mallory had already laid his plans by the time Edward Norton and Howard Somervell crawled back into Camp IV at the North Col. Somervell kept going down, back to the base camp, but Norton was exhausted and could not open his eyes, a 'blind crock' as he lay inside a tent for several days to allow his searing eyeballs to mend. He listened to Mallory's enthusiastic plan for himself and Irvine to climb, over two days, to Camp VI at 26,800 feet without oxygen (of which there was a limited supply in working order) and then push for the summit early on June 8. As expedition leader, he gave his support to the plan although he was in no condition to argue against it and would later concede that he had experienced a sense of foreboding.

At 7.30am on June 6 Mallory and Irvine set off accompanied by eight porters each carrying a load of twenty-five pounds (eleven kilograms) made up of oxygen cylinders, food, sleeping bags and fuel. The skies were clear and the wind subdued as they made their way comfortably to Camp V. Four of the porters then returned to Camp IV carrying a short note from Mallory: 'Things look hopeful.'

As Mallory and Irvine pushed upwards the next morning, John Odell moved up behind them to Camp V to act as support. The four remaining porters met him on their way down and passed another note from Mallory in which he laid out his plans for the June 8 assault. He intended to leave early to ensure he and Irvine had enough time to reach the summit and then make a safe descent back to Camp IV: 'It won't be too early to start looking out for us either crossing the rock band under the pyramid or going up the skyline at 8. Yours G Mallory.'

Conditions were almost still the next morning at 8am when Odell began climbing toward Camp VI. Back at Camp III John Noel had his telephoto lens trained on the ridgeline as instructed by Mallory's note. He would sit there for more than four hours and see nothing before giving up when clouds blanketed the view. Meanwhile Odell was making good progress. He was without oxygen but felt well enough to test himself against an extra climb as he neared the north-east shoulder. As he moved toward the top he glanced upwards to the summit, just as the clouds cleared, giving him a brief but clear view of the north-east ridge. What he saw and described in an official communiqué would be debated for the next ninety years:

> There was a sudden clearing of the atmosphere and the entire summit ridge and final peak of Everest were unveiled. My eyes became fixed on one tiny black dot silhouetted on a small snow crest beneath a rock step to the ridge; the black spot moved. Another black spot became apparent and moved up the snow to join the other on the crest. The first then approached the great rock step and shortly emerged on the top; the second did likewise. Then the whole fascinating vision vanished, enveloped in cloud once more. There was but one explanation. It was Mallory and his companion …

It would be the last sighting of George Mallory and Sandy Irvine alive.

* * *

George Finch was climbing in Corsica with Bubbles when the two men went missing, but had returned to London by the time the terrible news broke on June 21. Whatever differences they might have had in life, George had only praise for the bravery and legacy of Mallory, as he told the *Daily News*: 'Some will say that this sacrifice of human life is not worthwhile. I say it is worthwhile.

Such struggles keep alive that rejuvenating spirit of adventure without which any nation must decay.'

George also rushed through a reprint of his memoir *The Making of a Mountaineer*, published only a few weeks before, to include a chapter on the 1924 campaign and address what would become – and remain – the two biggest mysteries of mountaineering: What happened? And did Mallory and Irvine make it to the top?

George thought a slip or fall was unlikely, given Mallory's experience and also dismissed the idea that the two might have lost their way. The most likely cause of their disappearance and presumed death, he said, was a defect in the oxygen equipment:

> To be suddenly deprived of oxygen means a relapse into lethargy, that incapacity of doing more than drag one foot after the other, and even then holding up for every step to pant and pant in the almost vain effort to supply the lungs with sufficient oxygen to maintain life. It is there that I think one must look for the true cause of the loss of Mallory and Irvine.

And did they reach the summit? George thought not, because there had been no sign at the peak which could have been seen with field glasses from North Col.

More than ninety years later, even after the discovery of Mallory's body, the prevailing view has not changed – that they died during the ascent.

What might have happened if it had been George Finch and not Sandy Irvine who was with Mallory that day? Although it is a hypothetical question, there are some facts that are indisputable. George would not have been involved in the first two attempts without oxygen. As a result, he would have been fit for the attempt that began on June 6. Although Irvine was talented, there can be little doubt that the experience and passion of George Finch would have made him the preferred man to manage and, if necessary, fix the oxygen equipment high on Everest. He had done it before and managed to bring Geoffrey Bruce back alive.

Another significant point lies in the actions of the Everest Committee. In their desire to spurn George Finch, they not only ignored his offer to be involved in the redesign and construction of the oxygen equipment, but also delayed the work until it became a rushed job that resulted in leakages and malfunction.

Percy Unna would later accept responsibility for the administrative mistakes, but it was Arthur Hinks who should have been held accountable.

32.

A NEW LEGACY

There was something mysterious about the chemistry department of the Imperial College, London, an air of forbidding isolation and solitude, its ugly functional buildings – some little better than huts – linked to Prince Consort Road by a rough timber bridge and guarded by grim black sentinels: a 10-metre high gas generator and a monstrous riveted-iron gas tank.

The guiding principle of Professor William Bone, that the success of his department should be measured by what it produced in terms of research and students rather than its façade, only became more relevant as the world left the Great War behind and entered an era of rebuilding – economically, politically and socially.

Under Professor Bone, the purpose of the department was to seek answers to the undiscovered, so the professors and students were encouraged to immerse themselves in research, which he also believed should be the cornerstone of the teaching and learning process. George Finch and the rest of the staff embraced the philosophy with gusto.

Walking through the front doors of the main building was an overwhelming experience; it was a place of noises and smells, a place of high-pressure explosions and reactions; of the study by high-speed photography of flame movements in gaseous explosions; of the chemical constitution of coal and gas reactions in the blast furnace. The top floor was the domain of postgraduate chemical engineering, headed by Professors Hinchley and Ure, who would help found the Institution of Chemical Engineers. Professors Newitt and Townend ran the high-pressure laboratory below, a series of steel-walled rooms filled with compressors and enormous gas storage cylinders, an environment from which the occasional forgetful smoker was immediately ejected. The basement belonged to the coal and fuel laboratory of Professor Himus, a former power station executive who had turned to academic life and was beloved by his students, particularly when he fired up the head gas generator, dressed in his boiler suit and sweat rag, and wielded his three-metre long poker to stoke the fires, resulting in a great flame of water gas that occasionally burst beside the Queen's Gate.

George Finch, a rangy, slim and dapper figure in his dark suits, bow ties and pocket watch, had the entire second floor for his electro-chemistry laboratory. As a mountaineer, he'd been seen by some as a long-haired rebel, born in the wrong country and educated at the wrong university – an abrasive colonial who ridiculed those who could not match his fastidious drive for perfection and insouciant daring.

Yet in an academic these traits were respected, and Finch was highly regarded as a man who would not rest on accepted practice but would strive to find a better way; a man excited to explore the unknown in partnership with young minds who knew less and made mistakes, but loved him for his tolerance. Unlike the Alpine Club and the Royal Geographical Society, whose bureaucrats expected definitive answers and saw the world in black and white, the science laboratory was a place where answers were often grey and failure was simply the imprimatur to try again.

How could George's embracement of youth be reconciled with the man who had twice turned his back on children for whom he bore at least a modicum of responsibility, whether he was the natural father or not? In his mind, George Finch probably justified the decisions in terms of the financial aid he provided and that he was leaving the mother rather than the child. It was the truth, if an imperfect one.

Then again, this might have been his penance, for there was no sense of his legendary abrasive personality on show in the classroom. Instead, his students, including the department's first female student, who would top her class in the mid 1920s, would have fond memories of a teacher intent on engaging young minds, not only as an instructor but as a collaborator, continually devising new experiments that not only explored a relatively new and rapidly evolving science but doing so with ingenuity and versatility.

Just as he had proved in war and at the top of Everest, George Finch was a master of improvisation, turning part of the tunnel beneath Prince Consort Road into a dark room for his photography experiments and converting a mishmash of War Office surplus equipment into high-tension generators for research into electric discharge.

On another occasion he built an experimental car engine, prompting a string of complaints from the nearby Royal College of Music, where the symphony orchestra rehearsals were shattered whenever the engine roared into life. Similarly, the music students were in uproar when a rudimentary megacycle oscillator, built from spare parts to measure the speed of chemical reaction, filled the air with an undulating thrum that invaded, subliminally, the quiet tick-tock environment of their studios.

The mountain climber had brought his independent and rebellious spirit into the classroom, only here it would be appreciated. Among his students' favourite recollections was the day a number of them went to visit their lecturer in hospital as he recovered from minor surgery. They walked in to find George sitting up in bed reconditioning the hospital's supply of headphones, his only tools a penknife and a sixpence, with a halfpenny wedged in a slice of lemon as a test battery.

Perhaps the best example of George's devotion to young minds was the day he travelled to Yorkshire to plead with the father of a student who had decided his son's science course was a waste of time and money and that the boy should be working instead in the local coal mines. Such a journey – to persuade a man to allow his son the chance of a good education and stimulating career – was almost unheard of. It worked. The student returned to Imperial College the next semester, passed his course and had a long career as an industrial chemist.

* * *

The reporter from the *Westminster Gazette* was ushered into the neatly cluttered workshop where the two white-coated scientists waited. The newspaper, small but politically influential, had been invited to witness a demonstration of the dangers of potentially explosive chemicals packaged in the cartridge of a child's toy gun. George Finch, the younger of the two scientists involved in the consumer protection stunt, placed a mound of the contentious mixture of barium nitrate, magnesium and aluminum onto an anvil then stood back and watched his boss, William Bone, take a small hammer and rap the compound sharply. The reporter was startled by the crack of the explosion, amplified in the confines of the small room. The scientists smiled, their point made.

The resulting article, published a few days later, seems innocuous, unlikely to force a change in the law but perhaps sufficient to influence the thinking of policymakers and parliamentarians who were among the paper's modest but loyal readership. Even so, George Finch regarded the exercise as significant enough in his life to have kept a carefully cut out copy in his personal papers, alongside the headlines that lionised his achievement of standing higher than any man before him.

It was more likely a symbolic memento, serving as an acknowledgment that his life had changed and that he would probably never conquer the mountain nor stand on the roof of the world as he had hoped all those years before. But George was also determined to ensure that the bastardy would not dictate or sully his future – he wanted to leave a legacy by climbing very different mountains.

The first challenge was to be a family man. Years later, Bubbles would recall her husband's initial awkward attempts at fatherhood in a society that maintained clear parental demarcations and distinctive roles for men and women. Most memorable was the 'tight fit' as he shed his professional uniform of a jacket and bow tie to climb into Bunty's playpen and laugh with his daughter after arriving home from the college in the evening. It was clear that he wished to be a more 'hands-on' parent than Charles and Laura had been.

George would become far more comfortable with his role as Bunty and the two sisters who would follow – Paola Jean in 1924 and Felice George in 1929 – grew older and he took the family on climbing holidays, spending every Easter in Wales below Snowdon and one summer month in the Alps. In later years, after he had given up climbing, he rediscovered the sailing he had loved in childhood summers on Sydney Harbour and bought an ageing eight-ton gaff-rigged cutter named *Wasp*, big enough to sleep the family and guests, and sturdy enough to sail on the open ocean, which he did on typically meticulously planned and mapped trips across the English Channel to northern France. He captained his vessel with customary zeal, and enjoyed telling of the day in 1939 that he rescued a stricken yacht attempting a difficult channel and facing almost certain tragedy. George admonished 'the ass' owner in the hope he would never sail again.

Bunty would grow up to be her father's likeness in female form, tall and rangy with a physical adeptness that would prompt Geoffrey Winthrop Young to announce that she was the best female rock climber he had ever seen, nimble and sure-footed with a keen eye for finding routes over difficult terrain, just like her father.

Now aged ninety-one, Bunty still smiles fondly when recalling her father's encouragement to explore and discover the world for herself, as George had learned from his own father: 'George and I didn't climb together very often because by the time I was a teenager he had stopped climbing on medical advice. But that didn't stop him from making sure I was trained properly. I always climbed with people he trusted. He was always very careful. It was his trademark.'

Bunty's sisters would have different relationships with their father, whom they would refer to as George on reaching adulthood. The youngest, Felice, or Colette as she would be known in the family, has passed away, but Paola, now aged ninety, remains intellectually sprightly: 'I haven't answered to that name in my entire life,' she snaps with her father's famed bluntness, in a sharp reminder that she was always known as Moseli, after a family joke about the baby in the bulrushes.

It is unsurprising that she would butt heads with her father, as two strong-willed people often do: 'George and I got on well, as far as it went. He was open-minded about many things but could be rather dogmatic at other times, quite prepared to insist that black was white if necessary,' she remarked, reminiscing over a photograph taken of the two of them in the 1950s, enjoying lunch on an upper level of the Eiffel Tower, where George, his pale blue eyes startling even in a black-and-white image, is clearly intent on the discussion rather than the view out toward Notre-Dame, the scene of one of his first 'climbs' all those years before.

Another of the clutch of memories she keeps in her home is an image of herself with Bunty, aged perhaps eleven and twelve respectively, during their annual Easter holiday in Wales. Bunty is grinning triumphantly atop a rockface while Moseli stands beneath, sour-faced and clearly miffed: 'I threw a bit of a tantrum that day,' she laughs. 'I didn't take to climbing like my sister and our mother. Colette and I preferred the sailing we did after George gave up climbing. We loved it on the water when we were allowed to take the tiller.'

At home her father was a man of quiet purpose who rarely lost his temper and yet maintained an authoritative air that was not often challenged by anyone other than his equally strong-willed wife. He spent much of his time in the reading room, stocked with books notated with the date and place of purchase, like a travel diary of his life. It was where the household often gathered in the evenings after dinner to read, as other families might play board games. There was a piano in the house, which his daughters learned to play but George rarely touched, although he would often be seen reading music scores and listening to records played on a home-built gramophone.

George Finch may have revelled in the wilderness extremes of mountain climbing – sleeping under rough blankets in straw bunks, washing in tepid water from a tin basin, eating tinned peaches and drinking tea made from melted snow – but at home he was a man of comfort and refined tastes, invariably clad in a three-piece suit and watch chain, appreciative of fine red wine and a stickler for the formality of a sit-down meal with the family or friends.

As the family grew, they would move from their Kensington flat to a house in the green fields of Osterley on the western fringes of the city, and later George and Bubbles would move to Upper Heyford, a village in Oxfordshire, where George would branch into experimental gardening, including an early form of hydroponics, in which the garden was organised on scientific lines, with potatoes grown on plastic sheets, and the industrial quantities of runner beans he harvested were preserved in huge jars lining the kitchen shelves.

Everest was a subject to which he responded sparingly, a little like a soldier recalling conflict he'd rather forget. Despite his disappointments there were no regrets. He believed he would have made the summit if Geoffrey Bruce hadn't broken the glass valve, but it would not have been worth a man's life for him to have continued alone. It would have been ridiculous to risk Bruce's life and perhaps his own just to stand on top of a mountain. Some would read this as a pointed observation about Mallory, although, publicly at least, George would always remain diplomatic about his relationship with the man whose death only entrenched his iconic status.

Australia emerged in conversation on occasion, particularly in connection with George's fascination with snakes. If a visitor discovered on a shelf in the reading room the glass jar that contained a viper he'd caught with his bare hands and pickled in alcohol, he would use it as the launching pad for tales of his boyhood in the bush. He was wistful about his horse-riding and shooting abilities, the latter of which he kept sharpened by competing with some success in events at the Bisley shooting range.

By the late 1920s he had also taken up racing cars at the famed Brooklands circuit in Surrey, the world's first purpose-built race track and the venue where most of the land speed records were established early in the twentieth century. The girls would sit in the grandstand with their mother and watch their father spin around the concrete embankment in a 'crawler' he was always modifying in his backyard garage. It was a family joke that he was caught once driving at forty miles per hour along Park Lane. When he admitted the transgression to Bubbles she chided him for driving too slowly.

If Bunty was his chosen companion in the mountains, then Moseli was his frequent assistant in the workshop he created in an upstairs bedroom, helping her father with components that were too small for his large hands. In the workshop he built high-speed cameras, among other ingenious items, and undertook household repairs, once mending his own watch by making a new winder.

It was a place of wonder for a child. The room seemed Tardis-like, crammed full of salvaged items, building components and machinery, including lathes of various sizes that hummed quietly as George honed parts for his creations. It was the time when her father became most animated, Moseli remembers, talking excitedly about his latest highly complex experiments, all the while his tiny radio emitting its tinny sounds, which only seemed to add to the excitement of his work rather than be an impediment to his concentration.

And concentration is what set him apart from others.

The household revolved around their father, although Bubbles was hardly a subservient character; rather, she was the opinionated domestic powerhouse who doted on her husband and took delight and pride in managing affairs around him. It was far from an unequal relationship, as Bunty and Moseli remembered it, but that of two strong-willed and at times sharp characters, who found a balance that provided both with a sense of achievement. Bubbles adored climbing with her husband but barely tolerated the yachting trips. They went to a theatre in Oxford once a week and shared a love of music.

Inside his laboratory, however, George was in his own world.

33.

THE BEILBY LAYER

There would be some remarkable similarities between George Finch's challenges as a mountaineer and his career as a scientist. Just as the so-called golden age of mountaineering had spanned the latter half of the nineteenth century, when men thought they had conquered and seen all that was worthwhile only for climbers like Finch and Mallory to aim higher, so too the study of physics was beginning to stall toward the end of the 1800s as scientists began to believe they had discovered almost all there was to know.

But that would change as the new century dawned, sub-atomic particles were discovered and a wild-haired German named Albert Einstein revealed his extraordinary theories about time and space, challenging not only what was known but also what might remain to be discovered. Like George Finch, Einstein was a student of the Eidgenössische Technische Hochschule in Zürich and had returned to teach at his alma mater in 1912, just as George was about to graduate as the university's gold-medal-winning student.

The impact of Einstein's theories, first made public in 1905, was explosive and provided a wave of excitement that would encourage men and a growing number of women to take up the challenge of scientific discovery in the discipline of physics. Over the next three decades there would be innovative work on electrons and atoms, neutrons and positrons, x-rays, radiation, photo-electrics, alloys, heat radiation and crystals.

Quantum physics would emerge in the early 1920s, paving the way for atomic energy, lasers and computer technology. Some physicists began theorising about flying a rocket to the moon, while others marvelled at the intricacies of light and sound and the manner in which electrons travelled in waves. Often physicists in different countries and institutions would be working from the same set of theories only to emerge with exciting twists that would set off a new round of exploration. Industry leapt on board and began funding research it hoped would lead to practical applications.

George Finch could not help but be inspired. This was a world that embraced the notion that there was more to do, a world unafraid that new discoveries might make previous theories obsolete. He would look back decades later and assess the moment he embarked on his voyage of scientific discovery, offering a thoughtful vignette of his outlook and into his character:

> It is not for all men actively to practise a science and advance it. But its gifts are gratuitous and there is no one who need go in want of them, nor anyone who may scorn them wholly and call himself modern. For it speaks the universal language. Where it turns to gaze it puts a new dimension in the scene, deepening it with marvellous perspective. This science, this cool way of looking … into vast spaces carried away a mind that had been encouraged so far chiefly to institutional judgments and emotional understandings. It was all too easy to have opinions on books, music, architecture. But appreciation is an edge that dulls with repetition; emotion is inconstant. Science has no use for any of this; it requires instead a bracing impartiality.

George's first job at the Imperial College as a 'demonstrator' had been to design and manage a course on explosives, and a decade later, encouraged by William Bone, he embarked on ambitious studies of ignition and gas combustion in electrical discharges, focusing first on thermionic emission, the heat-induced electric charge observed by the iconic American inventor Thomas Edison when he watched an electric charge pass from a heated filament to a metal plate inside a table lamp. In essence, George Finch was setting out to build a better light bulb.

Unlike his mountaineering days, when he hardly kept a note of his plans or of their execution, George would meticulously record all the details of his experiments from first principles, as if he were preparing a lecture for a room full of lay people who required an explanation of even the reasons for the inquiry. In April and May 1920, as his excitement grew over the potential to tackle Everest, he also laid the groundwork for his experiments in a 200-page handwritten dissertation on 'the explosive process', detailing not only its importance in advancing industry in general, but emphasising the need to ensure the safety of workforces in industries like coal mining, in which deaths from explosions caused by the ignition of gas were all too frequent. Over the next five years he would produce dozens of papers on aspects of his research, each adding a layer of practical knowledge to an otherwise complex set of theories.

His interest in ignition would lead to studies of the reactions of gaseous mixtures and metal catalysts, the research taking him back to the work he did with Fritz Haber and Carl Bosch as a student in 1911, when he was involved in improving the process of synthesising ammonia with iron to produce fertiliser for commercial applications.

George's research now centred not on iron but on the use of other metals, including platinum, gold and silver, as catalysts to speed up the reaction of carbon monoxide and oxygen to form carbon dioxide, a mixture that would become critical in later years in the development of fuel cells and micro electronics, and lead to the development of catalytic converters in cars to eliminate carbon monoxide from exhaust gases. The science of heterogeneous catalysis would be particularly important to industry because it explored and harnessed the use of chemical reactions between metal and gas to make the production of energy more efficient.

George also began to study the properties of the Beilby layer, named after the Scottish chemist Sir George Beilby, who discovered theoretically in the early years of the twentieth century that mechanical polishing of metals disturbed their molecular surface structure and created a new layer which behaved like a viscous liquid, 'almost as if it had been melted and then smeared out like butter over the surface', as George would describe the process.

This had particular relevance for the lubrication of machinery and internal wear and tear in combustion engines. George looked at aeroplane engines and the mechanics of cylinders to understand the differences between the effect of the layer on cast iron and aluminium and why running in an engine helped to prolong the life of its moving parts. It would be painstaking study, his research continuing for almost three decades, through World War II, and finishing only as he prepared to retire in the early 1950s.

At times his research would attract media attention, his work distilled into clever, easily digestible bites, explaining, for example, his discovery that 'sapphires' formed inside car engines, the tiny stones created by heat and clustered on piston heads where they caused engine wear. The sapphires were so small that they could only be seen through an electron microscope.

At other times the reports would be more complex and serious. In December 1933 the Imperial College announced George's research into the Beilby layer. It was a significant industrial breakthrough because he had demonstrated what Beilby had deduced, one paper declared:

> The surface of polished metal is 'liquid'. This fact, established for the first time by a London professor, is likely to lead to important advances in the protection of iron and steel against corrosion, the manufacture of permanently stainless steel plating for motor cars and the use of lighter alloys in aircraft which will yet withstand the destructive action of rain and atmosphere.

George Finch was surrounded by and could hold his place among the best scientific minds of the modern world, perhaps best illustrated when he was invited by the Nobel Prize committee to be on the nomination panel for its physics prize. It helped to dull his anger at his treatment by Arthur Hinks and Hinks's cohorts as the lure of Everest faded and his climbing was reduced to annual visits to Switzerland and Wales.

* * *

When a nineteen-year-old George Finch was told by Artur Schnabel that he was not quite good enough to be a concert pianist, he simply stopped playing. Although there was a piano in his house George rarely sat down to run his fingers across the keys, instead content instead to listen to his daughters learn to play and to read sheets of music as he sat by the window in his reading room.

He now faced the same conundrum with mountain climbing, his dream of standing on the roof of the world denied by vindictive bureaucracy. He would give brief consideration to the idea of pursuing his own expedition, backed perhaps by American money, but the death of Mallory and clumsy diplomatic manoeuvres of the 1924 expedition, including instances of expedition members hunting animals against Buddhist law, put paid to that notion, and Everest disappeared as a target for almost a decade.

But climbing would not disappear entirely from George Finch's life. The intellectual pursuit of science was now his focus but he found that, unlike his dismissal of the piano, he could not simply prop his icepick in a corner of his tool shed, hang up his eiderdown jacket in an overlooked wardrobe of the guest bedroom and forget the exhilaration of an icy climb under moonlight, nor the peace of a breakfast of tinned peaches and condensed milk washed down with lukewarm tea.

It might have been different if Bubbles had not taken so enthusiastically to the sport, now wielding a pick with her name embossed on the head as they spent their Easters in Wales and month in Europe, usually based in Zürich at the Neptune Hotel and climbing around Zermatt and Chamonix.

George now carried not only a pocket camera but a 35mm film camera strapped to his back with the idea of making films on climbing techniques. He had been encouraged by the response to his memoir, *The Making of a Mountaineer*, which he'd published in 1924 and which diplomatically skirted details of his Everest triumph to concentrate instead on a combination of stories and instructions to encourage young climbers. In his preface he wrote: 'It is primarily for the members of the younger generation that this book has been written, in the hopes that by affording them a glimpse of the adventurous joys to be found in the mountains they may be encouraged to take up and try for themselves the pursuit of mountaineering.'

A second book, *The Struggle for Everest*, would be published only in German in 1925 because of the continued harassment and legal threats by Arthur Hinks. It would be another eighty-three years before the short book was printed in English.

True to his desire to encourage young climbers, by the mid 1920s George had begun a mountaineering club for Imperial College students, initially organising climbing trips in the Snowdonia region but eventually venturing to the Alps during the summer and including in the parties members of the Oxford University student club with which George Mallory had made his first climb.

In the summer of 1931 George took ten climbers with him to Europe, including Raymond Peto, whom he had introduced to climbing in 1923. The pair had become close friends since the younger man had completed his studies and he was now on leave from his position as a chemist at the Wellcome Trust's tropical disease research laboratory in Sudan.

The group had spent two weeks in the Gotthard Massif and Bernese Oberland in central Switzerland, tackling progressively more difficult ascents in the lead-up to their main target, the Jungfrau, which George and Max had first climbed in 1909. The weather had been mostly good, but had become unpredictable in the middle of the month, with periods of pleasant summer heat interrupted by several days of cold.

The changing conditions had made George wary of the potential for some of the icier slopes to have destabilised by the time they tackled the formidable mountain on August 19. All went well on the ascent, the group roped in four parties behind George. They reached the summit around midday, after more than five hours climbing, with plenty of time to rest and take in their splendid surroundings.

George took the lead again on the descent, while Peto, as the next most experienced climber, brought up the rear with two of his friends from university days, Robert Kershaw and William Downey. George led the party back via a rocky rib, which angled down to a safe rendezvous point called the Rottalsattel. It was a longer route than they could have taken, and required step-cutting, but George was worried about the snow conditions on an easier slope which he considered unstable because of the weather.

By mid afternoon George's group had made it to the rendezvous point, as had the two groups immediately behind who had followed in his footsteps, but there was no sign of Peto, Kershaw and Downey. The trio appeared soon afterwards, not on the route George had carefully carved. They were attempting to traverse the slope he had specifically warned them to avoid. Years of experience told him they were a step away from disaster, the snow thin and prone to collapse in the afternoon sunshine. Why had Peto made the decision, he wondered.

The men were too far away to hear his warning shouts and too focused on their task to see his urgent waving. All George could do was watch and pray as they inched their way toward the safer part of the mountainside, all the time edging closer to a precipice which fell away more than 1600 feet to the base of the mountain.

Then it happened; one of the men slipped. George was not sure who it was but the misstep pulled the other two off their feet and in seconds they were sliding uncontrollably toward the cliff edge. There was no sound, no screams of terror, as the men tried in vain to anchor their axes in the slope and stop their headlong slide as they disappeared from view. They were gone.

George Finch, shattered psychologically and blaming himself, led the search with four guides the next day. An avalanche had followed the men over the cliff and a second had fallen overnight. It was dangerous to search but George could not bear to leave the bodies of his friends behind. He placed one of the guides as a lookout for further avalanches while he and the others scoured the area at the base of the great cliff, using long poles to feel deep into the fresh snow. It took more than six hours, in between dashes for cover as a fresh avalanche fell from above, to find and dig out the three bodies.

George had witnessed death on a mountain before, his mind going back to the horrific plunge of the two Germans on one of his first climbs with Max, but this was different, and personal. Intellectually he knew the tragedy was not his fault, but it would be impossible to shake the sense of responsibility.

He would never climb again.

* * *

The idea that electrons move in waves had been proposed in the mid 1920s by the French physicist Louis de Broglie and was confirmed in 1927 by George Paget Thomson, a colleague of George Finch at the Imperial College, with whom he would work closely and who would later be awarded the Nobel Prize for his work.

George Finch preferred to talk in lectures and presentations about electrons behaving like fish, swimming uniformly in a school, but wriggling in desperation when removed from their environment. Waves, he explained, were akin to the audience being shown a series of photographs of mountain climbers in dangerous situations, prompting a range of responses from amazement to anxiety, dismay and relief.

George was in frequent communication with Thomson and by 1930 had shifted his research focus to electron diffraction – the movement patterns of electrons – in the hope that it would provide insight into surface structures and how metals bonded together. What he needed was a machine that would enable him to 'see' more closely the surfaces he wanted to understand.

Initial studies using x-rays had failed because uncharged particles pass through matter, so George decided to experiment with diffraction by firing charged electrons, 1800 times lighter than atoms, in waves at an object and then studying the pattern they created. As he would explain to students: 'X-rays tell us about the internal structure of a body but electron waves inform us about the surface because they cannot penetrate more than a few atoms deep.'

When George's request for college funding to design and build a machine that would enable him to study the surface patterns was rejected, he simply went home and built one himself. His creation would be called a camera even though the finely crafted collection of coils, diaphragms, pumps, vapour traps, rods and tubes resembled an elongated microscope, standing almost two metres tall. Although George designed it as a practical device, he built the finished object with the loving care that had defined the crafting of the Atwood machine, the eighteenth-century pendulum that explained Newton's laws of motion and had stood in his father's study all those years before.

The Finch camera, as it became known, was so technically advanced for its time that it would remain the standard until the 1950s – when George improved it himself in order to study thicker films. It used magnetic coils to focus a beam of electrons toward either a crystal or metal film, and then collected them as they diffracted to create patterns imprinted onto a photographic plate.

It was just a matter of time before George Finch's work would be recognised. In 1928 he was awarded Belgium's highest civilian honour, becoming a Commandeur in the Order of Léopold, which effectively made him a knight of the court. In 1936 he became professor of applied physical chemistry at the Imperial College and then spent 1937 as a visiting research professor at the University of Brussels, as a recipient of the prestigious Francqui Foundation award. On his return from Brussels in 1938, George was made a Fellow of the Royal Society.

But another, important, achievement remained hidden. George Finch had read *Mein Kampf*, Adolf Hitler's 1925 manifesto, and was aware more than most of the threat that Nazism posed. During his year in Brussels he would make at least three unannounced trips into Germany, ostensibly to visit academic friends. But his real purpose was to aid young Jewish scientists and students, to bring them out of Germany and find positions for them at the Imperial College or in companies like Imperial Chemical Industries and Ferranti International, for which he had become a part-time consultant.

George would never document his actions, part of a wider effort among London's scientific community to protect their European counterparts from the madness of war. He would do the same in Belgium during the war and its aftermath, finding opportunities for young scientists from Belgium whose shattered nation had lost most of its facilities and industries. He received no medal or citation for this contribution, nor would he have expected the recognition, although in 1941 George received a letter from the King of Belgium, Leopold III, thanking him 'for the unstinting assistance he kindly gave to Belgian refugee students in England enabling them to continue their studies'.

34.

F DIVISION AND THE J-BOMB

George Finch was too old to fight when World War II was declared in the autumn of 1939, although his expertise in explosives and ignition would become invaluable. Recruited by the Ministry of Home Affairs as a scientific advisor, his principal duty was to try to restrict the damage wreaked by the bombing raids of the Blitz that erupted a year later.

The situation was bleak. Between September 1940 and May 1941, mass Luftwaffe aerial raids were launched against sixteen British cities. London alone was attacked seventy-one times, at one point being bombed over fifty-seven consecutive nights. Twenty thousand civilians were killed and more than one million homes destroyed or damaged. Birmingham, Liverpool, Plymouth, Glasgow, Bristol and Hull were also targeted repeatedly. Aerial defences managed to stem, but could not prevent, the attacks and many city-dwellers fled the onslaught, seeking the relative safety of the countryside.

George's task was to limit the damage on the ground. Volunteer fire brigades were drilled and equipped to respond to the fires ignited by the bombs and the incendiary devices designed to spark flames on landing, but what was desperately needed was a better understanding of how the devices worked and how the fires spread.

George Finch not only took his role seriously but cherished it: among the collection of his personal effects is a soot-smudged white armband which identified him as a 'Fire Observer'.

By then, the family was living at Osterley and Moseli, a teenage schoolgirl, remembers accompanying her father as he headed out in the evenings when the air raid sirens wailed. It was with a mixture of excitement and fear that she watched her father, a cool and reassuring figure on the periphery of the devastation, advising the army of volunteers, largely middle-aged tradesmen and white-collar workers who formed the backbone of the Home Guard, on how best to deal with the fires. The next day George would return early to scan the smouldering remains for clues about the spread of the blaze.

George pored over reports written about the fires he didn't have time to attend, becoming increasingly frustrated that the official observers, although well meaning, were not properly trained. More scientists and engineers were needed to properly study the properties and behaviour of the fires sparked by the bombs. At his suggestion, a training college was set up in Brighton to teach fire marshals about the spread of fire with demonstrations designed to show the significance of heat and how it is transferred. A photograph of the ranks of scientific volunteer instructors eventually recruited reveals that on this occasion George Finch managed to get his own way.

Sharing his knowledge, George would begin his lectures with an anecdote in which he described asking an experienced brigade officer what his job was in dealing with a fire: 'He immediately replied, without thinking, "to put the fire out, of course",' he told his audience of volunteers. 'Yet nothing is further from the truth,' George would go on to say.

It was counter-intuitive, he told his audience, but they had to resist the temptation to attack the flames, instead working first to ensure that the fire could not spread. He described the techniques of containment, urging the volunteers to picture a series of compartments that, one by one, were made safe before the beast itself was corralled, cornered and tamed.

Finch also taught them to recognise the most dangerous fuel loads and the rates at which fire would spread on different surfaces. They needed to understand what he called the 'phenomenon of the passage of fire', to know the barriers that would stop or at least slow the chances of the flames jumping from one building to another and destroying an entire street of homes rather than a single dwelling. There were myriad complexities that could be solved by science, he told them, and it boiled down to how chemicals reacted in heat.

At the height of the Blitz, there had been a series of particularly destructive factory bombings; so large were the blazes that it was feared a new incendiary bomb had been deployed. George was called in to assess the situation and quickly realised that the link between the blasts was not the explosives but the buildings into which the bombs had been dropped. They were flour factories, and the bombs had broken open equipment and sent clouds of fine white flour into the air, which ignited in secondary explosions that were much more devastating than the original blast. George's solution was to place packets of inert materials around shop floors to counter the incendiary impact of the explosions.

Back at his Imperial College laboratory, he meticulously built scale models of furnished rooms and factories and created a series of experiments to track the way fire spread, 'preying on its surroundings and spreading like an infectious disease'. His notes show a desire to balance the specific findings based on scientific observation with language that allowed widespread understanding. It was 'man's wealth and most precious possessions in life' – that is, furniture and room contents – which provided the fuel, he noted. Finch's conclusions, which were credited with saving many buildings and lives during the war years, would later be adopted in the construction of new buildings, long after the war was finished. Just as he had challenged the comfortable stalwarts of the Alpine Club to countenance change, George Finch had pleaded for a co-ordinated approach to fire prevention in order to curtail the loss of life and destruction of homes.

In a speech delivered to the Royal Society in 1946 after the war had ended, he said knowledge had been too ad-hoc and research blindly ignored:

> The fireman can study the risks, the scientists can point out
> fire load, the architect can secure lines of escape and barriers
> to delay the fire, the legislator can check the irresponsible and
> help the ignorant, the manufacturer can give us steel furniture
> and woolen nightclothes for our children, and the ordinary
> man can exercise a little more care.

* * *

Science, of course, plays a varied and often conflicting role in war. Fritz Haber, a man of Jewish origin, invented the gases used to kill millions in the World War II death camps, while his scientific colleague, Carl Bosch, was shunned and shamed for refusing to join the German war effort. William Bone was also opposed to war, but recognised the need for scientific input, pragmatically negotiating for his staff to play their part in the war effort on the proviso that their work did not involve poison gas.

In the early years of the war, George Finch had concentrated his scientific effort on the defence of Britain, but in the late winter of 1942 he used the knowledge he had gained from the study of the German bombs that had caused so much devastation during the Blitz to design an improved weapon that could turn the attack on the enemy.

The Ministry of Home Security had broadened its work and created the Fire Research Division, or F Division, as it came to be known, within the Research and Experiments Department. F Division was led by Lord Falmouth, an engineer and board member of the Imperial College, who wanted George to join his team. George agreed and persuaded Falmouth to also recruit a former colleague, Professor Townend, who at one time ran the high-pressure laboratory at Imperial College and was now working at Leeds University. George was keen to collaborate with Townend to try to understand how radiation from magnesium contained in German incendiary bombs spread through buildings.

The two men's research revealed that the heat in burning timber rises vertically in a conical shape and that it is burning furniture in buildings, and not the explosion itself, that acts as fuel and heat to set alight floors and joists. This work would lead to a rethink of Britain's own bomb design, producing a weapon that would shoot out a horizontal rather than vertical flame on landing with the specific intention of spreading fire across floors to set alight as much furniture as possible. It was as logical as it was simple. And it would prove deadly.

George also experimented with the gas used to ignite the bomb's flames, working with Townend to produce a bomb filled with pressurised butane gas which produced a long and intense flame. The problem was supply and stability, the gas not easily available and much too dangerous to keep inside a military storage facility. The eventual answer lay with petrol sprayed outwards on impact via a combination of metal powder and oxide that was triggered by a fuse. The Jet, or J, Bomb was born.

Two years later, the British air force dropped J-Bombs during raids over Munich, Stuttgart, Bremen, Stettin, Rüsselsheim and Königsberg. Over the following eighteen months more than 800,000 J-bombs were manufactured and dropped on cities across Germany with the aim of demoralising the civilian workforce, just as the German Blitz of 1940 and '41 had attempted in Britain.

The bomb's success was announced publicly on August 23, 1944, with dramatic headlines that declared 'Bomb with 15-foot flame Britain's new weapon. Already used on Reich' and stories detailing the raid by 250 Lancaster bombers over Munich in April, which had devastated an area between the city's railway station and the River Isar. The centres of Stuttgart and Bremen had faced similar devastation as the raids continued through July.

In a bid to excite public imagination as the tide of war began to turn in favour of the Allied forces, the Ministry of War had released photographs and enough detail to reveal how the bomb, now known as the Flying Meteor or Super Flamer, worked. Dropped under a parachute to slow its speed and to ensure that it remained whole on impact, the thirty-pound (fourteen-kilogram) tube crashed through rooftops and fell only as far as the floor, where it could do the most damage. On landing, a detonator fired, in turn igniting a primer which forced a mix of methane and petrol through the tube to emerge in a sheet of flame that would burn for several minutes, creating enough intense heat to fell a brick wall.

'The Germans have no answer to this. They can't put it out,' Townend was quoted as saying.

Even so, the challenges were still coming thick and fast, all discussed in top secret behind the door of George's office, Room 441 in an unidentified government building, one of the many that line the stretch of Whitehall between Nelson's Column and the Houses of Parliament. It was here that George worked when not teaching at the Imperial College, here where he advised on the most effective arsenal to carry during bombing raids, and it was here, too, that he brought his meticulous logs and navigation maps from his yachting exploits in the English Channel and offered them to the intelligence division of the Admiralty.

George continued to refine the J-bomb, filling bomb heads with new combinations of metals designed to burn at high intensity on impact. He also worked to make aerodromes safe from crashing aircraft, recommending the use of cowled aircraft propellers mounted on trucks to help clear runways of burning fuel.

True to form, George did not suffer fools gladly, at one point remarking to a critic who dared challenge his conclusions:

> I find that the probability of the water freezing is of the same order as a regiment of monkeys banging away on a multitude of typewriters will produce the latest edition of the British Encyclopedia in time for me to consult it during my earthly span. Ergo, every time I repeat the kettle of water experiment I know – I do not expect – that the water will boil.

In January 1943 George had travelled to Newmarket, north of London, to talk to operational crews at No. 3 Group Bomber Command. The visit was to discuss general operations and safety, but in the course of conversation he became intrigued by the concerns of crews carrying 'photo flash' flares during aerial reconnaissance missions.

The flares were designed to light up the night sky momentarily to enable aerial photographs to be taken over enemy positions before darkness again enveloped and shielded the planes and crew as they made their way back to safety. But they were dangerous, constructed from an unstable combination of sodium nitrate and magnesium powder that was sensitive to friction, a dangerous proposition during a jolting flight compounded by vibrations from pounding anti-aircraft gunfire. George left the base determined to find a better and safer flare.

His experiments were swift and revolutionary, not just for British planes but American aircraft which would be modified to his designs. Instead of magnesium, George's charge used aluminum powder, a much more stable solution that also emitted a shorter and brighter flash and was far more effective for the job at hand. He tested the flares in the tunnels beneath the Imperial College, which he had previously converted into a dark room for high-speed photography.

Just as his advice on fire fighting would help revolutionise post-war housing construction, so too his photo flash would be adapted in later years to aid experiments in shock wave reflection which had implications for the design of heavy machinery, trains and rail tracks, buildings, bridges and shipping.

* * *

The success of the J-Bomb had drawn the attention of United States military officials, and in early November 1944 George was part of a high-level delegation on the way to Washington to discuss the bomb's use in America's war on Japan. Far from being anxious about the dangerous crossing, George was elated to be back in the thick of the action, as he wrote to Bubbles in a concise cable: 'Had splendid passage, enjoyed every minute. Putting on weight fast. Love you and all.'

He arrived in Washington armed with carefully written guidelines on diplomacy, which probably only titillated his irreverent and forthright nature. Americans didn't like to be criticised, particularly by a 'Britisher', the guidelines warned: 'Do not forget that the opinions of a government servant on national affairs carry more weight abroad than at home. Nevertheless, excessive enthusiasm, or an attempt to show that all criticism must be founded on ignorance or prejudice, provokes an unfriendly reaction. Be reasonable, therefore, as well as confident.'

But George Finch was there to impress: a tall, svelte and now craggy figure in his trademark bow tie among the uniforms of the top brass at the Pentagon who turned out to listen to his views on adapting the incendiary makeup of the J-bomb to suit the humid environment and lighter furnishings of Japan. The British contingent spent a month in the United States, attending briefings and conferences at venues up and down the east coast, including New York, the Eglin Air Force Base in Florida and Orlando, where George also lectured.

Far from posing any diplomatic problems, George Finch won over the Americans with his forthrightness. Among his papers are two poems written to him 'in admiration and friendship', one by a senior Navy Department official in Washington and the second by an anonymous author, but clearly treasured:

We all love the goldfinch
The bullfinch, the chaffinch;
They sing as they search for their 'gorge'.
But our love growing stronger
And deeper and longer
Goes to Finch who answers to 'George'.

Amid the acclaim came further recognition. On November 21, as the delegation flew back to Washington from Orlando, word reached them that George had been awarded one of the Royal

Society's highest individual honours. The Hughes Medal, named after the Welsh-American inventor David Hughes who built the first crystal radio receiver, printing telegraph and microphone, is awarded each year for discoveries in the field of physical sciences.

George had been officially acknowledged for 'his fundamental contributions to the study of the structure and properties of surfaces, and for his important work on the electrical ignition of gases'. The second-choice Everest mountaineer, Nobel Prize judge and unseen war-time advisor had finally been recognised in public in Britain as the genius he had always been.

Bubbles broke the news by cable. The award would be presented on November 30: 'Please be there,' she implored. He didn't make it. The US mission was far more important than individual honours, he decided, arriving home two days after the ceremony, important enough even in war to be reported in *The Times*.

The accolades would continue as the war ended and the various departments and advisory boards were disbanded and civilian life resumed. The United States Embassy in London expressed its thanks and asked George to continue offering advice; the vice-president of the Ordnance Board, Air Vice-Marshal Bilney, insisted that advances in knowledge of fire 'are very largely due to you personally'; and there was an offer from the British government of a position as Britain's senior scientific advisor, which George turned down to return to academic life.

Lord Falmouth, who had run F Division and consistently backed George's views, at times against loud opposition, provided the tribute George treasured most. The viscount had lost one son and seen another severely disfigured during combat, yet took the time to write: 'Your advice and assistance have been of the greatest value in dealing with the many problems which we have had to tackle. All kinds of new problems were arriving daily as a consequence of the actions of the enemy ... [your work] was of the utmost importance ...'

At the beginning of the war, George Finch had been frustrated at being refused permission to fight, but by the end it was clear that his scientific contribution from home was far more valuable than being a frontline soldier.

35.

'WHOSE SON AM I?'

Bunty Finch met Cynthia Wood in the late summer of 1942 when the two young women found themselves sharing a bedroom as new recruits of the national security agency MI5. They became great friends and, as life slowly returned to normal after the war, Cynthia, whose own father had died when she was young, found herself increasingly involved in Finch family events and coming under the watchful, paternal eye of Bunty's father, George.

Cynthia, now in her nineties, observed a careful and organised man driven by his intellectual interests but the antithesis of the isolated, haughty academic she had been expecting. She recalls that Finch would joke about his students at the college, saying that if they were struggling in their studies, he would always ensure they were given the chance to 'scrape through' the course if they helped him clean the bottom of his yacht, *Wasp*, which was moored on the Lymington River near Southampton.

Cynthia found herself hurled headlong into a new and exciting world:

He had a way of talking to us about complex and interesting things without being boring. I remember clearly him telling me why the thumb was the most important digit because it set us apart from other animals. He took Bunty and me to a ball at the Dorchester one year and gave me my first glass of Château d'Yquem and then talked to me about it.

We went with him to a lecture at the Royal Society one night. Until then I'd had nothing to do with science but this intellectual world was riveting where nobody cared if you were well bred but if you had brains and wanted to use them. He was a man with a very broad vision and in many ways it was unfortunate that he lived when he did because he would be very, very acceptable now. He was also very modest; confident but modest.

The only darkness Cynthia remembers was when Bunty and her sisters found out about their father's first marriage and the existence of Peter:

> Bunty was upset at first, perhaps for her mother's sake, but I think more so because it had been a secret all those years. I just thought he'd had a colourful life; after all it had all happened before he had even met Bubbles. And who could blame them? George was a charming man and very good looking. He had the most amazing blue eyes.

* * *

If George Finch ever regretted his decision to separate a young boy from his mother then he never expressed it, even when that same boy, now a man on his way to becoming a West End and Hollywood star, turned up on his doorstep thirty years later, seeking answers.

In the grey early winter of 1948, Peter Finch, a theatrical actor and already with a number of movie credits to his name, arrived in London at the encouragement of the stage legend Sir Laurence Olivier, who had been impressed by Peter's theatre performance in Sydney and promised to take him under his wing, 'if you ever come to London'.

It was a big risk for the 32-year-old, particularly considering his established fame in Australia, where he had been named actor of the year for the previous two years in the biggest medium of its time – radio. And the leap into the unknown was to become even stranger when, a few days before he and his wife, the ballerina Tamara Tchinarova, were due to sail, he received a telephone call from his Aunt Dorothy, who wanted to see him before he left. When he arrived at her house in North Sydney she gave him a packet of letters, saying they would tell him about his mother and father.

Peter began opening the letters when he boarded the *Esperance Bay*, and by the time she sailed out through the heads of Sydney Harbour he had decided to track down George Finch and Betty Fisher. Dorothy, who had been a frequent presence in his early life, had told him that her brother could be found at the Imperial College in Kensington. But she had no idea where he might find his mother.

Peter and Tamara arrived in London on November 17 and checked into the Regent Palace Hotel, on the edge of the theatre district, where Peter hoped to find work. Before he could think twice, Peter had telephoned the Imperial College and been put through to Professor George Finch who, although surprised and clearly not warned by his sister, took the call in his stride and arranged to meet Peter and Tamara at the hotel three days later.

In the days before he met the man he believed was his father, Peter travelled to Cambridgeshire to visit the ancestral Finch stronghold at Little Shelford. Charles Finch had told him stories of the family and its roots, and even if there were questions about his belonging, Peter felt comfortable there, in a melancholy moment even contemplating being buried in the church graveyard when he died.

He was about to be disappointed. Tamara could still sense the awkwardness in the cramped hotel room when she described the meeting with George Finch in an interview thirty years later. The professor appeared on time – 'tall, straight, handsome, grey-haired and very thin' – and decided to go up to the room rather than meet downstairs, perhaps unwilling to risk his dirty laundry being washed in public. 'It was very awkward as there weren't enough chairs so one of us sat on the bed,' Tamara said. 'He was very dry and abrupt in his speech. It was a very inarticulate meeting … full of undercurrents without any real communication. Peter was full of questions which the professor evaded answering.'

The trio moved downstairs for tea. That lasted barely thirty minutes as the conversation stalled on the banal: what Peter was doing in London and how long he might be in the country. 'We just had self-conscious conversation about everything and saying nothing,' Tamara remembered. 'And then … he left.'

Peter Finch would tell friends about the meeting, including Enid Lorimer whom he'd known at the Theosophist Society headquarters in Sydney. It left Peter conflicted, unconvinced that the mystery had been solved and wondering why he had become collateral damage of a bad marriage. The older man's reception seemed cold, measured and totally rejecting: 'I'm sorry to disappoint you, young man, but you're not really my son,' George had said.

'Whose son am I then?' Peter challenged him.

The reply was unyielding: 'Better ask your mother.'

And so it went on, the budding actor who was about to become a Hollywood movie star desperate for answers and the famous mountaineer and scientist unemotional and determined not to explain himself until the subject turned conclusively to his first wife. Then his calm demeanour suddenly cracked. Although more than three decades had passed, it was clear that George still felt wronged by Betty Fisher's disloyalty and that it was this that had led him to take the boy, albeit with good intentions, and wreak such an awful revenge.

Behind his namesake's apparent dispassion, however, Peter hoped that there was a measure of regret. He knew from the letters he'd read on the ship that George Finch had expressed affection for him, not just as an innocent victim of a bad marriage but as 'rather a dear little fellow'. What Peter didn't know was that it had been protests from Gladys May that prevented George from raising Peter himself. At least, that was the kindest view that could be drawn from the events that followed George's divorce from Betty Fisher.

'He must have burned up a lot of his valuable energy putting the knife into my mother,' Peter told Lorimer. 'Was it a dog-in-the-manger attitude on George's part, or were they all really convinced I was a Campbell? I was passed along the line of Finches like a football through a rugby team. From age two to age fourteen I changed hands faster than a dud pound note.'

But the meeting wasn't the last they saw of each other, according to Peter's only son, Charles, who says the pair rendezvoused several times afterwards, sometimes walking together along the Thames in conversation – 'walkabout' as Peter put it. There was a rapprochement, if limited and private, as George attempted to repair some of the damage of his actions without complicating family life with Bubbles and the girls, and Peter tried to make sense of his life: 'In my father's mind he was climbing the mountains of life, just as George had climbed Mount Everest,' says Charles, whose mother, the South African actress Yolande Turner, was the second of Peter's three wives. 'There was definitely dialogue between them; I know that for certain. Ultimately there was a great deal of affection between them.'

Charles, named after Charles Edward Finch, also believes that George was his real grandfather:

My father died believing that George was his real father, and that's what I believe. His mother [Betty] told him that when they met in 1948.

It's almost as if the family has been under a curse; this question mark over whether George was my grandfather. One of the things that sticks in my mind is my father's insistence, his anger in a way, [directed] to my mother that, yes, George was his father.

My take is that George was a very vain man who was outraged and embarrassed at the way his first wife had behaved. He took my father from his mother for two reasons: because he believed that Betty could not take care of him and because he believed the boy was his real son.

Despite everything, my father loved George and was proud of his achievements. This is from a man who lived his life as a Buddhist with no desire for earthly chattels. But it was important for him and so it is important to me.

* * *

The veteran Australian actor Ronald 'Trader' Faulkner was a close friend of Peter Finch and felt compelled to write a biography about his mate's strange life. Now a sprightly eighty-six, Trader still climbs the stairs to the sixth-floor Kensington flat he bought in 1950 soon after he went to London to try his luck on the stage.

He shakes his head sadly at the thought of his mate who resorted to alcohol to hide his fragility – a little like his mother: 'I don't know who was his real father. I suspect it was Jock Campbell but the dates suggest that it could be George, although less likely.'

Then there is the question of where Peter's genius as an actor was created. George Finch saw himself as a serious man and Jock Campbell carried many generations of military service in his genes. Betty Finch was theatrical in a sense, but it was the flamboyant Laura Finch whom Peter admired who best understood and nurtured his artistic flair.

Peter Finch died in January 1977 from a heart attack. Later that year he won an Oscar for best male actor, the first ever awarded posthumously, for his portrayal of the enraged news anchorman Howard Beale in the movie *Network*. Particularly memorable is the scene in which he delivers an impassioned soliloquy, exclaiming: 'I'm as mad as hell, and I'm not going to take this any more!'

Trader Faulkner is emphatic about his friend's motivation for the famous line: 'There is no doubt that the inspiration behind that speech was his own life. He was still crying out for answers.'

36.

CONQUERED

When he came to power in 1950, the first Prime Minister of India, Jawaharlal Nehru, knew his country needed to establish itself as a modern society with a vibrant and developing economy. Industrial development was a vital part of his vision, and Nehru believed that one of the key elements in unlocking India's vast potential in this area was the establishment of a national centre for scientific research.

The National Chemistry Laboratory of India was built on a 200-hectare site on the outskirts of Poona – 'on a beautiful, breezy and healthy plateau in close proximity to the educational institutions of the city', as the announcement of its establishment would declare with pride. More than one hundred scientists were employed to make a mark internationally across a broad range of disciplines, including chemical engineering, biochemistry, physics and electrochemistry.

Six Nobel Laureates attended the opening of the laboratory, and by the end of 1951 the centre had been fully staffed and the National Council of Scientific and Industrial Research was looking for an eminent scientist and administrator to lead its research division. Nehru insisted on making the final decision himself. He chose George Finch.

Whether there was any previous connection between the two men is uncertain. They were about the same age and Nehru had studied natural sciences at Cambridge before spending some years in London as a young lawyer. And George Finch and William Bone had been instrumental in encouraging young Indian scientists to study at the Imperial College as early as the 1920s.

There was, however, a strange connection through the theosophist movement. Annie Besant had been a friend of the Nehru family, and Nehru had joined the movement and been influenced by its teachings as a young man. Then there was George's hippie-like mother, Laura, who had continued to spend most of her time in India until her death in the 1940s and had been involved in the Indian nationalist movement as a devotee of Mahatma Gandhi.

Whatever the connection, Nehru was aware of George Finch and his scientific work, and knew that he was ready to retire, as an Emeritus Professor, from the Imperial College after a career spanning almost forty years. George accepted Nehru's offer with glee. Although he had only been to India once, fleetingly, for the 1922 Everest expedition, he felt an affinity with the country and jumped at the chance to be involved in the development of a research facility.

When George and Bubbles left London in September 1952 on board an Air India flight, the pilot, apparently under instructions from Nehru, set a course which took the plane directly over the top of Mont Blanc as a tribute to the professor and his wife. George would recall the experience: 'It was a beautiful clear day and for a few joyous moments we looked down on the Aiguille du Goûter, the Tacul and Mont Maudit, the Innominata and Peteret routes spread out below. It was a sight that quickened the heart.'

They were celebrated on their arrival at an official reception hosted by Nehru, who would become a frequent visitor to the apartment above the laboratory at Poona, where the Finches would live for the next five years, on occasion bringing his daughter Indira Gandhi and his grandson Rajiv, both future political leaders of India.

India would also unexpectedly take George back to his carefree boyhood as he spent weekends hunting and fishing in the company of his adoring hosts. For the first time since he left Australia as a teenager, George felt drawn to the country of his birth and began planning a trip home.

But first there was Everest. George and Bubbles had only been in Poona for three months when he received a letter from Colonel John Hunt, an army officer and mountaineer, who had been chosen to lead the ninth British expedition to conquer Everest. The party was leaving on February 12, 1953, and Hunt, whose own mountaineering exploits had been inspired by George Finch's adventures, wanted to pick Finch's brain about strategies on the mountain. George was only too pleased to give his opinion and repeat the theories that had been so utterly ignored in 1924:

> My dear Hunt,
>
> I have read your problems with much interest. You are our chosen leader in absolute command in the field and, as such, I would like you to consider the following suggestions. Past expeditions have always thought in terms of two, three or even four attempts. But if it were only possible to pick out the best assault party [of only two or at most three men] the lift above 21,000 feet could be greatly reduced by using the rest of the climbers and porters sacrificially in the sense that their job would be to carry loads up to as far as say 27,000 feet where the highest camp would be established; and then to return as quickly as possible to advanced base so as to

make as little inroad as possible on the supplies deposited in
the camps they established. Members [climbers and porters]
of the sacrificial parties should go ... straight through to
South Col [26,000 feet] with 2lb of oxygen per man and
return unladen the same day. The real point is that the
chosen assault party must go lightly laden from Advanced
Base. It would be splendid if a sacrificial party could equip
oxygen at 28,000 feet. The generous oxygen consumption
I have suggested should be reserved only for the assault
party – the sacrificial parties should only use O_2 at about
half their rate – given that is more than Bruce and I used.
Don't forget the hot liquids [and plenty of them]. But how
you will manage this is a problem – but it is nearly as critical
as oxygen. I'll meet you in Bombay and hope you'll be able to
stay with me in Poona for a day or two.

      Yours sincerely

      Geo Finch

* * *

Although he had been dumped from the 1924 expedition and its
preparations, George had remained a prominent and vocal figure
on the sidelines over the years as continued attempts were made to
conquer Everest.

It would be nine years after the deaths of Mallory and Irvine
before another mission was mounted, and Arthur Hinks was still
at the helm in April 1933 when the fourth British expedition
sailed under the leadership of Hugh Ruttledge, a civil servant and
compromise appointment when Charles Bruce, Geoffrey Bruce
and Edward Norton all turned down the role. 'The lot fell to me,'
Ruttledge would write of a campaign that got no higher than

Edward Norton's mark from 1924, although it found Sandy Irvine's abandoned axe.

The team had taken redesigned oxygen tanks with them, although reluctantly, as borne out by the bitter remarks of Francis Younghusband that he had regretted siding with George Finch on the issue before the 1922 campaign. Ruttledge wasn't keen either, specifying that the oxygen would only be used above the North Col and even then only in an emergency. The crates were never opened.

George Finch had retired from climbing by now, his misplaced guilt over the death of his friend Raymond Peto compounded by poor health as a result of his war-time malaria. But his brain and tongue were as sharp as ever as he weighed into the debate on future expeditions and how they should be managed.

He signalled his intent in October 1934 when asked by the weekly magazine *The Listener* to review Ruttledge's book on the 1933 expedition. George was typically forthright. While not criticising Ruttledge directly, he insisted that a climber, rather than a civil servant, should have been in command, a decision he blamed on the Everest Committee with the none too subtle observation: 'A committee is a peculiar organisation which can and frequently does, in its dealings with individuals, act untrammelled by the dictates of consciences.'

His comments about oxygen were equally blunt; he labelled the expedition's stance as a 'wretched state of indecision' and added: 'Oxygen should be used full blast … or utterly tabooed on moral or material grounds or indeed for any reason which the wit of man can conceive. And if the prospective Everest Committee cannot decide one way or another then sack the lot!'

A reconnaissance mission returned to Everest in 1935, this time led by the climber and coffee grower Eric Shipton, who had been a member of the previous attempt, and included a young Nepalese porter named Tenzing Norgay. But the monsoon season had set in by the time the party arrived and no serious attempt was made on the mountain.

The committee had still not heeded George's words when they met to decide the composition of the 1936 expedition that again would be led by Ruttledge. Shipton and Tenzing Norgay were again among the team, but yet another early monsoon season put paid to any chance of making a serious attempt on the summit. Amid the frustrations, opinions about the use of oxygen were beginning to shift, albeit slowly. Oxygen tanks were taken and this time used as the party crossed the Tibetan Plateau, as a means of acclimatisation. Ruttledge would report: 'We came to the conclusion that considerable benefit could be obtained from its use but it is still far too heavy and research is being made to find a more convenient and more dependable apparatus.'

But it was not enough for George, as he told the *Morning Post*: 'Our present position is that we are beginning to look ridiculous. Unless we put up a better show it will be difficult to argue that we are justified in keeping Mount Everest to ourselves.' Until then Britain had managed to control access through its colonial power in the region, but it was clear that the situation would eventually change.

There would be one more expedition before war intervened. In 1938, Bill Tilman, a decorated war hero, adventurer and close friend of Shipton, would lead a party that again included Tenzing Norgay. Tilman favoured small parties (like Shipton) and was a vocal opponent of oxygen, although he agreed, under sufferance, to take two oxygen sets: one an open-circuit set based on the system designed by George Finch, and the other a new closed-circuit system, which was potentially more efficient because it excluded outside air.

Tilman would use neither, but another climber, an engineer named Peter Lloyd, tested both during the expedition, yet another attempt foiled by poor weather, and returned to tell the Royal Geographical Society that he believed oxygen would prove to be the difference between success and failure: 'I have a lot of sympathy with the sentimental objection to its use, and would rather see the mountain climbed without it than with; but, on the other hand, I would rather see the mountain climbed with it than not at all.'

It would be the last British attempt for thirteen years, as World War II raged and China invaded Tibet, shutting off access to the north face. A new strategy was required and in 1951, after several rogue attempts by individuals and a growing interest by American and European climbers, a fresh British reconnaissance mission was launched under the leadership of Eric Shipton to assess the possibility of climbing via Nepal and the mountain's southern face.

In the lead-up to their departure, the team members visited Snowdonia for a training camp where they were introduced to George Finch, now aged sixty-three. Cynthia Wood was there with Bunty and recalled the occasion: 'The weather was misty and the rain fell softy and I remember that we all walked up what George called the cow path to the summit of Snowdon. I don't know the specifics of what they talked about but it was clear to me that there was an enormous amount of respect for him.'

George Finch had finally come in from the cold.

* * *

John Hunt had been offered the leadership of the 1953 expedition after the Everest Committee lost faith in Eric Shipton, whose demise was clearly a result of the British desperation to reach the summit before a team from another nation claimed the glory. With

Indian independence in 1947 the borders were thrown open. There had been a Swiss attempt in the spring, which fell just short of the summit, and the French were due to mount a campaign in 1954. This might be Britain's last chance to claim the prize and Shipton was seen as too indecisive; he had even admitted that he was bored with Everest and disliked the nationalistic race to the top. He also remained emphatically anti-oxygen.

By contrast John Hunt embraced the idea of technology, as he later wrote:

> Whereas it is certainly true that knowledge of man's power of acclimatisation to extreme altitude has been largely contributed by climbers on Everest, the futile controversy over the ethics of using oxygen, and the failure to accept the findings of pioneers in its application, handicapped for thirty years the introduction of the method which promises to revolutionise mountaineering.

Hunt's expedition reached the new base camp beneath the southern face on April 12, 1953, and over the next few weeks established a series of camps ever higher on the mountain. By May 21 they had reached the South Col and pegged Camp VIII at just under 26,000 feet. Hunt was broadly following Finch's strategy of using 'sacrificial' climbers, including himself, to continue to push camps higher and higher to make the final assault an easier proposition.

There would be two assault teams, and on May 26 the first pairing of Charles Evans, a brain surgeon, and Tom Bourdillon, a physicist who, with his father, Robert, had developed the closed-circuit oxygen system they wore, pushed upwards, aiming for the summit. The two men managed to reach the lower, south, summit at 28,707 feet and came within a few hundred feet of the final summit before being forced to turn back, exhausted and defeated by oxygen-equipment problems and lack of time.

Behind them John Hunt and a sherpa named Da Namgyal had established another camp at 27,395 feet, where they were joined by the second assault team, Edmund Hillary and Tenzing Norgay, again following George Finch's blueprint. On May 28 Hillary and Norgay, aided by the 'sacrificial' climbers George Lowe, Alf Gregory and the sherpa Ang Nyima, moved further upwards to a ridgeline at 28,000 feet and camped for the night.

At 6.30am the next morning the beekeeper from Tuakau in New Zealand and the feisty and persistent Nepalese sherpa began their own assault, this time using the open-circuit oxygen system. They had reached the South Summit by 9am before tackling the 50-foot-high rock and ice spur that would become known as the Hillary Step, treating it as a chimney and inching their way up the inside with their backs against one wall and feet against the other.

At 11.30am on May 29 the two men reached the summit, stopping long enough to take photographs and search for any sign that Mallory and Irvine had made it to the top. Hillary then buried some sweets and a small cross in the snow while Norgay made a food offering to the mountain. The two men stood on the roof of the world for barely fifteen minutes.

Asked later about his thoughts at the time, Hillary was succinct and pragmatic: 'I did not have much time on the peak to think about the achievement. When you get there you are thinking about the return – if there is time, if the oxygen will last and whether the route will still be all right. The real moments of happiness come later.'

News broke back in London on June 2, the same day as the coronation of young Queen Elizabeth, and the few known details were reported by *The Times* with the note: 'They were using portable oxygen apparatus of the open-circuit type.'

George Finch was in Delhi three weeks later to greet the returning heroes, as Hunt reported:

It was a particular delight in Delhi to meet again George Finch, veteran of the 1922 expedition and pioneer of the use of oxygen for climbing purposes. His presence among us at the time was the more welcome in that we were so anxious that the tributes with which we were being showered should be shared with those who had shown us the way. As one of the two outstanding climbers of the first expedition to make a definite attempt to reach the summit of the mountain in 1922 – the other was George Mallory – and as the strong protagonist of oxygen at a time when there were many who disbelieved in its efficacy and others who frowned upon its use, no one could have better deserved to represent the past than George Finch. We saluted him.

Hunt made no bones about the importance of oxygen to the campaign: 'Among the numerous items in our inventory I would single out oxygen for special mention. Many of our material aids were of great importance; only this in my opinion was vital to success. But for oxygen … we should certainly not have got to the top.'

The Royal Geographical Society president James Wordie was equally emphatic when he addressed the society's annual general meeting. The ascent of Everest had finally broken down the society's prejudice against oxygen, as *The Times* noted in its report of his speech:

Mr Wordie said that any doubts about the use of oxygen were finally removed by physiologists who said that no human behaviour at great heights was normal and that the power

of thought and reason was no longer possible. Professor GI
Finch who was the pioneer in advocating oxygen in the
attempt on Everest in 1922 must take a great share in the
credit for the success of the method.

George Finch was not in London to participate in the celebrations.
He was in Poona, teaching the next crop of scientists.

37.

RECOGNITION AT LAST

In December 1959 George Finch was elected the thirty-third president of the world's oldest mountaineering organisation, the Alpine Club of London. Scott Russell, by now a respected mountaineer himself, watched the reaction to his father-in-law's triumph amid the Georgian splendour of No. 74 South Audley Street, Mayfair, the club's latest premises: 'My grandfather must be turning in his grave,' one member said of his relative, a prominent anti-Finch figure, adding: 'I am delighted.'

The public acceptance of George was complete. He had lived to see, and play a significant role in, the conquest of Mount Everest by climbers using artificial oxygen. In 1957 he became chairman of the Everest Foundation that had replaced the defunct and lopsided committee run by his enemies, and he had now been chosen to lead the club whose antiquated principles he had dared to question and whose leadership had despised him and sought his ruin.

There was no glee in George's response to his ascension. Whatever his personal failings, he was a man who looked ahead rather than to the past. There were no scores to settle. He had always been willing to trade strong opinions in public but had never expressed regret or bitterness in any of his writings or media interviews about the way he had been treated. Although he professed to dislike confrontation it was not in George's nature to take a backward step and, as his father had taught him when he dropped him into Sydney Harbour as a three-year-old, he would always fight his own battles.

No journalist had ever asked why George Finch had been excluded from the 1924 expedition and George had diplomatically ignored the issue in his own books. He had refrained from crowing when Everest was finally conquered, instead expressing relief and conceding that, given the right circumstances and the right climber, it might also be possible to ascend without oxygen.

As much as this determined looking forward was a strength of George's character, it was also a curse, demonstrated most sadly by the severing of his bond with his brother, Max, never to be repaired, and the hidden failures of his first two marriages. It was easier to simply move on and forget.

He would make an oblique reference to this in a speech he gave around this time: 'Memory is that part of the mind which stores up information and guides the search for forgotten data; but it also performs that merciful and alleviating role of forgetting past disappointments, unhappy events and hardships.'

* * *

The Alpine Club election capped a satisfying return from India after five years managing the Poona laboratory. In typically pragmatic fashion George had left comprehensive notes for his successor, not touting his own achievements (during his tenure the laboratory published 350 papers, produced 46 patents and served 65 industries), but outlining a strategy for the future and what he believed still needed to be done, step by step. He also included an assessment of his staff and senior pupils, pointed in parts – just as his assessment of his colleagues had been on the road to Everest thirty-seven years before.

The importance of George's work in modern India could be judged by the swathe of correspondence that arrived at the Finch home each week, frustrating Bubbles who prided herself on managing her husband's professional affairs. He would return to Poona in 1964 at Nehru's request to review the country's scientific and industrial progress and make further suggestions.

George Finch was in his early seventies when retirement finally beckoned. His daughters were married and grandchildren would soon be abundant. He and Bubbles had bought a sprawling old farmhouse in the Oxfordshire village of Upper Heyford, where George created a new workshop, experimented with hydroponics and even attached special plumbing to the house so water softeners might ease Bunty's arthritis.

His range of interests continued to be broad: he called for lead-free petrol decades before its introduction, fretted about the 'creeping Americanism' he feared was undermining society, and deplored socialism as a 'beggarly creed', noting this last opinion on the inside cover of Jakob Burckhardt's *The Civilization of the Renaissance in Italy.*

Music remained a cornerstone of his life, and he was happiest when he sat deep in an armchair listening to music. Once he was even drawn to the piano he had abandoned to play a duet with Cynthia Wood – 'beautifully from memory', as she recalled. George and Bubbles attended the Glyndebourne Festival Opera each year and always sat in the same front-row seats at the Oxford Playhouse whenever a musical production was mounted so George could read the score and follow the music.

Francis Russell, son of Scott and Bunty Russell, remembers the brilliance, generosity and foibles of a grandfather who refused to stand on ceremony: 'I knew that other boys' grandfathers did not expect to be addressed as George,' he recalled fondly of a man who loomed as a giant to a small boy, especially under the low ceilings of Heyford.

Their house held special memories for Francis who was eight when his grandparents returned from India. The hall was hung with prints of photographs taken by George in 1922, his many books stacked neatly in numerous bookshelves around the house, along with treasured souvenirs and gifts – a Tibetan prayer wheel, bronze statues from India and a Chinese watercolour of a snake among them. His numerous medals were showcased in a glass-topped box, including the Olympic gold medal, although George always eschewed official recognition of his deeds. Outside, there were vegetable gardens, a barn for his workshop and an ancient wisteria beneath which George would sit in the summer in the teak chair he used at Everest base camp.

'Sometimes George talked of his boyhood: of being taught by his father to swim in Sydney Harbour; of panning for gold in the Blue Mountains; of the horse that after one long expedition when he himself was asleep took him back to his father's station. Although he had loved his father, he talked little of his mother.

'There were many things about which George did not talk: his first wife, or his second; the ruse by which he beat the German ace pilot who had learnt how to destroy the British observation balloons during the Thesalonika campaign. Although he sometimes referred to work on counteracting German bombs, he never mentioned his contribution to the J Bomb.

'They had an endless stream of visitors, not just fellow mountaineers but Indian scientists he'd mentored and old friends like Vincent Ferranti and Guy Smith-Barry. At Christmas they were bombarded with cards from rajas and maharajas with exotic names.

'A novelty in his life was the television. But the gramophone was not supplanted in his affection. He listened much to Beethoven, but the music I most associate with that time is Schubert's Quintet in C Major (Op. 163). This was played repeatedly. Its exquisite beauty is surely the musical counterpart to the taste of [his favourite wine] Yquem and when I hear the one or sip the other it is of George that I think.'

Canny as always when it came to money, George bought a van rather than a car to avoid Purchase Tax and drove himself to and from London at least once a week to attend the seemingly endless rounds of meetings and speeches, and only reluctantly relinquished his driver's licence at the age of eighty.

The one-time outcast from the London Alpine establishment had now become a key voice at its core, a member of numerous scientific committees and organisations and a member of the exclusive gentlemen's establishment the Athenaeum Club in Pall Mall, which drew its membership from prominent figures in science, literature and the arts. The outsider was now firmly on the inside.

He may have mellowed, but George's forthright nature flared occasionally such as the day he chastised a senior Alpine Club administrator for his 'Francophobe' views about a proposal for a joint English–French attempt on Everest: 'I regard this circular document as ill-considered, unworthy of the Alpine Club and politically damaging,' George wrote. 'It should be withdrawn with all speed and every possible step should be taken to prevent leakage of its contents.'

A fellow scientist, mountaineer and photographer, Basil Goodfellow, who served as George's vice-president during his tenure, noted: 'Those who came to know George Finch only in his later life soon realised that the fire in his character, of which one had long been aware from familiarity with his writing, was, if mellowed, far from extinct.'

George would celebrate his election by admitting to the Alpine Club an old friend, Sir Arnold Lunn, a famed alpinist who previously had been denied membership because his family 'made money out of climbing', by operating a ski and travel business. As president George would be a champion for inclusion and breaking down the nationalistic barriers he believed had stymied the early attempts on Everest – at the expense of men like his old friend Marcel Kurz, whom he continued to see during his occasional visits to Switzerland.

George regarded nationalism as a noxious weed, making his feelings known during his valedictory speech to the club in 1961, after his three years, the maximum allowed, at the helm:

Like all adventurers we mountaineers are rebels, forever seeking to extend the frontiers of knowledge. But the search for new knowledge stagnates in isolation; it can flourish only where there is freedom to exchange experience and ideas. Thus we rebel against the growth of nationalism which, from seeds sown in Napoleonic times, has today become a terrifying exuberant weed. I like to hope that we are on the winning side, for I know of no association of mountaineers where nationality is a bar to membership. Nor are we bothered with a nationalistic competitive element for which the appropriate and highly effective weed killer is ridicule.

George would also prove vital to the ageing club's financial survival, calling on the coterie of wealthy friends he had made over the years through climbing and science to support an institution he once thought was irrelevant because of its antiquated views. Although he embraced his role as a respected elder statesman there were the occasional, if subtle, reflections on the flaws of his old foes, as in 1966 when he delivered a speech at the centenary celebrations of the Swiss Alpine Club in Geneva:

Mind, the most precious attribute of man, achieves nothing unless it is exercised and so put to use. It is only then that perception, reason and memory collaborate in that overall potentially constructive intellectual activity which is thought. But it is precisely here that we meet with serious difficulty because, of all forms of human activity, thinking is by far the most unpopular. Many people leave it to others to think for them; the so-called thinking of some makes no real appeal to reason and so ends up in idle speculation. And there are many other ways of sterilising the mind.

This would be George's last public speech. Entitled 'Men and Mountains', it was a sweeping appraisal of his twin careers that somehow dovetailed one into the other: 'both reveal new horizons opened up by the adventure of discovery'. At one point George ventured back to that moment on Mount Canobolas, high above his hometown of Orange, that had so inspired him: 'The mountains draw their devotees from the young who seek nothing more than adventure and experiences wider than those offered in the plains – and they are rewarded beyond their dreams.'

He argued for change to be embraced because 'the growth of knowledge never stands still' and pleaded with young climbers to pause occasionally, to bivouac at the tops of mountains and enjoy their moment of triumph with a tin of peaches, drenched with condensed milk and chilled with a handful of snow, 'where there is time to forget one's resentment of yesterday's hardships and so to accept the trials and tribulations of the present'.

Then there were the mountains themselves, some of which, quite apart from Everest, he had never climbed:

Ever since I first saw the Weisshorn it has been to me the loveliest of all mountains and yet I have never climbed it. And why not? Somewhere I had read a description of its summit as consisting of three sharp white ridges meeting in a perfect point. I have always felt that, if I ever got to the top, it would be to find the lovely picture trodden out by brutal feet and the mountain shamed and desecrated by the sordid leavings of previous climbers.

Others were old friends:

The Tödi, for instance, with its jewel of a glacier nestling hard under the tremendous precipices of the Bifertenstock, has drawn me to its summit twenty-two times. On the last occasion – it now seems a farewell celebration – a large party of cheerful Swiss with bulging rucksacks joined my wife and myself on the mist-shrouded summit. From their sacks they produced a concertina and sundry other instruments and for two happy hours we sang gay songs in praise of the mountains.

* * *

As he prepared to step down from the presidency of the Alpine Club, George and Bubbles decided to spend a few days in the Ogwen Valley in northern Wales. They had been there many times over the years, often staying at the Pen-Y-Gwryd Hotel. The granite and slate-topped building was once a farmhouse, then a coaching inn, before being transformed into a snug base for those who wanted to climb Wales's highest peak, Snowdon.

George had come here to write his valedictory speech in the shadow of a mountain that was a pimple compared to the Alps, let alone the

Himalayas, and yet the place still held important memories. It was here, soon after arriving in London, that he had met George Mallory at an Easter gathering organised by Geoffrey Winthrop Young. They were rowdy annual events at which sixty or more climbers would spend a week testing themselves against each other on Snowdon's crags.

Edmund Hillary and Tenzing Norgay had trained here in early 1953 before conquering Everest. Through the 1930s and '40s George had brought his daughters here to introduce them to climbing, although he stepped back from any hands-on role, fearing it would be as fraught as a parent trying to teach a child to drive a car. Instead, he watched proudly as Bunty took to it with ease, scrambling up cliffs without hesitation.

It was youth who held the key to the future of mountaineering. He had always known it, in his early battles with the establishment and his joy in taking inexperienced climbers on difficult ascents. There had to be a way to foster and encourage youth, with all its potential and enthusiasm.

One morning as he drove alone along a valley road, George stopped for a young man who was clearly struggling with climbing gear and a giant rucksack. He was heading for Milestone Buttress, a challenging 250-foot climb at the base of a mountain, the Tryfan, still six miles up the road. George offered him a lift.

They chatted as George drove, the young man filled with enthusiasm for the task ahead and completely unaware of whom he was talking to, much less what George Finch had achieved. He wanted to learn to climb and had 'all the gadgets', he told the older man who helped him unload and lift the rucksack over the fence between the car park and the base of the rock.

'Are you going to carry the rucksack up with you?' George asked politely, wondering if the young man realised the difference that such a weight would have on the climb.

'Oh no,' he replied. 'I'm leaving it down here. It's perfectly safe and I want to repeat the climb several times this morning to get the practice while the weather's good.'

George watched, bemused and slightly worried, as the young man tied one end of the rope he carried around his waist, a pointless act given that he was climbing alone.

'It's more like real climbing this way,' he explained, sensing George's eyes on him, then after a moment's hesitation asked: 'Would you like to climb with me?'

It was George's turn to be taken aback. 'I'm sorry, but I'm too old for that sort of thing.'

'Pity. It's great fun. You should try it.'

EPILOGUE

George Ingle Finch, 'the boy from Down Under', as he described himself in a scrawled late-life memoir, died at home peacefully on November 8, 1970, succumbing to pneumonia. He had recently turned eighty-two.

Most British newspapers published obituaries, among them *The Times* which devoted two columns to an overview of his life and many achievements. It concluded, simply: 'He was one of the two best Alpinists of his time – Mallory was the other.'

Such had been their partnership, it came as no surprise to the family when Bubbles lasted for just two years more, dying of a heart attack following her morning bath. Although George had made some dubious decisions regarding relationshps, Agnes Johnston, the petite Scotswoman with the bouncy curls, had proved to be his perfect partner in life.

And what a life! It is difficult to know where to begin in assessing his legacy. One could cite the Everest ascent in 1922 as his greatest achievement, but he would almost certainly disagree. George Finch was a rare physical specimen, able to hold his breath until he passed out as a test of his prowess, one of the great technicians on a mountainside, and confident enough to back his own judgment against bullying elitists.

But ultimately it was his intellect and curiosity that shone brightest; he proved his ingenuity in two world wars and was the driving force and spur-of-the-moment genius behind an oxygen system still used today, as well as the designer of warm, lightweight winter clothing, the forerunner of the ubiquitous puffer jacket that can be found in any high-street store. He was a champion of youth, as he proved when climbing mountains, rescuing Jewish students caught in political crossfire or in the classroom engaging young minds. Most of all, he was a brilliant scientist, at the forefront of research that led to some of the most significant breakthroughs in industrial chemistry of the twentieth century.

The enthusiastic boy who chased wallabies up Mount Canobolas and was inspired by the view could never have conceived the truly sweeping prospect that lay ahead.

29

THE BASTARDY OF
ARTHUR HINKS

In the late autumn of 1935 a young man named Scott Russell arrived at the rooms of the Alpine Club in Savile Row to introduce himself as a prospective member. His mid-morning timing was deliberate, as the club was largely empty before noon when the other members would begin filing in for lunch and an afternoon of reminiscing. The club was usually filled by late afternoon, particularly on Tuesdays when there was an evening lecture.

It was unnerving for the fresh-faced 22-year-old to be ushered into the first-floor lounge and reading room, the wood-panelled walls lined with bookshelves filled with accounts of the splendid adventures of members over the eighty years since the club's founding in 1857. There were a few stalwarts around and Russell found himself chatting with the Honorable Sydney Spencer, a 57-year-old former club secretary and librarian and now vice-president.

Spencer was pleasant enough and curious about the young man's background. And Russell obliged; after all, he needed to convince the club committee of his climbing pedigree if he were to be adopted as a member. Russell was London-born, he assured Spencer, but raised at the bottom of the world in New Zealand

ACKNOWLEDGMENTS AND NOTES ON SOURCES

I would like to thank Francis Russell, George Finch's grandson, his mother, Anne (Bunty), and sister Virginia, who granted me access to family archives and were kind hosts through the process of researching. Likewise, George's other surviving daughter, Moseli, and her son Nanda were generous with their time, as was family friend Cynthia Wood.

I should also acknowledge Tony Ingle-Finch, grandson of Michael, who was generous in sharing information about his family, and also mention the descendants of Bryan Ingle Finch, who did not want to contribute, for understandable reasons. Memories can be difficult. Details of events past are often scant and confusing, making interpretation of motives difficult, particularly when they have to be placed in the context of the time, place and social norms.

My main sources for the book were the private papers of George Finch, an amazing array of formal and less formal documents and photographs, including his handwritten diary of the 1922 Everest expedition, and his many scientific papers and speeches, all of which echoed his brilliance, determination and complexity.

Archives are an integral part of a historical account, given that most of those involved or who witnessed his life have since passed away. I thank Glyn Hughes, archivist at the Alpine Club, and the Alpine Club office staff for arranging access to the club records, minutes, papers and letters; and the Royal Geographical Society archival staff for their patience and help during my visits delving into their fascinating records. The records at the British Library proved helpful for filling in missing pieces about George's battle with officialdom, as were files held at Cambridge University, where access to the letters of George Mallory was organised by Catherine Sutherland and made available by the Masters and Fellows of Magdalene College. I would also mention the amazing resources at the British National Archives at Kew in London.

My main literary references were George Finch's 1924 memoir, *The Making of a Mountaineer*, republished in 1988 with additions by his son-in-law Scott Russell; and his 1925 book, *Der Kampf um den Everest*, republished in 2008 as *George Ingle Finch's The Struggle for Everest*, edited by George W Rodway.

My readings included the award-winning *Into the Silence* by Wade Davis, a patient, scrupulous and wonderfully written book about of the early Everest expeditions and the men behind them. *Finch, Bloody Finch* by the late Elaine Dundy and *Peter Finch: A Biography* by Trader Faulkner helped in piecing together the story of Peter Finch. I also referenced the official accounts of the 1921 campaign by Colonel Howard-Bury and the 1922 expedition by Charles Bruce.

Other books I consulted include *The Life and Murder of Henry Morshead* by Ian Morshead; *After Everest: The Experiences of a Mountaineer and Medical Missionary* by Theodore Howard Somervell; *Hired to Kill* by John Morris; *The Epic of Mount Everest* by Sir Francis Younghusband; *The Story of Everest* by Captain John Noel; *The Wildest Dream: A Biography of George Mallory* by Peter and Leni Gillman; *The Mystery of Mallory & Irvine* by Tom Holzel and Audrey Salkeld; and *The History of Imperial College 1907–2007: Higher Education and Research in Science, Technology and Medicine* by Dr Hannah Gay.

Newspaper archives have also been important, particularly those of *The Times*, which was a sponsor of the early Everest attempts, as well as Trove in the National Library of Australia, and websites such as Ancestry.com. I have also read numerous reports published in the *Alpine Journal*, as well as academic papers, including 'George I. Finch and his pioneering use of oxygen for climbing at extreme altitudes' by JB West published in the *Journal of Applied Physiology*, May 2003; and *A Record of Shelford Parva*, by Fanny Wale (1908).

Finally, I want to thank Richard Walsh, who realised that George Ingle Finch was a man whose incredible life story had not been fully told. I am also very grateful for the support of Shona Martyn, Amruta Slee, Mary Rennie and my editor, Amanda O'Connell, at ABC Books/HarperCollins in Sydney. To my wife, Paola, thank you for your patience, encouragement and suggestions; also to my friend Andrea Dixon for her support and ideas with the early draft.

Robert Wainwright
February 2015, London

Robert Wainwright was born in Western Australia but now lives in London with his wife, journalist Paola Totaro, and their family. His previous books include the international bestseller *Sheila: The Australian Ingenue who Bewitched British Society*. He has written about Rose Porteous, Ian Thorpe, Justin Langer, Martin Bryant and the murder of Caroline Byrne. Robert is fascinated by characters – good and flawed – and what drives them. In George Ingle Finch, his maverick mountaineer, he found an outstanding personality: complex, ambitious and volatile.